Frank Chance's Diamond

Frank Chance's Diamond

The Baseball Journalism of Ring Lardner

Edited by Ron Rapoport

Essex, Connecticut

An imprint of Globe Pequot, the trade division of
The Rowman & Littlefield Publishing Group, Inc.
4501 Forbes Blvd., Ste. 200
Lanham, MD 20706
www.rowman.com

Distributed by NATIONAL BOOK NETWORK

British Library Cataloguing in Publication Information available

Library of Congress Control Number: 2016031018
ISBN 978-1-4930-8099-1 (paperback)
ISBN 978-1-4930-8100-4 (e-book)

∞™ The paper used in this publication meets the minimum requirements of American National Standard for Information Sciences—Permanence of Paper for Printed Library Materials, ANSI/NISO Z39.48-1992.

"A considerable body of first-rate Lardner is entombed in back-number magazines and disintegrating newspapers."

—Matthew J. Bruccoli and Richard Layman

Contents

Introduction

In 1914, an editor for the *Chicago Tribune* suggested that Ring Lardner, who had covered the Chicago Cubs and White Sox for the paper for several years, use his imagination and write a baseball story to be printed in the feature section. Lardner submitted a story in the form of a letter from a vain, clueless, but somehow endearing pitcher named Jack Keefe to a friend back home. But the editor thought Lardner's misspelled words, shaky grammar, and use of the vernacular were out of place in his section of the paper and rejected it. Undaunted, Lardner sent "A Busher's Letters Home" to *The Saturday Evening Post*, where it was printed and created a sensation.

The public demanded more "busher" stories, and by the end of the year, Lardner had written another five. Two years later, they were collected in the book *You Know Me Al*, which was the first, and some have called the greatest, baseball novel ever written. By then a teenager in Oak Park, Illinois, Ernest Hemingway was signing articles for his high school paper "Ring Larder, Jr.," while in England, Virginia Woolf, who didn't know the Polo Grounds from Buckingham Palace, was calling him the best prose writer in America even if "his language is not English."

But Lardner's stories did more than find an audience. They also established baseball as a fit subject for literary fiction. Serious American novelists such as Bernard Malamud, Philip Roth, Robert Coover, Mark Harris, Don Delillo, Chad Harbach, and others would use their imaginations to follow Lardner into ballparks and locker rooms and emerge with stories of their own. These writers, and Lardner himself, all owe a profound debt to his baseball journalism and his fascination with the men who played the game.

Lardner was a journalist his entire working life. From the first articles he wrote as a sports reporter at the *South Bend Times* to the regular columns of radio criticism he wrote for *The New Yorker* until just a few months before he died, Lardner never abandoned his roots.

Many fiction writers begin their careers working for newspapers or magazines, but when their novels or stories become successful, they leave journalism behind or return to it only occasionally. Not Lardner. For all intents and purposes, he pursued parallel careers, turning out the short stories that secured his place in American literature while continuing as a journalist all the while.

Between 1913 and 1919, Lardner wrote more than 1,600 "In the Wake of the News" columns and other articles for the *Chicago Tribune*—which is to say he wrote virtually every day—while at the same time publishing such classic stories as *You Know Me Al*, *Alibi Ike*, *Gullible's Travels*, *Champion*, and more. This is an astonishing output, and the fact that the overall quality of his *Tribune* columns remained so high, says Lardner's biographer Jonathan Yardley, "must be counted among the extraordinary accomplishments of American journalism."

In 1919, Lardner moved to Long Island, where for the next eight years, he wrote more than 500 columns for the Bell Syndicate, most of them as a regular weekly "Letter to the Editor." They were syndicated to more than one hundred newspapers around the country and reached some eight million readers. He wrote about World War I, Prohibition, politics, social conventions, family life on Long Island, opera, the theater, and any other topic that came into his mind. Occasionally, he wrote extra pieces for the syndicate on the major events of the day. He covered the World Series; heavyweight championship fights; political conventions; the inauguration of Warren G. Harding; a disarmament conference held in Washington, D.C.; an America's Cup in New York; and more.

In assessing the sheer volume of this output, one question arises: Where did he find the time? Lardner was not a recluse working in a lonely garret. He had a wide circle of friends; was an avid golfer, bridge player, and theatergoer; a regular at the Algonquin Round Table; a frequent traveler; a prolific letter writer; a loving husband; and a devoted father of four sons. For many years, he was also the bemused lord of a manor in Great Neck,

Long Island, where titans of business and show-business celebrities lived in close proximity, and where the party scene, which moved from lawn to lawn throughout the night, was so relentless that Lardner's neighbor and drinking companion, F. Scott Fitzgerald, moved to France, where he could get some work done. Lardner was also a drinker of legendary proportions—he and another neighbor, a silent movie actor named Tom Meighan, called themselves "two-bottle men"—which may have contributed to his death from tuberculosis at the age of 48.

Lardner's ubiquity in print made him one of the most famous people in the United States, on a par with Calvin Coolidge, Charles Lindbergh, and Babe Ruth. And more than any other journalist before or since, he was bigger than the stories he covered. Since his Bell Syndicate columns were accompanied by sketches from the prominent cartoonist Dick Dorgan, in which he was prominently featured, his face was familiar to the public too. So when the *Indianapolis Star* wanted to tell its readers it would be publishing Lardner's coverage of the 1925 World Series, it simply ran his picture under the headline "No Need to Introduce This Guy."

Lardner got his first newspaper job, so the story goes, when Edgar Stoll, the editor of the *South Bend Times* came to his home in Niles, Michigan, in 1905, looking for his brother. Rex Lardner, who was four years older than Ring, had established himself at the *Niles Daily Sun*, and Stoll wanted to hire him. But Rex was out of town, and Stoll asked Ring whether Rex had a contract with the Niles paper.

"I said yes, which was the truth," Lardner wrote years later. "I asked how much salary he was willing to offer. He said twelve dollars a week. Why? 'Oh,' I said, 'I thought I might tackle the job myself.'" When Stoll asked if he had any writing experience, Lardner said he often helped Rex, which was, he admitted, "far from the truth."

Lardner, who had failed at a number of jobs and had not enjoyed any of them, was then working as a meter reader and collector of bad debts for the Niles Gas Company. ("I never heard of any good ones," he wrote.) He was ready for something more interesting and was not about to let the truth get in his way. The following week, he reported for work at the *Times*, where he covered everything from high school sports to Notre

Dame football, with some general news, court reporting, and society and theater news thrown in. He never received a byline, but it was the best on-the-job training a 20-year-old reporter could have.

Lardner would summon up the memory of his days in South Bend a few years later in articles he wrote for the *Chicago Tribune*—his first "Memoirs of a Baseball Scribe" is one example—just as he wrote a number of pieces about leaving South Bend for Chicago, as depicted in the second "Memoirs of a Baseball Scribe."

Lardner's first job in the big city was with the *Chicago Inter-Ocean*, where he wrote his first article on Major League Baseball in 1908: "Twenty-Six Cubs Will Be Taken On Southern Journey." He does not appear to have met any of these Cubs, nor would he write about them again until the following year when had moved to the *Tribune*. But the article is noteworthy on two accounts. First, it adopts the jocular tone he would seldom abandon when writing about baseball—Vickburgers and Vicksburgerines, indeed—and second, a look at the Cubs' roster in the closing paragraphs gives an indication of who Lardner, and his readers, were dealing with.

These were the Cubs of Tinker to Evers to Chance. They had played in the last three World Series and won the last two and were the reigning lords of the game. But beyond their prowess, the team contained some great characters who soon came to enjoy Lardner's dry wit as much as he enjoyed them. Players like Frank Schulte, Jim Schekard, Heine Zimmerman, Mordecai Brown, John Kling, Ping Bodie, Peaches Graham, and others were storytellers, practical jokers, poker players, drinkers, and all-around lovers of fun who made numerous appearances in Lardner's work. The players and reporters mixed freely on their long train rides together, and Lardner took copious mental notes.

Nor did the players seem to object when Lardner made them figures of fun. They enjoyed his satirical parodies of popular songs, which he sang while accompanying himself on the piano, and regarded him as one of the boys. Before long, Lardner was putting his words, often expressed poetically, into their mouths in stories for the *Tribune* that are some of the most fanciful baseball journalism ever written. The players didn't mind that either and often conspired with Lardner in running gags that lasted for weeks and strain all credulity by today's standards.

The one thing Lardner's fiction and journalism had in common was his use of the vernacular, which depends on such literary aberrations as ungrammatical dialogue, misspellings, haphazard punctuation, and odd abbreviations. He must have driven his copy editors crazy. And indeed a comparison of his Bell columns as they appeared in various newspapers around the country shows that some editors "corrected" what he wrote. Thus, "instants" became "instance" and "happly marred men" became "happily married men."

Hugh Fullerton, the Chicago baseball writer who helped Lardner get several jobs early in his career, tells of a spring training trip they took with the Cubs to a small southern town where a telegraph operator had trouble transmitting their copy. When Fullerton asked if it had finally been sent, the operator said, "Yours went all right, but that other fellow's was awful. It took me an hour or more to correct his spelling." To the extent Lardner learned of these and other outrages, they must have driven *him* crazy.

When Lardner took over the "In the Wake of the News" column at the *Tribune* in 1913, he inherited what had previously been little more than a collection of notes about sports. But almost from the beginning, he indicated that he wasn't interested in simply stretching boundaries. He meant to break them altogether. Buried near the bottom of a column barely a week after his "Wake" debut was an item bearing the title, "The Pennant Pursuit. A Novel. [By the Copy Boy.]"

"As Vern Dalton strod passed the jymnaseium one day in April, bound for the college ofice, where he was going to make arrangmunts for entring the college next fall, the ball nine composed of 20 (twenty) or more members came out on its way to the athletic feild. O said Verne I wonder if Ill ever have a posichion on that team and figth for the glory of my ama mather, but he did not have much hope because his parents had said he must devoat all his time to study. (To be continued.)"

This was Lardner's first shaky attempt at using the vernacular in print and would soon be followed by many more, including "The First Game," which was ostensibly written by "A Athlete" and was a direct precursor of Jack Keefe's habitual self-centered whining in the busher stories.

A year later, Lardner dared those reading "In the Wake of the News" to follow him into the depths of "Cubist Baseball," a delightfully eccentric commentary on various current baseball topics that the author Douglas Robinson says is a parody of a book of poems by Gertrude Stein.

Lardner's ascent at the *Tribune* was a circuitous one. Looking for more money—and because he was about to be married, a less itinerant lifestyle—he left the paper late in 1910 to work for *The Sporting News* in St. Louis. He lasted there only three months before leaving in a dispute with his bosses, but he made the most of them, turning out 10 "Pullman Pastimes" articles, which gave his first extended look at the lives of ballplayers and reporters on the road. As such, they gave a hint of what his short stories would be like. He then moved to the *Boston American*, where he covered the Boston Rustlers—they would become the Braves the following season—who had another colorful bunch of players.

Another disagreement with management led to Lardner's resignation during the 1911 World Series, and he returned to Chicago. He was 27 years old and had worked at five different newspapers. It had been a remarkable apprenticeship, one that pointed him in the direction of bigger and better things.

Lardner went to many World Series while working in Chicago, and later, for the Bell Syndicate, and his coverage over the years shows his development as a writer. Early on, he proved his mastery of the straightforward game story. His accounts of key games in the 1909 and 1912 World Series, for instance, are expertly constructed, full of keenly observed detail, and, in the description of Christy Mathewson's loss in the latter, heartbreaking. Similarly, Lardner's description of the first game ever played at Forbes Field in Pittsburgh shows he could write a sweetly evocative piece when called upon while his story on the Cubs' clinching the 1910 National League pennant demonstrated the creativity that would always be one of his hallmarks.

But once Lardner took over the "In the Wake of the News" column at the *Tribune*, his approach to the game quickly changed. Nothing was off-limits now, even if it meant he would often leave writing about the games themselves—and including such nonessentials as the final score—entirely behind.

At future series, Lardner would write "Friend Harvey" letters to his editor about his travel plans, make fun of play-by-play accounts, pretend to interview befuddled fans, send up wartime propaganda, write in fractured French, talk about his golf game, comment on what the umpires were wearing, and more. Of all these, his articles during the 1922 Series must be counted as his masterpiece. He wrote five columns about his quest for a fur coat for his wife, and I could not resist including them all.

Lardner's coverage of the 1919 World Series deserves special mention. The legend is that he quickly became aware that his beloved White Sox were throwing games to the Cincinnati Reds, and he is said to have called Eddie Cicotte, one of his favorite players, to his hotel room after a game he had lost and demanded to know what was going on. He also collaborated with his *Tribune* colleague James Crusinberry on the lyrics to a parody of a popular song of the era that began "I'm Forever Throwing Ballgames."

Yet none of Lardner's suspicions appeared in his coverage of the series. While Crusinberry wrote several articles in which White Sox manager Kid Gleason, sensing that something was amiss, agonized over his team's poor play, Lardner wrote one lighthearted story after another. The closest he came to mentioning the scandal, which would not come to light until the following year, was a cryptic reference in a column that appeared October 9 in which he said he was examining a baseball used in a game and that "it looks soiled on the northwest side and I will worry my life away wondering who put a dirty finger on that ball which I have got and my children will still have it after me."

In the years that followed, Lardner occasionally said that the Black Sox scandal destroyed his interest in baseball, but this is an exaggeration. He knew that gambling had long been a part of the game and that there had been a number of suspicious occurrences in previous years. Lardner himself often bet substantial amounts on the games he covered and his son, Ring Jr., wrote years later, "the way he spoke about the event later gave me the feeling he was at least as concerned about losing a substantial bet . . . as he was about the moral turpitude of the players."

What did decrease his interest in the game was the arrival of Babe Ruth and the lively ball, a subject he discussed at length in "Br'er Rabbit Ball" and "Why Ring Stopped Covering Baseball," though it should be noted that he covered four more World Series after writing the latter. In a letter to the legendary New York Giants' manager John McGraw when both men were nearing the end of their lives, Lardner did not sound like a man who had turned his back on the game that had defined his life.

"Often I have wondered whether you ever enjoyed the feeling of security and comfort that must be a manager's when the reporters assigned to his club are 'safe' and not pestiferous," Lardner wrote of some of the managers he had written about, "a gang such as (Frank) Chance and (Fielder) Jones and Jim Callahan were surrounded with for a few years in Chicago, and I don't say that just because I happen to be one of the gang. . . . The managers referred didn't wince when they saw one of us approaching. They were our friends and we were theirs."

Lardner's commitment to journalism and short stories has led to an ongoing debate over what might have been. Did it distract him from concentrating on his fiction? Did it keep him from writing the Great American Novel? Did it ultimately consign him to a lower place in the pantheon of American writers than he otherwise might have earned?

Edmund Wilson, one of the leading critics of the era, expressed these concerns after some of Lardner's early work was republished in a book. Wilson admired the stories, but wanted more. "Will Ring Lardner, then, go on to his *Huckleberry Finn* or has he already told all he knows?" he asked. . . . "Here is a man who has had the freedom of the modern West no less than Mark Twain did of the old one. . . . If Ring Lardner has anything more to give us, the time has now come to deliver it."

Fitzgerald also weighed in after Lardner died in an otherwise affectionate tribute to the man with whom he had spent so many companionable hours in Gatsby country. Lardner's achievements fell short of his capabilities, Fitzgerald wrote, because "During those years, when most men of promise achieve an adult education, if only in the school of war, Ring moved in the company of a few dozen illiterates playing a boy's game. A boy's game, with no more possibilities in it than a boy could master, a game bounded by walls which kept out novelty or danger, change or adventure. . . . However deeply Ring might cut into it, his cake had the diameter of Frank Chance's diamond."

But Lardner had no interest in novels. After one chapter, he wrote to Ring Jr., he "would be even more bored than the reader." He was content spending his life writing the short stories that secured his place in American literature, the theater pieces and song lyrics he enjoyed, and proving, in the journalism that has been entombed for too long, just how deeply a writer who loved baseball beyond measure could cut into the delicious cake that was Frank Chance's diamond.

A Note to Readers

Ring Lardner's fiction has been reprinted and anthologized many times over the years, but the only two books devoted solely to his journalism—*What of It?*, published in 1925, and *First and Last* (1934)—are now long out of print. Among the anthologies that contain some of his nonfiction, only *Ring Lardner: Stories and Other Writings* (2013), which leans heavily toward his short stories, was published in the last 40 years. So the time seems right for a fresh look at his baseball journalism, one that includes his early newspaper work, his Bell Syndicate columns, and his magazine articles.

In disinterring the archival tombs that are the only places where much of Lardner's journalism can be found, a few problems were encountered. Occasionally, Lardner would be in a hurry to meet a deadline and drop a word or compose a sentence that made no sense. These are hazards every journalist encounters, particularly those who work for newspapers where the rush to get papers on the street often resembles a fire drill. He was also inconsistent in his usage. He variously rendered the New York Giants' ballpark, for instance, as Polo Grounds, Polo grounds, polo grounds, Polo's grounds, and pologrounds. And his haphazard use of commas could lead to consecutive sentences like these: "If you are in the Monday Opera 500 club, you belong. If you ain't you don't." Also, the editors at the various newspapers that ran Lardner's Bell Syndicate columns sometimes differed on exactly what he had written. I have relied on my best judgment to resolve these issues, and I apologize for any mistakes I may have made.

Like any good journalist, Lardner often made reference to people and events that were in the news at the time. Since the time was close to a century ago—more than a century in some cases—a number of those references are now obscure. I have supplied footnotes for some of them, which I hope will offer some useful context, as well as explanatory notes at the end of some of the pieces.

It should also be noted that nearly all the articles and columns in this book are presented as they were written. A few of Lardner's accounts of baseball games have been made shorter by leaving out his lengthy description of the play-by-play. This was a convention of baseball reporting in the era before radio and television revolutionized sports reporting, but it makes for tedious reading today, a fact that Lardner acknowledged in his parodies of the form. I have indicated these and a few other cuts with ellipses. Also, I have changed some of the headlines—and written a few for the "In the Wake of the News" columns that didn't have them—to make them correspond more closely to the subject matter.

Ring Lardner Tells His Sad, Sad Story to the World

Omaha World-Herald, Bell Syndicate, June 8, 1924

THE BEST OF MEN WILL BREAK INTO VERSE AT TIMES. IT NOW BECOMES Ring Lardner's hour. Ring, you must know, is striding toward Cleveland right now to help "cover" the republican national convention for the World-Herald. On the eve of the big conclave, he steps to the front of the stage with the following, which he entitles, "An Autobiography."

Hardly a man is now alive
Who cares that in March, 1885,
I was born in the city of Niles,
Michigan, which is 94 miles
From Chicago, a city in Illinois.
Sixteen years later, still only a boy,
I graduated from the Niles High School
With a general knowledge of rotation pool.
After my schooling, I thought it best
To give my soul and body a rest.
In 1905 this came to an end,
When I went to work on The Times in Souse Bend,
Thence to Chi, where I labored first
On the Inter-Ocean and then for Hearst,
Then for the Tribune and then to St. Lews,
Where I was editor of Sporting News.

And thence to Boston, where later a can
was tied to me by the manager man.
1919 was the year
When, in Chicago, I finished my daily newspaper career.
In those 14 years—just a horse's age—
My stuff was all on the sporting page.
In the last five years (since it became illegal to drink),
I've been connected with The Bell Syndicate, Inc.
I have four children as well as one Missus,
None of whom can write a poem as good as this is.

RING LARDNER

Memoirs of a Baseball Scribe (Part 1)

Chicago Tribune, July 15, 1915

GRAND RAPIDS HAD A THIRD BASEMAN WHO THOUGHT THAT WATER was created for chasing purposes only. But for his insatiable thirst for something stronger this man would been in a big league—a star in it. He might even have "gone up" if he could have got enough liquid refreshment at night. But no; he had to have it in the morning, which, as every player is supposed to know, is iunethical.

He had a whip of steel and a fast ball as smoky as most pitchers.' He preferred warming up with some catcher to practicing in his regular position.

South Bend, where I first reported the pastime for gain, had two press tables. They were in front of the grandstand, on the field. Mine was a few feet from the visitors' bench and the rival sheet's close to the home dugout.

John Ganzel's Grand Rapids team came down for a series and the third baseman proceeded to light himself up the minute the club got in town. By game time he was so bad that Ganzel wouldn't allow him to play. Being near the Grand Rapids bench, I heard the torrid dialogue between manager and man. Ganzel came over to me at length and asked that I print nothing about the matter. Being agreeable in those days, I promised to pass the story up.

The rival sheet's reporter, however, had no such request from Ganzel and ran half a column of the stuff, with pictures. It was in his paper the next afternoon.

The afternoon after the next afternoon I took my place as usual and proceeded to write down the batting order in my massive score book. I was interrupted by a sharp pain in the shin. A ball had struck me, and the ball had been thrown by the steel whip of the Grand Rapids third baseman. He was doing his customary warmup stunt and one of his shots had escaped his catcher.

The catcher, Dan Howley, was standing directly in front of me, not ten feet distant.

"Move over a little, will you?" I said. "I don't want to get killed."

Dan moved to a position which made mine safe except from a ball thrown deliberately at me.

And right away there was a ball thrown deliberately at me.

I ducked and the ball whistled past my ear.

"What are you trying to do?" I yelled at the third sacker.

"You'll find out if you set there long enough," he said.

The ball had bounded back off the screen and he had recovered it. Taking careful aim, he shot at me again. Howley was quick enough to get his glove in front of the ball, and divert its course.

"Cut it out,—!" said Howley. "You'll get in trouble."

"I don't care if I hang," said—. "I'm going to get that bird."

Howley picked up the ball and held it. The third baseman went to the bench to secure another ball. Failing to find one, he grabbed a bat and let fly. The missile fell short.

"Give me that ball," I said to Howley. Howley gave me the ball and, standing up, I threw it as hard as I could at my friend. If it had hit him in a vulnerable spot it might have hurt him. But he caught it in his bare hand and it came back several times as fast as it had gone. It missed its target by inches.

Ganzel and the other Grand Rapids players were returning to the bench from their practice. I summoned Ganzel.

"—is pegging at me," I said. "You'd better make him cut it out."

— came over to the table.

"This is the guy [he didn't say guy] that knocked me in the paper," he said.

Howley interposed.

"No, it ain't," he said. "It was the other fella."

"It don't make no difference," said—. "They're all alike."

"You lay off'n my ball players!" said Mr. Ganzel.

"It was the other fella," repeated Howley.

"Whoever it was," said Mr. Ganzel, "you lay off'n my ball players or you'll get killed. I'll do it myself."

Grand Rapids had lost two straight.

"The next time you tell me not to print a story I'll run it on the first page," I said.

"You do and see what happens to you," said Mr. Ganzel. "I got a notion to fix you now."

The arrival of Chief McWeeny (Jim) and a short speech by him saved my young life.

I shed few tears when——guzzled himself out of baseball and when Manager Ganzel suffered worse than death—the management at Cincinnati.

Lardner told this story somewhat differently in 1931 in an article for the *Saturday Evening Post.* In that version, the aggrieved player became angry when Lardner, the game's official scorer, called an error on what he insisted was a hit.Omaha World-Herald, Bell Syndicate, June 8, 1924

Memoirs of a Baseball Scribe (Part 2)

Chicago Tribune, July 28, 1915

There came a day in the late summer of 1907 when I was taken violently ill with big league fever.

"I'm going to Chicago for Labor day," I told my boss.

"You have fine taste," said he.

But it was not for pleasure that I was going.

I went, or came, and on my arrival called up a friend who had the honor of knowing Hughey Fullerton personally to speak to. On Labor day morning my friend escorted me to the newspaper office where Hughey was working. If we'd known anything about the metropolitan newspaper business we never would have sought Hughey at his office in the morning. Our ignorance took us there, and there, for some queer reason, was Hughey.

"Glad to know you," I said.

"Glad to know YOU," replied Hughey, with no regard for the truth.

"This fella," said my friend, "wants a job on one of the papers."

"What line?" asked Hughey.

"Sporting," said I.

"Well," said Hughey, "I don't know of any openings just now, but if you'll go out to the game with me, we'll talk it over."

That day was one of the most enjoyable in my existence and doubtless the most boresome in Hughey's.[1] He wasn't writing baseball at that particular time and he put in an off-day at the Sox park purely as an accommodation to a busher whose dissertation on the national pastime must have been as entertaining as brown pop.

A canvass of the representatives of the various papers developed nothing in the way of a job and Hughey could have been forgiven if he had dismissed me permanently from his mind. But at the parting he said:

"Try to get up for the world's series, and maybe we'll have better luck."

And it was at the fourth game of the series in Detroit, that he introduced me to Duke Hutchinson, sporting editor of the I.O., and Duke, in an unguarded moment, engaged me.[2]

A week later I reported at the I.O. sport desk for duty.

"Sit over there," said Duke. "You'll find shears and paste in that drawer." So I sat over there and opened that drawer. A large rat jumped out.

"Eighteen-fifty a week isn't a bit too much for this," I thought.

"That's Ben," said Duke. "You'll like him when you get better acquainted."

Notes

1. Lardner is being disingenuous here. Hugh Fullerton, one of Chicago's most distinguished baseball reporters, was impressed by his baseball knowledge and became a mentor who recommended him for several jobs.

2. Years later, in a piece for the *Saturday Evening Post*, Lardner embellished the story of his hiring at the Chicago *Inter-Ocean*, quoting Duke as asking, "Have you figured how you're going to live in Chicago on eighteen-fifty?"

"I can get on the wagon."

"You can get on the wagon," said Duke, "but nobody can work for us and stay there."*Omaha World-Herald*, Bell Syndicate, June 8, 1924

Twenty-Six Cubs Will Be Taken on Southern Journey

Chicago Inter-Ocean, Feb. 2, 1908

The world's champion Cublets went so far last summer and fall that the training trip laid out for them seems short by comparison. The West Side bugs are rather glad than otherwise that their favorites will not stray a long way off. It will be an easy matter to secure daily tidings of the world beaters' doings when they are as close to civilization as Mississippi.

Mr. Chance will load his likely stable on an Indiana bound rattler March 3. The car will first hesitate at West Baden, where the champs will bask in the baths for ten more or less sunshiny days. Very little actual work will be done at the Hoosier resort, the stop there being almost solely for the purpose of dragging the kinks from twenty-six frozen backs.

On the 14th, the band will ramble southward toward Vicksburg, Miss., where it will be loudly welcomed by all the Vicksburgers and Vicksburgerines. The inhabitants of this sedate city have been saving up all winter to make a big noise when the Cub flyer toots its station toot. Vicksburg is said to be the ideal spot for training, particularly at times when snow, sleet, and chill blasts kindly remain absent.

The champs will sojourn in Vicksburg until the 24th, playing exhibition games with the natives daily, or at convenient periods. On the 24th the Chicagoans will again take to the road and will play in Meridian on the 25th. The monotony of the saunter homeward will be broken by the following stops.

Montgomery, Ala, March 26 and 27.

Atlanta, Ga., March 28 and 30.

Chattanooga, Tenn., March 31 (with Toledo).

Birmingham, Ala., April 1, 2, and 3.

Memphis, Tenn., April 4 and 5.

Nashville, Tenn., April 6 and 7.

Evansville, Ind., April 8.

Terre Haute, Ind. April 9.

Fort Wayne, Ind., April 10.

Indianapolis, Ind., April 11.

Dayton, Ohio, April 12 and 13.

From Dayton the team will go to Cincinnati, where the opening game of the real fight is slated.

Manager Chance will not be burdened by a large assemblage of hopefuls on the trip South. The team which swallowed the Tigers whole will be re-enforced by only five youngsters. These will be Catcher Evans, Outfielder Elston, and Pitchers Walsh, Merker, and Donahue.

Of this quintet Evans is a recruit from the Virginia league club. He was some slugger with the Southerners and was also considered one of the best relievers in the organization. Outfielder Curt Elston hails from Lancaster, of the Ohio and Pennsylvania circuit. He is touted as cute on the bases, a skillful trapper of flies, and a trusty batsman. There are a few other good qualities which this youth is said to possess, but no one seems to know what they are.

Martin Walsh has been heard of before. He is a brother to the famous Edward[1] of the same name and about the same size. He was seized from the Danville team, where he made an enviable record and was the source of many misgivings amount the batsmen.

The two other young pitchers are Chicagoans by choice. John L. Donahue is a former member of the stout Spaulding semipro team and Albert Merker heaved for the Swing aggregation of the Commercial league. They have both been the object of several major league scouts' admiration for some time past and are said to ripe for fleeter company.

Twenty-six Cubs will be in the party when the start is made for West Baden. They are as follows:

> Pitchers—Brown, Reulbach, Lundgren, Frazer, Overall, Pfiester, Walsh, Donahue, Merker, and Durbin.
>
> Catchers—Olis, Kling, Moran, and Evans.
>
> Infielders—Chance, Evers, Zimmerman, Howard, Tinker and Steinfeldt.
>
> Outfielders—Schulte, Sheckard, Slagle, Hofman and Elston.

Note

1. Hall of Famer Ed Walsh, who pitched 13 years with the White Sox and would win 40 games in 1908 and complete 42. His brother Marty never made it out of the minors. *Omaha World-Herald*, Bell Syndicate, June 8, 1924

The Peerless Leader Takes Charge

Chicago Tribune, March 4, 1909

WEST BADEN, Ind.—Jack Pfiester and a miniature blizzard were almost simultaneous arrivals at this treacherous place today and their coming was about the only instance worthy of note. Jack was greeted with a smile by Manager Chance. The snow was not.

It appeared in time to dispell all thought of gamboling on the green, so gambling of less strenuous, but more costly nature was indulged. Southpaw Floyd Kroh, who called with four kings[1] in a battle last summer, proved conclusively he had been putting in a hard winter of practice at the indoor national pastime and has added to his deposits of the Bolivar bank.

Mr. Pfiester was "called" by the peerless leader for not coming earlier to training quarters. As he is three ounces overweight, he will have to work night and day to get in shape for the first brush with the Giants. He says his arm has felt good all winter and that he has tried it out a trifle, not curving them, however. He came up from Cincinnati, a three hour and a half ride, which always takes five hours.

The athletes were hustled out of bed at seven bells and taken out to a covered promenade, bundled in heavy sweaters. They were hustled three miles around the track and then sent to breakfast. In the afternoon most of them varied the monotony by a hike to French Lick and a bath in the rejuvenating waters.

Jimmy McAleer and his fat Browns had stolen away in the night, bound for permanent training quarters in Texas. Rube Waddell left in his wake various broken hearts and bottles. He also left a note saying he would pitch all the games in the next world's series against the Cubs and would call in all the fielders. This had a discouraging effect on Chance, and he does not know whether or not it is worth while to continue training.

Orvall Overall[2] was the hardest worker of the day and he took off four pounds, leaving only a paltry 220 to carry around with him. Frank Schulte did not put in an appearance, nor did Jimmy Sheckard. In the latter's case, Chance received a letter telling him that James had started for Hot Springs and would join the crowd there on Sunday.

The manager has to watch Jimmy Archer continually, because the latter has discovered an outlaw cave which sometimes is called the Archer cave, and the P.L.[3] is afraid he will jump to the outlaws. Overall and Brown wish he would, as there is no chance of their winning a pool game or bowling match as long as he is in the camp.

If there is a cessation of snow, uniforms will be donned tomorrow. The 7 o'clock Marathon race has been ordered again, but Chance is not satisfied to let his youngsters and "oldsters" get away with nothing but that. If the blizzard continues and keeps the men off the playing field, a long dash over the hills will be added to the program. And there are some hills in these parts. A. Bert Semmens, standing on the top of one of them, looked down and saw Overall and thought it was Jimmy Slagle.

The Badger fight for the benefit of Catcher Malone is scheduled for tomorrow or Friday night. This squad has little time to stay in Indiana, and whatever is due to be pulled off must happen soon. The bunch will leave these parts Saturday for Hot Springs, and West Baden will be left without excitement until Tuesday, when the rest of the Cubs and Pittsburgh batteries will blow in.

There is no telling whether Acting Manager Tommy Leach will consent to let his pitchers work with the Chicagoans, as the latter thus would be given an opportunity of learning in advance what new deceivers Maddox, Willis, and the rest have.

F. Chance has admitted he would not stay among the oranges. "I wouldn't miss our fun this season for all the fruit in California," said the P. L. "Of course, there is sure to be something beside fun, for I think the Giants, Phillies, Reds, and Pirates will be hard to beat. But our reception the first time we appear at the Polo grounds will be worth sticking around for. If you want to add any pet names to your vocabulary just open your ears and listen to what these 'bugs' call me and the rest of the boys when we make our entrance. We'll be about as popular there as a distillery in West Baden."

Floyd Kroh is sure to be as well received as Chance or any of them, for there are two Polo grounds fanatics who did ground and lofty tumbling stunts when he swung his long left arm in a mixup that followed Merkle's generous act,[4] but Kroh will meet the onslaught cheerfully if he is but given an opportunity to work against the tribe of McGraw.

First blood was reported today. Jimmy Archer showed up late in the afternoon with a dislocated cheek, caused by a disagreeable tooth. The jaw is to be lanced tomorrow, and in the meantime Jimmy is forgetting the pain with a long succession of strikes and spares.

Notes

1. Lardner transferred the fact that Floyd Kroh "called with four kings"—an unforgivably conservative play in poker—directly to *You Know Me Al.* He altered the facts a bit, though, perhaps thinking that nobody would believe any poker player would stand pat with such a good hand. In the story, Jack Keefe stands on four sevens and wins fifty cents.
2. The mention of Orval Overall should not pass without notice. Overall was the winning pitcher in the game that clinched the 1908 World Series. He remained the last Cub pitcher to claim that distinction for the next 108 years.
3. Short for "Peerless Leader," a nickname Charles Dryden, then the highest-paid sportswriter in the country, gave to Frank Chance. Lardner, a devoted fan of Dryden, trailed around after him so much that the players called him "Charlie's Hat."
4. "Merkle's generous act" refers to perhaps the greatest mistake ever made in a World Series Game, the failure of rookie Giants runner Fred Merkle to touch second base on a play that would have won the game and sent his team to the 1908 World Series. Amid great controversy, the game was replayed, and the Cubs won and went on to win the Series. *Omaha World-Herald*, Bell Syndicate, June 8, 1924

Record Crowd Opens Forbes Field

Chicago Tribune, July 1, 1909

PITTSBURG,[1] PA.—Before the biggest crowd that ever saw a ball game the world's champion Cubs beat Fred Clarke's Pirates on Pittsburg's beautiful new field this afternoon, 3 to 2. A throng of 30,338, or ninety one more than the former record, paid their good money to Messrs. Dreyfuss and Murphy, and there were at least 5,000 more who came in on invitations from the president of the Pittsburg club.

If there had been no ball game at all the masses of sweltering humanity would have paid for their coming, for the stands on Forbes field look out on some of the prettiest scenery to be found in Pennsylvania. And the stands themselves are pretty enough to draw sightseers even if there were nothing else for them to see.

A sight of the crowd was worth a journey to the park, although said journey is anything but comfortable. From early in the forenoon until the game started the masses of people crowded their way into the beautiful suburb, Bellefield, and fought for points of vantage.

The women came dressed as if for the greatest society event of the year, and perhaps it was for Pittsburg's year. Gorgeous gowns, topped by still more gorgeous hats, were in evidence everywhere. Most of the gowns were white and formed a pretty combination with the prevalent green of the stands.

Beyond the outfield fences Schenley Park and some of the handsomest buildings of the Carnegie institute were visible. The stands, themselves constructed almost entirely of Pittsburg steel and concrete, completely surrounded the field and yet were not big enough to hold the mammoth crowd.

There was an overflow from first base all the way around the outskirts of the yard to the home of Jap Barbeau and Harry Steinfeldt.[2]

Policemen were scarce, but the throng, disappointed though it was by general appearance and the final outcome of the game, was a peaceable assemblage and was just as polite as it looked. When most of Pittsburg's inhabitants and excursionists from the surrounding cities and villages had found seats either in the boxes or stands or on mother earth, Prof. Nerillos' military band began attracting much attention to itself by parading toward the home bench. There the usual line of athletes was formed and the procession started for home plate.

At that point the Cubs themselves, officers and magnates of the two big leagues, including President Pulliam and Acting President Heydler of the National league, President Dreyfuss of the Pittsburg club, and President Ben Shibe of the Philadelphia Athletics, who came over to see whether or not Barney had anything on him in the way of a ballyard, joined the crowd and started for the flag pole. Then, without any of the usual accidents, the stars and stripes were hoisted with a pennant bearing the words "Forbes Field," trailing a little below.

When the ceremonies at the flag pole had been completed the procession came back to the playing field and the two teams took their fielding practice amid more noise than ever has been heard in Pittsburg or the adjacent locality. When the gong rang for the beginning of the game, John Morin, director of public safety, which in English means chief of police, appeared in the middle of the diamond and looked bashfully up at the third deck of the box seats. There was seated Mayor Magee, and he threw the first ball on to the field. Director Morin caught it neatly and journeyed to the pitchers' mound. From the slab the strong arm of the law hurled it almost over the plate and into the waiting hands of catcher Hackenschmidt[3] Gibson. After that all human obstacles disappeared from view and the battle was on.

Notes

1. From 1891 to 1911, the official spelling of the city's name was changed to Pittsburg. Only after pressure from a U.S. Senator from Pennsylvania on the United States Geographic Board was the final *h* restored.

2. Third baseman for the Cubs and Pirates, respectively.

3. A nickname George Gibson earned the first time he walked into the Pirates' dressing room, causing Honus Wagner to shout, "Here comes Hackenschmidt," referring to George Hackenschmidt, a famous wrestler of the time. Gibson was just under six feet tall and weighed 190 pounds, about average for a major leaguer today and an indication of how much professional athletes have grown.Omaha World-Herald, Bell Syndicate, June 8, 1924

P.L.'s Team Leads Arabella to the Altar

Chicago Tribune, Oct. 3, 1910

CINCINNATI, Ohio—The wedding of Miss Arabella Cinch to Mr. Chicago Cub occurred this afternoon at the first Cincinnati Pastime church, Mr. Garry Herrmann officiating. Ed Reulbach was best man and Harry Gasper bridemaid.

For some reason or other, several pews were vacant. But the guests who were present were charmed by the beauty of the ceremony. One of them was so charmed that he gave vent to his enthusiasm in loud conversation with Usher Brennan, and was led down the aisle and out of church by a policeman. The simple bat ceremony was to have been used, but it was decided at the last moment that it [was] too simple. So a bunch of Cincinnati friends of the bride and groom enlivened things by throwing some old and new boots at the happy pair right while the service was going on. Seven red boots were collected by the janitor after it was all over.

The marriage was the culmination of a long and romantic engagement. Mr. Cub met Miss Cinch down south last spring and it was a case of love at first sight on both sides. Miss Cinch's parents were agreeable, but rivals for the fair lady's hand tried to break off the match several times after the engagement was announced.

In July last, Mr. Pittsburg Pirate became a dangerous suitor and it was predicted freely that he would come between the engaged pair, for Mr. Cub was losing some of his good looks by a series of accidents and illnesses. However Miss Cinch finally made up her mind that she would rather marry Mr. Cub disfigured than Mr. Pirate handsome. Mr. New

York Giant hung around until the last moment hoping she would prove untrue to her first love, for he, too, was enamored of her, though he really was not in her class. But he knows tonight that it is all over with him and he may as well join with the rest in congratulating the newly weds.

A wedding breakfast at the Havlin hotel followed the ceremony. The parents of the groom, Mr. and Mrs. Chance Cub, signed for all the refreshments, which certainly were some refreshments, believe them. The young couple will remain in Cincinnati until Tuesday night. Then they will go on a honeymoon trip to Chicago and will pass one day at the end of the week in Pittsburg before finally settling down to light housekeeping. They will be at home at Polk, Lincoln, Taylor, and Wood streets.

In other words, the score this afternoon was 8 to 4 in favor of the Cubs. The latter gave Harry Gasper an awful trimming and did some mean things to Bill Burns after Harry had been chased. Furthermore, the Reds did all the awful fielding of which they are capable, and they are capable of a great deal. Ed Reulbach had everything he ever had in his life, and it's remarkable that the Reds hit him as hard as they did.

The P.L., seated on the bench, thought they must be getting the signs, not in any illegitimate way, however, so he had Kling and the big pitcher switch their signals two or three times, but the switching didn't seem to do any good. However, it didn't make any particular difference whether Edward was hit hard or not, for Gasper, Burns, and the Cincinnati defense were a strong enough combination to offset any heavy batting on the part of the home folks.

The Cubs were not shy with the stick themselves. They grabbed off thirteen base knocks, of which three were made by Henry Zimmerman, successor to John Evers. Steinfeldt really hit the ball harder than any one else on either club. He drove runs in with two singles and was the victim of two swell catches by Paskert and Miller of long, vicious swipes.

The victory gave the pennant to Chicago beyond peradventure. The Giants can win all the rest of their games and the Cubs can lose everything else on the schedule and it won't make a bit of difference, so far as real results are concerned.

This is Mr. Chance's fourth pennant in the five years that he has been the Peerless Leader. He is proud of the accomplishment and proud of the team. Also, he is looking forward to a night of sweet sleep, something he hasn't enjoyed in a month.

This is a true statement. The P.L. has been worrying his head off because of the condition, or lack of condition, of his men especially his pitchers, and he was the most tickled gent in Cincinnati when this game was over and the flag was cinched.

In 1907 and 1908, after nailing the bunting Chance and his wife divided between them a bottle of wine. Subsequently, the Cubs copped the world's championship. So you can bet that Mr. and Mrs. P.L. had a cold bottle tonight, and it was the same brand they had consumed in other years.

No he isn't superstitious. He said after the game that the number thirteen had made it possible for him to lead his club to the championship. It was his thirteenth year with the Cubs he had berth No. 13 and locker 13 all through the season. When there was a twelve section sleeper he took the drawing room and numbered it 13. Once more, no, he isn't superstitious.

Now that the strain is over, the Chicago players will have to go on working pretty hard. They will be asked to practice every morning here, at home, and in Pittsburg. Some of the regulars, Kling, Steinfeldt, and Sheckard, for instance, may be allowed to sit on the bench and watch some of the games, but the pitchers will keep on working in turn unless the P.L. gets a hunch that some of them would do better resting. Hank Weaver will have a chance to butt in, and so will Frank Pfeffer and Tom Needham.

But we mustn't forget the feature of the afternoon's doings, which was the champion long distance triple play of the age. It helped Ed Reulbach out of a deep hole and Jimmy Sheckard was the hero of it, because he started it with one of the prettiest throws he ever made.

In the third inning, Egan singled to center. Corcoran was hit by a pitched ball. Gasper laid down a hunt. Zimmerman was slow to cover first and Reulbach's throw was bad, so the bases were full with none out. Miller lifted a fly to Sheckard and it was a pretty long one, too. The fleet Egan started for home as the ball was caught. Sheckard's peg hit bottom just at the edge of the infield grass. It skipped straight into Kling's hands without wasting any time and Egan was tagged out. Corcoran was afraid to go to third on the play and Gasper, who had started for second, was forced to turn around and hike back to first. Kling's relay beat him there and Archer did the rest of it.

Pullman Pastimes

Frank Schulte Is His Own Entertainer

The Sporting News, Jan. 12, 1911

Never an ardent devotee of poker, never much of a reader of magazines nor novels and never a singer with enough confidence in himself to give the entire public the pleasure of hearing his voice, Frank M. Schulte, alias "Schlitz," alias "Bud," alias, "Wildfire," alias "Schultz," is thrown on his own resources when the Chicago Cubs are journeying hither and thither. And they certainly are some resources. Mr. Schulte careth not whether he has an audience. When he is in the mood to talk, he will talk and talk loud, and he isn't particular whom he criticizes nor who is listening to his monologue. Mr. Schulte is at his best after the Cubs have lost a hard game. He likes to win, all right, but he doesn't see why defeats should be the cause of tears or post-mortems.

Aboard the sleeper after one of these defeats, for which two or three slips were responsible, there are gathered various little knots of athletes telling each other how it happened, how the beating could have been averted, and mourning and wailing over the unkindness of fate. In his seat all alone, or with a willing listener, sits Mr. Schulte.

"The boys seem to forget there'll be a game tomorrow to play. They act as if this was the last one they ever were going to get into. The pennant is lost now, and there isn't a chance for us to cop the World Series money. Let's hope the White Sox don't finish first. A city series with them will net the boys enough to worry through the winter on. They didn't trim us today because they played better ball. Oh, no! There never was a day when any team played better ball than these ten-time champion Cublets. Rigler called everything wrong and the luck was dead against us from the start.

"You saw Jack Murray hit that one out of the ball yard? Well, that's no credit to Murray. He had his eyes shut or was talking to someone back in the grandstand when he let that one loose. He didn't meet the ball square. Oh, no! The ball hit his little fingernail and bounded off over the fence. Besides, Edward (that's Reulbach) intended to get him to bite on his fall-away. Edward didn't want to get the ball over the plate. No, Edward was blinded by the dust and he pitched within Murray's reach when he really thought he was throwing to catch Doyle off second.

"Yes, and Schulte played that ball wrong, too. He ought to have left the park and stood on the approach to the elevated station. Then, you know there was a high wind blowing. Otherwise, that would have been a foul fly that Archer could have eaten up. But the pennant's gone now and we might as well arrange a barnstorming tour of some kind."

Then, if feeling particularly good, Mr. Schulte breaks into song, so softly that he can't be heard more than two seats away.

"Kidney stew and fried pig's feet—
"That's the grub I love to eat.

I guess there's no use of our going to Boston at all, the way luck's breaking against us and with all the umpires in the league ordered to give us the worst of it, we haven't a chance to take a game, even from the Doves.

"Heard a lot of talk about the champagne wine.
"But a great big stein of beer for mine.

"Here, boy, bring up that pair of cobs. Born and bred in the Rockies, sound as a dollar, catch him around the collar, hit him with a bootjack and—sold for 40 dollars to that gentleman right over there.

"Fancy foods I leave alone.
"For they ain't the kind of grub I'm used to getting down home.

"Never mind, boys. There'll be another ball game tomorrow and Schulte will play right field and bat third. Three cheers for the national pastime!"

This is followed by a few moments of staring out the window into the dark night. Then, if he is one of his rare poetic moods:

"This baseball season soon will end,
Or else I'm a liar;
Then I'll go back to Syracuse
And drive my old Wildfire.
Against the fastest horse there
My old Wildfire will go
And show his heels to all of them
Upon the pure, white snow.
How glad I am the time is nigh
When reins and whip I'll wield;
'Tis easier to drive a horse
Than run around right field."

Another five minutes of staring out into the gloom. Then: "Kind of looks as if the Athletics would cop that other piece of bunting. Well, if we can recover from today's hard luck and disaster and win a few more ball games on the field and forget the ones in front of the hotels, we may still climb up to that old pennant pole.

"Just let Edward get that fall-away perfect and teach Leonard (King Cole) that the plate is only a couple of yards wide, and the swatters are not all eight-feet-two like himself, and let Harry McIntire slip that old spitter across a couple of times and John Pfeister ease a few hooks over with that left soupbone of his and pitch the bones of big Orvie's arm together and have Mordecai warming up back of the clubhouse all the time and Rich rolling a ball around in the palm of his hand, and maybe we'll get there yet.

"Course, there's not much chance for us against all that hard luck and with all the umpires leagued on the other side, but those old Cublets never quit.

"Say, if we should happen to win out against the umpires and scorekeepers and the president of the league and the President of the United States and all the governors, that World's Series would be pretty soft for us, wouldn't it? The Athletics would probably forfeit the games when they knew we were going to play.

"I've heard a lot about this Eddie Collins. I've never seen him, but I wouldn't be surprised to find out that both his legs were cut off just below the waist and that he didn't have any arms and was stone blind. Harry's spitter will make him look sick. He's never seen any good spitball pitching. He's only been up against Ed Walsh. And those Philadelphia catchers can't be much account, either. Why, Detroit runs wild on them. Yes, it does. The Tigers never get less than 46 runs against the Athletics. I guess they must just waltz around those bases.

"Talk about Coombs and Bender. What would they do with Artis or Joe or the P.L. or Frank Schulte up there?

"They've never seen any good batters except guys like Cobb, Crawford, Speaker and Lajoie. No, I guess we'll probably scare them so that they'll refuse to play."

More looking out the window.

"Put on your own gray bonnet
With the big 'C' upon it
And we'll board the Pennsylvan-i-ay.
In the town of Philly
We will knock them silly
On that first World's Series day."

"What's the matter, Joe? Some one have a pat hand? Must have grabbed 'em off the bottom, sure. Don't let them get the best of you."

But, just to argue, suppose we did get into that World's Series, and the Athletics refused to run out of the park and Bender and Coombs didn't make any attempt to faint, and Thomas and Livingstone didn't tell Mack their arms were broken, and suppose Harry's spitter wouldn't break and Orvie's arm was as badly broken as I am, and Collins should happen to catch hold by accident, of course, of one of Leonard's fast ones and we should lose a game or two or three or four. I guess we'd go off and die then. There wouldn't be anything left in life. Of course, they'd offer us the losers' end of the money, but we wouldn't accept that. No, it would be much better to starve to death. What do you think about it, Mr. Kling?"

Mr. Kling is Mr. Schulte's roommate and each is so doubtful about the sincerity of any of the other's remarks that their conversation is a guarded affair.

"Lay off me," returns John. "Your job is to get out there in right field, catch 'em when you can reach 'em, chase 'em when they go past you, throw 'em when you get 'em and hit 'em when they're over. You don't belong in the real mechanism of the team and you talk a lot too much for an outfielder. You and Hoffman and Sheckard ought to pay to get into the ballpark."

"Yes," is Mr. Schulte's comeback, "and I guess you can lay off the rest of the season. You won't have anything to do if we should happen to get into that World's Series. Just as soon as O'Day says, 'Brown and Kling for Chicago,' the Athletics will tie their legs together for fear they might forget and try to steal a base or two. You can play pool with your right hand during the games, because it will be easy for you to do all that catching and throwing with that big mitt.

"Sing, sing. What shall I sing?
I'll sing you a song about Johnny G. Kling
When Collins starts stealing the bases on him, he
Will holler to Archer, 'Help, Jimmy! Help, Jimmy!'
I wish it would hurry up and be midnight, so I could go
to bed."

Pullman Pastimes

Dawson's Reform Credited to Two Cubs

The Sporting News, Feb. 2, 1911

Last year the Cubs had mighty good-looking youngsters on their training trip; "good-looking" referring more to their athletic ability than their facial beauty, although some of them might have been classed as comely. They showed so much merit in the practice down at New Orleans that Manager Chance had to do a lot of thinking before letting them out; in consequence, they stayed longer than is usual. Some of these recruits were not "city broke" and it became the duty of the veterans to teach them things about street, parlor and table manners.

One pitcher in particular—we will call him Dawson because it's such a pretty name—was new to the habits and customs of the great world. It's a safe bet that he never saw a hotel before he went to West Baden. We're too tired to look it up but we firmly believe he must have stayed at home while his bush league team was traveling and his home must have been a cave. At any rate, he didn't know how to start putting on any clothes but his baseball uniform and his use of table weapons was original, to say the least. The man who made seven million dollars on that combination necktie and mop invention would have been able to sell this recruit any amount of these goods, provided the ties were flaming scarlet and pale pink with heliotrope stripes.

Now, ball players are not a mean lot at all. When something like this breaks in, they carefully refrain from hurting its feelings by unkind remarks. Rather, they go about the work of reform in the most gentle manner possible. Among themselves they will ask "Where did this circus get the new clown?" or "Where is the sword swallower from?" But they don't fling their superiority in his face. However, it generally becomes necessary to take action to make the poor object human, especially when he demonstrates at the outset that he and a bath tub are only casual acquaintances.

To return to Mr. Dawson, Schulte and Sheckard appointed themselves a committee of two to make a man out of him. They got along so well that he was able to consume a meal of victuals without adding anything to the color scheme of his trousers before he was sent back for "more seasoning." Which reminds us that Charley Dryden originated this one on him: "Why did Dawson get this pepper and salt suit?" "I'm sure I don't know, Mr. Dryden. Why DID Mr. Dawson get that pepper and salt suit?" "So he could wear it two seasons."

There was a quick jump out of Montgomery one afternoon and dinner had to be eaten on the way to Birmingham. Sheckard, Schulte and Dawson sat down at the same table, design on the part of Schulte and Sheckard and accident on Dawson's, for he didn't care what celebrities dined with him. The two celebrities ordered large steaks; so did Dawson.

Sheckard came right down to the point while the meat was on the fire.

"Frank," he said to Schulte, "I've been watching you eat for three years and I haven't been able to catch onto the way you do it. Why, you can finish in ten minutes a meal it would take me an hour to eat. And it's all because you have the knack of getting your food all in a bunch and then getting it all in your mouth in a hurry. You could really leave the dining room after the first mouthful and then go back in the other car and finish your supper at leisure."

"Yes," admitted Schulte, "I know I don't waste any time at table. I learned a long time ago that it doesn't pay. I attribute my speed to the ease with which I can use a knife and I'll bet there isn't another man on the ball club who can get a plate full of food from the table to his mouth as fast as I can without spilling a lot of it."

The dialogue was continued until the waiter returned. Then the lecture became an illustrated one. Before he had eaten anything, Schulte ordered some wheat cakes and when they came he started a wonderful exhibition of the conservation of time. Three wheat cakes, a quarter "chunk" of a large steak and four or five French fried potatoes were rolled up together by the aid of a knife and fork and delicately conveyed to the mouth, the knife alone being used for cartage. There wasn't room for all of it between the right fielder's lips, but most of it made an entrance and the balance was suspended on the knife until available space within the mouth was found.

Mr. Sheckard expressed his admiration of the feat. But Dawson just looked. It's one cinch that he was disgusted, for he didn't wait to finish what was before him. At breakfast in Birmingham next morning, he sat with the manager and Joe Tinker and Archer and it was noted and reported that he had become acquainted with a fork and was getting more friendly with it every moment. Ever and anon, he looked at Schulte's table, then turned away with an expression of horror. Frank of Syracuse and James of Columbia got no credit for their labor, but they had started Dawson on the road to "recovery."

"We saved his life," remarked Sheck. "If he had kept up that clip he surely would have cut his face open from ear to ear before the real season started. And he never would have made a good pitcher with only half a head."

"Oh, I wouldn't make it as strong as that," replied Frank. "There are two or three good pitchers right on our club who get along with no heads at all."

Mr. Dawson was now a friend of the fork, but he was a stranger to the barber. He shaved himself, but he hadn't endured a hair cut since Methuselah was a messenger boy. At this time, the real Cubs were playing the exhibition games, the young team having done its heavy work during the New Orleans stay. But the young pitchers were still being used.

"Dawson," said Sheckard one night, on the way from Birmingham to Memphis, "the chances are you'll work part of the game tomorrow. Chance told me that he was going to play first base. Now, two pitchers have been let out on this club for a peculiar reason: Their hair was so long and thick that P.L. couldn't see across the diamond to Steinfeldt. You know, he gives Steiny all the signs—what hop to take a ground and all of that kind of thing. If his vision is obscured, it makes him so sore that he not only releases the man responsible for his anger, but usually scalps him. If I were you I'd sell about 75 cents worth of that lettuce."

This drew a smile from the ordinarily glum countenance of Dawson, but he was relieved of half his hair the next morning and much improved in appearance.

A discussion of the cost of Pullmans came up on the way from Memphis to Nashville. Harry Steinfeldt said they were built at an approximate cost of $20,000 apiece and Ed Reulbach said they were worth at least three times that sum. Inasmuch as neither athlete had the faintest idea of what he was talking about, this debate proved very interesting. The youngsters, including Dawson, listened to it breathlessly at first, but even their interest waned when the debaters got down to such prosaic arguments as the cost of the soap used. Seeing that enthusiasm was lagging, Mr. Hofman felt it his duty to revive it.

"Boys," he said, "you ought to see the sleeping cars over in Persia where I used to live. They cost 8,000,000 pesos each; that's about three billion dollars in our money. The climate is much warmer there and there are no roofs on the cars. Every berth is built out in the open air and each one is 200 miles from its nearest neighbor. The space between is filled with beautiful beechnut groves, gardens of underground moose plants and lakes of hair tonic. The porters always travel around the cars in electric runabouts and it takes the slow ones two years to make up all the berths. Wire screens are built over the berths, but at that, the occupants would die of suffocation it they didn't carry strychnine guns with which to shoot the elephants that try to make their beds on top of these screens."

"Yes," added Mr. Sheckard, "and the dining cars they use over there are nothing short of miraculous. You could put three deserts of Sahara into one of them and still have room for the forests with which they are decorated. The waiter rides in on a camel to take your order and he can't serve you inside of eight years, even if both he and the camel get humps on them."

To all of which the kids listened intently; and they probably wondered if insanity was the keynote of success in the big leagues.

The Rustlers Go Marching Through Georgia

Boston American, March 15, 1911

AUGUSTA, GA.—JUST A WEEK AGO TO-DAY THE RUSTLERS ARRIVED at Augusta and it is the opinion of every man on the squad that the week has been well spent. Up to yesterday the weather was ideal, and there is no reason to believe that yesterday's chilly unpleasantness will be repeated. But the cold air and slight mist failed to stop the Regular rehearsals and it will take a lot of worse weather than that to break up Manager Tenney's plans. The men were up early this morning ready for another hard day's labor. The usual morning batting and fielding practice was on the card with a game between the Regulars and Yanigans[1] booked for the afternoon.

Manager Stouch of the Augusta team informed Tenney that it would not be probable for his club to meet his team before Saturday, but this did not bother Fred much, as the present system is rapidly rounding the athletes into form.

The news that Pitcher Cecil Ferguson would not be with the Rustlers was heard with sorrow in camp for Fergy is a great favorite with the other players. Also, he is recognized as a good pitcher and the Rustlers realize that they can't probably be as strong without him as with him. Ferguson thinks his services are worth more than his contract calls for and he is reluctant to give up his job as salesman for a Boston plumbers supply house.

It must be a pretty good job he has if it can keep him away from the pastime which pays salaries that are not to be sneered at. The bunch is still hoping he will change his mind and it is probable he will be unable to resist the call of the game when the real season opens.

Poet Collins,[2] being informed that President Russell[3] was tired to death with the showing so far of his recruits, thought it proper to express William Hepburn's sentiments in verse. So he took his pencil in hand and dashed off the following masterpiece:

"Hurrah, hurrah," the magnate said, said he,
"Hurrah, hurrah," they all look good to me,
"Right now I'd like to bet we will finish one or two or three,
"While we are marching through Georgia."

Mr. Collins said the word "Marching" should be capitalized, explaining that it meant spending the month of March, just as Wintering means—"Oh, well, you know what it means."

The five athletes, Clark, Burke, Perdue, Collins and Rariden, who had their heads shaved,[4] have been dubbed the "convicts," and they certainly do look the part. Mr. Burke is sorry he fell for it now, but his sorrow won't hasten the return of his hair, which was one of his chief beauties. Wilbur Goode desires to inform the public that his name is pronounced just plain "good," to rhyme with "would, if he could," "stood," "hood," etc. He has been called "Goodey," "Gooda," and lots of other things and has stood for the mispronunciations long enough. He says he can't see why it is so hard to get it right, for no one ever thinks of saying "Josh Clarkee," or "Bill Burkey." The "e" in all those names is silent, as in hippopotamus. Speaking of a hippopotamus, Hub Perdue announces that he is good enough to pitch in the National League or the American, and that it will take some hard luck to keep him away from a regular berth on the staff.

Hub hasn't had a chance to exhibit any real pitching powers to date, but he surely possesses confidence, ginger and a sense of humor three times very valuable to a big league slabman.

Yesterday's game, which went to the Yanigans in six innings, 4 to 2, was marked by the fact that one pitcher worked the full route for the defeated Regulars. The pitcher was Buster Brown. He didn't exert himself a great deal but was glad to learn that he felt no ill effects from his trial gallop. Hub Perdue pitched the first two innings for the Yanigans and Chick Evans finished it up. Hub was in a tight place in the first inning and a double play saved him a lot of trouble.

Two weeks later, in a dispatch from Roanoke, Virginia, Lardner described the aftereffects of a 34–0 victory by the Rustlers over Greensboro.

Sunday at Greensboro was necessarily quiet. It would have been quiet anyhow from choice, for the players were so weary from Saturday's chase around the bases that they had no pepper to do anything but just sit around.

Peaches Graham remained in his apartments and conversed with the rats. One of them, a big fellow, told Peaches that he was a catcher on the Rodent team that plays a bunch of field mice every Saturday for a pound of cheese. His name is Trap, probably because he is a rat catcher. The manager on the team is the Pied Piper of Hamlin and he and Trap are having a disagreement over salary. So Peaches and the Rat had much in common to discuss.

Hub Perdue stood up all day because he had slept on what he called a tombstone and his feet having extended several feet over the end of it, were not as badly bruised as the rest of his body. However, there was one nice thing about that hotel. It gave you plenty to eat and the plenty was good, too, but as Hub said, you couldn't sleep in the dining room. There must have been a private eating place for the rats, for they didn't disturb the athletes at their meals.

Bill Sweeney took advantage of the holiday to catch up with his business correspondence. You know Bill is the company in the J.M. Sweeney Company, of Newport, Kentucky, which makes and sells various patent medicines. Among its productions are pills that cure colds, grippe, charley horse, mumps, measles, croup, rheumatism, gout, diphtheria, whooping cough, toothache and warts.

Notes

1. A scrub or backup player.
2. Second baseman Bill Collins.
3. William Hepburn Russell, owner of the Rustlers.
4. Lardner had noted the shaved heads a day earlier under the heading "Society Notes."Lardner told this story somewhat differently in 1931 in an article for the *Saturday Evening Post*. In that version, the aggrieved player became angry when Lardner, the game's official scorer, called an error on what he insisted was a hit.Omaha World-Herald, Bell Syndicate, June 8, 1924

I shed few tears when——guzzled himself out of baseball and when Manager Ganzel suffered worse than death—the management at Cincinnati.

The First Game

By A Athlete*

Chicago Tribune, Sept. 28, 1913

WE OUGHT TO OF TRIMMED 'EM. WHEN EGAN, THE BIG SLOB, SAID I WAS out at second he musta been full o' hops, the big boob. I like t'know where he was at las' night, the big bum. Some o' them umps oughta be on the chain gang, the big boobs.

Matty pitched wrong to Collins. That little bum couldn't hit a curve bull with a mattress. Matty's been pitchin' long enough to know how to pitch, but sometimes he pitches like a damfool. I wisht he'd let me tell him somethin.' But d'ya think he'd listen to me? He knows it all. He oughta knew he didn't have speed enough no more to get one past that guy.

Wisht Mac had let me wallop when I had the big Indian three and nothin' that time. 'Member? Merkle was on third base. I looked 'round and Mac gives me the sign to take one. That's rotten baseball, I think. I took one that I could of hit out o' the park. Then the big Indian hooks one on me and I missed. Then I'm lookin' for another hook and he comes with a fast one. And the Catfish calls me out. That last one was a foot outside. If I'd a known he was goin' to call it on me, I'da hit that one out o' the park. The big bum.

Then there was that third innin' decision, when Egan calls me out at second, the big slob. Barry missed me that far. I wouldn't lie about It. He missed me that far. If I'da been out, I'd never opened my clam. But Barry missed me that far. The big slob. He was lookin' out in right field

*Unassisted.

somewheres. Barry missed me that far. Bet if you was to go to Barry now and ast him, he'd come through and say he missed me that far. The big rummy. I'm glad we don't have them umpires in our league. No wonder Milan steals bases. He's probably out all the time, but the umps is lookin' out the window. Why Barry missed me that far.

I ain't no pitcher, but I bet I know as much about pitchin' as some of them pitchers. Ja see what Matty handed Collins? He slips him a fast one right over the heart when all he had to do was hook one and Collins woulda fell dead. Matty's been pitchin' fifty years and he don't know no more'n a baby. McGraw'd oughta tell some of them guys somethin.' But no, he sits on the bench and don't say nothin' till the inning's over. And then it's too late.

'Member when Merkle was on third base? I'da busted 'er up right there if Mac had let me alone. But he makes me take one when I had the big Indian three and nothin.' That first one came right over and I coulda hit it out o' the park. But, no, I had to stan' there and take it. Then he comes across with a hook and I missed it. And then I'm lookin' for another hook and he comes with a fast one and Klem calls it on me. The big rum. It was a mile outside. But if I'd knew he was goin' to call it on me, I coulda hit it 'way out o' the park. Some o' them umps oughta be on the chain gang.

How long's this Egan been umpirin'? I thought Finneran was the worst I ever see, but this Egan's got him skun. Didja see what he pulled on me? Mac tells me to steal and down I goes. Schang makes a perfect peg, but I give 'im the hook and Barry missed me. Egan says: "Yer out." I says: "What fer, you big rum?" He walked away. He knew damwell what I'da said to him if he'd stuck around. He walked away and didn't give me no chance to say nothin.' Barry missed me that far. The big, no-good slob.

Matty's been pitchin' a hundred years, but he don't know no more about pitching 'n some kid. He goes and hands Collins a fast one when the old hook woulda knocked him dead. His fast one ain't what it was. It's straight as a string and it don't hop. But he goes and slips it to Collins and that's jes' what Collins was layin' for. At that, it was a wild pitch. It was six feet over Collins' head, but he was jes' lucky enough to meet it. No wonder them Athletics wins the pennant every year. I never seen a team have the luck break for 'em like it does for them big slobs.

We'da got 'em, though, if Mac'd left me alone when Merkle was on third base. The big Indian had me three and nothin,' and I wanted to take my wallop. I knowed he wouldn't have nerve enough to hand up three hooks, and I knowed the first one was a-goin' to be a fas' one. But I looked at Mac and he shook his head no. He makes me take the first one and it's a straight one, right over the heart. Then the big Indian hands me a hook and I swung at it 'cause it'd been a strike anyway. Klem was callin' 'em all strikes anyway. So I swung and missed, and then he comes back with a fast one when I'm lookin' for another hook, and the stuff's off. I took it and Klem says it's a strike. Mighta knew he'd call 'em all strikes. It was that far outside.

Bender pulled a boner at that. He oughta walked me and took a chance on Larry. But he got away with it, the big lucky slob. But he never woulda got away with it if it hadn't a-been for Mac and then Klem callin' that third strike on me.

An' didja see what Egan done to me? Where'd they get them umpires. They oughta be peddlin' eggs, the big boobs. Barry missed me that far.

We'll get 'em tomorrow. Big Rube'll make 'em quit like dogs, the big, lucky rums. They was ready to quit today, only Egan and Klem wouldn't give 'emno chancet.

Watch me tomorrow. Plank's pie for me. I'm liable to knock a couple men dead in them bleachers. We'll fix 'em. the big, lucky slob. Rube'll make'em look sick.

Ja see that doll in the box back o' our bench? She couldn't keep her eye off o' me. We'll get 'em tomorrow, the yellow, quittin' dogs.

Cubist Baseball

Chicago Tribune, June 9, 1914

A SELDOM.

A White Sox base hit, a base hit with a man on third base is a seldom. Is strange to. Is a curiosity. Is sincerely fainting to fans. Why not once in awhile? Or why? The time to make a base hit a White Sox base hit is too late or later. The whole thing is unconscious.

THE PITTSBURGH.

A Dutchman and first place first place in April May. No sooner. A series a series with New York was abominable. A little speed is a necessity altogether but not a necessity because it did not. Now where are they at? The system of pitching curving hurling no good where speeding base running and weakening at bat is absence. Hopelessly now maybe and maybe hopeful and worrying because knocking.

THE SPITBALL.

The spitball is nastiness and not talk about is polite. It breaks it breaks red it breaks red it breaks white it splashes. Batting hitting and fielding throwing erring red erring is spitball fault. Suppose a miss and running stealing. Catching throwing wilding and center field. Scoring and is spitball fault. Suppose disease germ and contagion making everybody sicking and doctor bill. Abolition is leading.

A ANNUNCIATOR.

Might as well say enthusiastically hull house hot house grapes Lou Houseman Frank John Henry Van Dyke dog house summer house house of correction. Might as well say anything nothing unintelligent unintelligible. Buy a program a program five cents.

THE FEDERAL.[1]

Butt in butt in butt in. Spend filthy and make everybody else spending I should worry. Expenses up flagpole high tree high sky high and receivings down low down well down hell down. Welcome. The Federal. How long. Cause a whole thing joke.

A DISASTROUS.

Umpire is disaster. Rotten. Awful rotten. Get rid of them all is favorable. All wrong system is all wrong. Decide plays should be by fans by fans in the stands by fans in the bleaching.

FUNGOS.

Nothing flat nothing quite flat and more and more round rounder. Not smaller nothing smaller and more small than regular bat longer and narrower and fuller and thicker and thinner. White Sox can hit fungos.

CHARLIE MURPHY.[2]

He was president is he president? Out or In? Say sell out maybe sell out maybe not sell out. If not sell out ought to have solding. If not solding out maybe running million back into shoestring and maybe lose shoestring too. Contemplation miserable. Weeping writing arithmetic.

A SWEATER.

A sweater is a sweet and a sweeter a hat and a hitter. An undercoat and an overcoat and a banquet. A sweater is more comfort comfortabler than a collar in winter snowing and not in summer shining. A world's champion an Athletic a Philadelphia sweater is ugliness, homeliness like whole world's champion uniforming. Why not Athletics buy new suits new uniforming new sweating sweaters? Poverty.

A GEORGIA.

Crack a rib crack a pennant hopes. Ty Gers is Ty Cobb. Ty down grandstand or Ty steal it. Detroit first place crack a rib third place heal a crack rib second place going up. Suppose he dying buried. Where is Detroit then? In Michigan.

THE WEST SIDE PARKING.

All the seats are needing renewing. A white dress is ridiculous. A peanut a peanut a popcorn a pop a cigar a tobacco chocolates and bon bons. Aisles narrow corns. Pillars, invisible. Beautiful, beautiful, beautiful, beautiful. $800,000.

A ONE HIT.

Nothing a one hit is nothing minus. A White Sox pitching monotonous. Everybody's doing it. There is no gratitude in similar. Scant glory and a sore souper. Aching arm and vacuum of victories. Benz a bear Scott a skillful scamp and Cicotte a cyclone. Succotash. One hit and no hit simply unexcitement and mildly without consequence. More victories.

ROLLIE ZEIDER.

A hook a hook a hook a Hoosier hook a prominent proboscis a promontory a preeminence a peninsula. But a good guy a funny fella a perfect poker player a bear base runner and a hook slide. A hook.

Notes

1. The Federal League began operations as a competitor to the American and National leagues in 1914, which led to a rise in players' salaries for a brief time. The league ceased operations after two seasons.

2. Despite owning the Chicago Cubs when they won their only two World Series titles, Murphy became widely disliked and eventually sold the team.

RING'S ALL-STARS

Peaches Graham

Nine Men in One

Boston American, May 28, 1911

"You know," remarked the Sporting Editor, "we get out a Sunday paper once a week, so you needn't sit there doing nothing just because there's nothing in sight to do. There's a certain amount of space to fill and you're supposed to be one of the fillers. How about interviewing a catcher?"

With that, he turned away without giving the reporter a chance to reply. So the poor slave knew that it was up to him to make the perilous journey to the Rustlers' clubhouse again and run the risk of arousing the displeasure of one or more of the idols of the town. The necessary nickel was borrowed with no little difficulty, but the journey to Walpole street was made without mishap.

As luck would have it, the only occupants of Mr. Neary's hotel, aside from the proprietor, were Messrs. Rariden and Graham, whom the reporter recognized as catchers by their receptive attitude. The Rariden party looked far less formidable, so it was to him that the reporter spoke first. But the result showed clearly the truth of the old saw—"Appearances are deceiving."

"What do you want, boy?" came from the lips of G. Graham, whose countenance now looked kindly by contrast with that of his brother artist. "Perhaps I can do something for you if it isn't too hard, and if you refrain from asking foolish questions. If you have come to find out find out how to catch, you're wasting your time. I'm a baseball team—do you get me? A BASEBALL TEAM."

"There he goes," remarked Mr. Rariden, as he started out the door, while the reporter wondered how anyone ever got sufficiently familiar with him to call him "Bill."

"That's what I am—a baseball team," screamed Mr. Graham, and the reporter, anxious to humor him, smiled and nodded sympathetically.

"I won't be interviewed on how to catch," the famous athlete continued. "That's just like trying to tell how to enjoy a sirloin steak—one's as simple as the other. But if you'll give me all your attention and not misquote me, I'll tell you how I became a baseball team and some of the things I did when I was one."

The reporter was cute enough to know that it was too late to stop now, so he produced a cigarette paper and prepared to take notes, and the nine ballplayers in one got the following out of his system:

"First and foremost, even you must have noticed that I am called 'Peaches,' not merely 'Peach.' Why? Because I'm plural. Ty Cobb is sometimes spoken of as the 'Georgia Peach,' but never as the 'Georgia Peaches.' That's because he's just a fielder and only one peach. I'm a catcher, a pitcher, four infielders, three outfielders, one utility man and one pinch batter. That's why I'm Peaches, a whole crop of them.

"I ought to speak of myself as 'we' and 'us,' but if I did, folks probably would call me conceited. I started playing professional ball when I was four years old. You know I was born in Persia and came to this country in one of the old fashioned balloons when I was a little over two. For the next year and a half I worked as a drummer on a street car, selling transfers, but the pay was small, a little over $140 a week, and that was just enough to keep me in collars.

"Our trolley line passed a ball park in Spring Valley, Ill., and it was there that I first saw the national pastime. The Spring Valley team used to play the Kewanee club once every Saturday and two or three times on Sunday. There was great rivalry between the two towns and sometimes pools of as much as 18 cents were up on the games.

"My entrance into the sport was the old story—one of the stars hurt and no one to take his place. I volunteered and played shortstop one day so much better than the star that they sent the latter to jail for thirty years.

"Well, it happened that there was a contagion of croup in Spring Valley that year and every ball player on the local team was taken with it except me. I had my throat removed before I came across the ocean.

"The manager was in an awful fix, or thought he was till I came to the rescue. He had all those games scheduled with Kewanee and had posted a forfeit of $2,300,456 to insure his playing them.

"That night the epidemic hit the town, he came to me and said:

"'Peach'—I was only one, then—'I'm up against it right. I've got some ball games booked and no players.'

"'Manager,' I answered, 'why do you say you have no players when I'm still here?'

"'But you can't play the whole game,' said he.

"'Try me and see,' said I. For in those days I had more confidence than money.

"So the posters advertising the next day's game were left up, and when the hour for the battle arrived the park was crowded. Every fan present was a doctor, for all the rest of the people had croup. The Kewanee team came on the field joyously for the players thought the series would be forfeited. You can imagine their astonishment when they saw me in uniform. Their astonishment turned to alarm when they witnessed the spectacle of one man going through fielding and batting practice and warming up to pitch besides.

"Perhaps batting practice was hardest for me to master because it came first. I hadn't yet worked up the full speed of my legs by running, so I had to pitch slow ones from the box so I could get to the plate in time to pick up a bat and hit at them. It didn't do to miss any swings or foul off any for that meant I had to run back to the grandstand and tire myself out.

"I was so fast on my feet by the time the bell rang for my fielding practice that it was simple for me to hit a ground ball or a fly and then run to one position or another and field it. I completed my preparations by acting as catcher to warm up to the pitcher, and as pitcher to do the warming up.

"The game being played on the Spring Valley grounds, the Kewanee team was first to bat. I cut loose two fast ones at the first hitter. He missed them both. The effort of getting from the box to the catcher's position was proving terribly wearing and I knew I couldn't stand it long. So then and there, I invented a new delivery, which I called the Round Trip. It was thrown with a caressing, beckoning motion. When the ball wasn't hit, it came right back into my hands.

"You can imagine that this delivery was a great saving of energy. I couldn't use it continually, else it would lose its power to deceive, but I signed myself for it six or seven times an inning.

"The Kewanee hitters were helpless before me for eight innings. Meanwhile, I had been unable to score a run myself. The hit and run play was my favorite, but you must know it was hard to pull off. To accomplish it I had to start from first toward second, or second toward third, while the pitcher was winding up and at the same time dash for the batter's box, so I would be on hand when the ball came up to the plate.

"The result was I couldn't get set to swing. Several times I missed connections at the plate and the catcher would throw me out at some base or other because I had been obliged to stop short on my journey on the base lines to return to bat.

"So the count was 0 to 0 when the ninth inning came. In Kewanee's half my real troubles started, for the opponent began to bunt. It took me by surprise and eight runs were scored before I thought out a way to spoil the play. I finally did it by mastering the pop-up delivery, which forces batsmen to hit little pop flies.

"I wasn't feeling exactly gay when I finally got the side retired and went in to try to overcome that lead of eight runs. But the owner of the team had bet a pound of chocolates on the result, and I knew I was as good as dead if I failed him in this crisis.

"Did I get the nine tallies? Yes, I did and not by hitting them over the fence, either, although I could tell you I did that and get away with it. I beat Kewanee at its own game—I began to bunt.

"First I laid down a perfect one and easily beat it out. Then I bunted another one and sped for first, yelling at the top of my voice, 'Second base, second base.'

"The pitcher, who picked up the ball turned to throw to second but no runner was trying for that bag. Then he started to throw to first. I immediately changed my course and started for second. He did finally throw to first, and the first baseman made the catch just as I landed at second.

A big argument followed. Kewanee claimed it had one out.

"'But who's out?' I boldly asked.

"'You are,' was the reply.

"'Where and why am I out?' said I.

"'At first base because the ball got there before you did,' said they.

"'How do you figure that?' said I. 'I left first base as soon as the succeeding batter bunted, and here I am safe at second. Nobody tried to get to first, so there was no play there.'

"Well, the umpire and the Kewanee players finally had to admit the force of my argument. The game went on and on the next bunt the pitcher unhesitatingly threw to third. I dashed to first and no effort was made to stop me. Thus the bases were full and the rest was simple, so long as I could keep the bunts on the ground.

"I succeeded beyond my wildest dreams. All I had to do then was lay down nine straight bunts and just touch the plate with my foot after each one, thus scoring one tally at a time until I had nine.

"The Kewanee boys were a pretty sick looking lot when it was all over. But the Spring Valley owner was tickled to death and that night, on the way home, he took a crisp dollar bill out of his pocket and handed it to me. 'This is a loan,' he said, 'but there'll be no interest.'

"There isn't much left to tell. I beat them three more games and then they quit coming. Finally it got so bad that no team would play at Spring Valley unless I left town. So I left and since then I have been forced to play only one position at a time, which, as you may imagine, is pretty tame sport."

"A posse of cops is on the way here," remarked Jimmy Neary.

Mr. Graham paid no heed.

"Yes, sir, I have played first, second, third, fourth and fifth and all the outfield positions, and I have pitched and caught."

"And what do you like best to do, Mr. Graham?" asked the reporter.

"Smoke a pipe," said they.

Ping Bodie's Monologue

Chicago Tribune, Oct. 3, 1913

If you live on the south side you undoubtedly have gathered from the billboards the info that Frank Bodie has sold his soul—i.e., decided to go on the stage. If the city series is over before Oct. 10, which we earnestly hope and pray will be the case, Ping will open a four days' engagement at the Alhambra on that date. If the city series is not over by Oct. 16, which heaven forbid, Ping will appear the first three days of the following week. So reads his contract, which also provides that his stunt be a monologue, duration not set, subject matter, baseball.

The management assures us that Ping will not be the only thing on the program. The subject, baseball, is a broad one, as is the monologuist. But the chances are that Ping will confine himself to those details or phases of the sport with which he is most familiar. He might talk interestingly on "Pilfering the Pillows" or "Sliding Into the Sacks." However, without having seen him for some weeks—not since he accepted the theater's generous offer—we guess that his real theme will be "Inside Ball" and that he will handle it about as follows:

"I can sure hit that old pill.

"Some of you smart guys say I'm solid ivory. Do I look like solid ivory? Or solid anything?

"I don't pull no more boners than some of you smart guys. But Ping's to blame for everything. If Buck misses a fly ball Ping had oughta run in and caught it. It wasn't Buck's fault. It was Ping's. If I'm on first base and they give me the hit and run and I go down, and Larry misses his swing and I get throwed out twenty feet, it's 'Whadd'ya think o' that big bonehead trying to steal?'

"I don't have to play ball in this league. If they don't want me, why don't they can me? I know where I can go and play ball, in the bushes where they pay the money. Couldn't hurt my feelings by canning me. I wish they would let me out. I should worry.

"I can sure hit that old pill.

"I guess I'm a bonehead. I don't know anything. But the guys that talk that way about me are sitting on the bench while I'm out there working and winning ball games. How many games would we have won from Philly if Bonehead Bodie had been on the bench?

"I don't have to play ball. I can go out there to San Fran any time I want to and get a job. But I'll be playing ball long after some of those smart guys have got the can.

"If I'm so rotten, why do the play me? They've got a lot of fellers sitting on the bench, doing nothing. They don't have to use me. Let 'em put me on the bench. Iskabibble.

"I can sure hit that old pill."

One of the most feared sluggers of the 1910s, Frank Stephen Bodie was nicknamed Ping for the sound of his fifty-two ounce bat hitting the era's dead ball. When he played with the Yankees, Bodie was Babe Ruth's first roommate and delivered a classic response when asked about the arrangement. "That isn't so. I room with his suitcase."

Matty

The American Magazine, August 1915

What kind of a pitcher *was* he? Where do you get that "was" stuff? When he's through it'll be time enough to talk about him like he was a dead corpse.

Oh, yes, I've heard all that junk they been pullin,' but wait till he comes acrost with four or five good games in a row! Then you won't be able to find nobody that even suspected he was done. The boys that's been writin' subscriptions on his tombstone will pretend as if they was just jokin' and really knowed all the time that he was the same Matty, only a little bit slow about gettin' started.

He's been all in a whole lot o' times before this, if you b'lieved what you read. They was namin' his pallbearers as far back as 1909, and they been layin' him to rest every year since, but when they've drove back down-town from the cemetery they've always found him standin' on Main Street, big as life and wonderin' whose funeral it was. You've heard the old sayin' that a cat's got nine lives? Well, boy, Matty makes a cat look like a sucker.

They called in a special doctor to look him over last time their club was West. He couldn't sleep and they was a pain in his left arm, and his neck kept stiffenin' up on him. The special doctor says it was some kind o' nervous trouble. Great stuff! If Matty was goin' to be bothered with nervousness I guess it would of happened before this. If he was nervous every time he had a chanct to be, he'd of broke both legs ten years ago, knockin' his knees together.

Besides, do you think a stiff neck and a pain in the left arm and unsomnia is goin' to stop him from pitchin'? His brain ain't diseased and he's still got the same right hand he always used. And as for the not sleepin,' I never noticed him out there on the field with his eyes shut.

So give him a chanct. The year's still young yet. Leave him get warmed up and then give him a good look. This spring was hard on old soupers. You can't expect a bird that's been hurlin' the pill in the big show fifteen years to set the league afire in June when May mistook itself for Feb'uary. Don't talk like he was gone and ask me what kind of a pitcher was he. If you want to know what kind he is, I'll try and tell you.

You're just bustin' in, kid, and I don't know if you're there or not. But if you don't want to be huntin' a job as floorwalker or night watchman somewheres in a few years, the best thing you can do is find out all the bad habits Matty's got and then get 'em yourself. It must be a awful strain on McGraw, handlin' this bird. Unless he keeps his eye right on him, he's li'ble to sneak up to his room some night and play a game o' checkers. That ain't all, neither. If McGraw is ast out to somebody's house or to go to the theayter, he don't enjoy himself on account o' worryin.' How does he know that Matty ain't smokin' a see-gar or lappin' up a dish of ice cream? Mac can't never leave the hotel without bein' a-scared that Matty'll buy a magazine and read it. And I s'pose that oncet or twicet a season he goes all to pieces and chews a stick o' gum.

I don't know if the job o' managing him is worse off the field or on. When he's out there in the box he seems to lose his head entirely. With the bases loaded, they's always a chance that Matty'll make a guy pop out instead o' whiffin' him. Then, with a man on first base and nobody down and the batter sent up to bunt, he's li'ble to forget he's a pitcher and try to do a little fieldin.' You can't never tell. Maybe he'll run in and grab the bunt and force a man at second base, instead o' standin' still like a see-gar sign and hopin' somebody else'll do somethin.' Yes, sir, I bet McGraw don't sleep a wink on the road, or to home neither, from frettin' over this guy and wonderin' how he can learn him somethin.'

They's a flock o' pitchers that knows a batter's weakness and works accordin.' But they ain't nobody else in the world that can stick a ball as near where they want to stick it as he can. I bet he could shave you if he wanted to and if he had a razor blade to throw instead of a ball. If you can't hit a fast one a inch and a quarter inside and he knows it, you'll get three fast ones a inch and a quarter inside and then, if you've swang at 'em, you can go and get a drink o' water. He plays a lot o' this here golf, and I bet if they'd let him throw at the hole instead o' shootin' with a club, he'd stick 'em in there just as often as he wanted to from sixty foot away.

I ain't tryin' to make you believe that he don't never fail to pitch where he's aimin' at. If he done that, he wouldn't be here; he'd be workin' agin the angels in St. Peter's League. But he's got ten to one better control than any guy I ever seen, and I've saw all the best o' them. If one o' these here Af'can dodgers[1] seen him comin,' he'd either quit his job or fix it up for a A.D.T. boy[2] to notify his widow, 'cause even iv'ry'll crack if it's hammered steady enough.

I s'pose when he broke in he didn't have no more control than the rest o' these here collegers. But the diff'rence between they and him was that he seen what a good thing it was to have, and went out and got it, while they, that is, the most o' them, thought they could go along all right with what they had. Well, you don't see many o' Matty's schoolmates pitchin' in the league now, do you?

Matty didn't never take the trouble to tell me nothin' about himself and how he got wise. Maybe he seen in the Bible where it says about you should not ought to ride a good horse to death. That's it, ain't it? He's just like one o' these here misers. They get a-hold of a lot of money and then they don't let none of it go, except just enough to keep 'em from starvin.' Instead o' money, Matty got a-hold of a curve ball and there here fadeaway and a pretty fair fast one and a slow one and a bunch o' control, and then he locked it all up and took a little bit of it out to spend when nec'sary, only most o' what he's been spendin' is control, which he's got the most of, and which it don't hurt him none to spend it.

Take him in a common ordinary ball game, agin a average club, and every day pitchin,' and what he's tryin' to do is stick the first one over so's he won't have to waste no more'n one ball on one batter. He don't stick it over right in the groove, but he puts it just about so's you'll get a piece of it and give the Giants a little easy fieldin' practice. If the Giants gets a flock o' runs and goes way out in front, he'll keep right on stickin' that first one over, and maybe he'll allow a little scorin.'

But if the guy workin' agin him is airtight, and the game's close, and you get a couple o' men on and a base hit'll do some damage, he unlocks his safe and pulls out some o' the real stuff he's got and lets go of it. Maybe the curve he'll show you ain't as good as some you've saw, but it'll come where you can't get a good hold of it. Or if it's a fast one you don't like, that's what you'll get, and even if it ain't as fast as Johnson's, you'll find that it comes past you a couple of inches higher or lower or this side or that side of where you could wallop it good. Or maybe you'll see this fadeaway that he got up himself, and it's about as easy to hit as this here Freddie Welsh.[3]

That's the way he works in a reg'lar game, when they ain't much dependin' on it. He don't really pitch till he's got to, and then he sure does pitch. The rest o' the time, he's puttin' that first one where they either got to hit at it or have a strike called on 'em, and leavin' it to the guys back of him to take care o' what's hit. That's why he's been good so long and that's why he's goin' to be good a whole lot longer. And McGraw's smart enough to help him save himself. You don't see Matty pitch one day and warm up the next. When he's pitched his game, he's through till everybody else has tooken their turn, except oncet in a while, when the race gets hot, and then maybe he works a innin' or two and pulls out one o' the other guy's games, besides winnin' his own. But that ain't often. He ain't never tried to make no Walsh[4] out of himself, and if he had tried, the Giants might maybe of win one more pennant, but they wouldn't have no Matty round to keep 'em in the race for another.

McGraw treats him just right to keep him a-goin.' But I don't give Mac no credit for that. He'd be a sucker if he didn't. It's pretty soft for a manager to be able to set down by the fire in January and say to himself: "Well, we got to win ninety-five games next season to cop. That means that Marquard, Tesh-er-eau and my young fellas must grab seventy between 'em. Matty's twenty-five is already in." When it comes to a World's Serious, that's diff'rent. If the Giants wins it, it means more dough, not only for the players but for the owners o' the club. And as soon as it's over, Matty's got five months to rest up. So he's in there about every other day, and he ain't savin' himself neither. He's still tryin' to get that first one over, but they's a lot more stuff on it than when he's pitchin' a reg'lar season game. He ain't so willin' to let guys get on the bases and he's ready to do more work himself and leave less to his club. Well, the Giants hasn't set the world afire beatin' the clubs in our league, but where'd they of been in any one o' them Serious's if 'twasn't for Matty? And if you want to make them Ath-a-letics or the Boston Red Sox either one give you the horse laugh, tell 'em Matty's easy to beat.

He's been beat in every big Serious he's been in, except in 1905, when he was still a kid. You know what he done then, don't you? He worked three o' the five games and if goose eggs had of been worth a dollar a dozen, the Ath-a-letics could of quit playin' ball and toured the world in a taxi. As I say, he's been beat in all the other big Seriouses, but I seen the most o' them and I'm tellin' you that most o' the games he lost was a crime.

You know, kid, I'm with our league all the while and pullin' for 'em whatever they're up agin. But they's been times when I felt like as if we should ought to be ashamed to take the money, when I couldn't holler none over winnin' because I was feelin' so sorry for this big guy we'd beat and didn't have no business to beat. A man can't have no real time celebratin' when he knows that if the luck had of broke even, he'd be payin' off. At least, I can't.

I wisht you could of saw him tryin' to hold a jubilee that night in Boston a couple o' years ago. The Red Sox winnin' give me a even two hundred bucks, but all the while I was spendin' it, I felt like as if it didn't belong to me. Honest, I'd of almost gave it back and seen the Boston club licked rather than to of saw 'em win me the dough the way they did. If I'd of stayed in Chi and just read about it in the papers, it wouldn't of been so bad. But to be right there and see him get robbed o' that decidin' game, and the honors that should ought to of been his'n, was enough to upset my stomach and take all the joy out o' the two hundred.

You remember how it was: They'd win three apiece, and the Giants was full o' the old con-feed-i-ence, while the Boston club's dauber was way down in their shoe. They'd had the Serious all but won, three games to one, and then New York had came along and evened it up. McGraw has Matty ready and Stahl[5] uses this young Bedient, who'd pitched a whale of a game a few days before, but was nothin' but a kid and up agin a tougher proposition than a kid should ought to be ast to face.

Well, I'll have to slip it to young Bedient. He was about as nervous as if he was pitchin' to the batters in practice. You'd of thought, to watch him, that it was a exhibition game and that the only crowd there was a few hundred rubes from Jones's Crossing. He wasn't a bit scared, and he give 'em a awful battle. The Giants got a run off'n him; I don't remember when or how they done it. Anyway, they done well to get a run and the bugs should ought to of throwed their money at him when he was tooken out.

I think it was the eighth innin' when Bedient got through. The run scored off'n him was the only one o' the game, 'cause Matty was workin' like they ain't nobody else can work. With that "1" up on the score board, it looked all over. I didn't think they'd tie it up in a thousand years. Well, in Boston's half o' the eighth, or seventh, maybe it was, Stahl or Wagner happened to get a hold of one and cracked it for two bases. They was down to the tail-end o' the battin' order and I think one was out before the ball was hit. Whoever the guy was, he was left there till they was two out and it come Bedient's turn to hit. Stahl took him out and sent up this Henriksen. He was a new one on Matty, and it's a good thing for him he was. The count come to two and two on him and then he reached outside the plate and cracked one down the third base line. It was a two-bagger and the score was tied up. Hooper went out and the innin' was over. The crowd went crazy, but, honest, I figured that was the last run the Boston club would ever get and that it was just a question o' time till the Giants grabbed another and settled it.

Stahl sticks Woodie in to pitch and they was no scorin' did on neither side in the ninth. But in the tenth, Murray catched one o' Woodie's fast ones on the nose and drove it a mile into center field. It come near clearin' the whole works and bein' a home run. It didn't make no diff'rence, 'cause Merkle was there with a base hit and Murray scored. They was two down when Meyers come up, and he hit one just as hard as he ever did in his life. The ball come right at Woodie and hit him in the side. He was game enough to pick it up and throw it to first base, but I bet he couldn't of pitched another ball if his life had of depended on it.

They helped him off'n the field and they was a pretty sad lookin' gang. They figured just like me: That they'd been lucky to tie up the score in the seventh or eighth, or whenever it was, and that they had about as much chance as a rabbit o' doin' it again.

Then come the mess that spoiled my meals for a week, and me pullin' my head off for Jake and the boys. Jake sends Engel up in Woodie's place for two reasons: because he's a better hitter, though Woodie ain't no bum at that, and because Woodie prob'ly couldn't of walked that far. Well, Engel sends a fly ball to center field and it should ought to have been the one out. But it wasn't. Snodgrass drops it and Engel pulls up at second base. Now they're playin' for one run and Hooper goes up to sacrifice. I never seen no better pitchin' than Matty done to him, and they was no more chance of him buntin' the first two fair than they was o' hittin' 'em out o' the park. I think he missed one entirely and fouled the other one. Then Matty gives him one that he couldn't meet right and he flies out to center. Snodgrass held onto this one. Well, I guess Matty must of gave Hooper everything he had, 'cause when Yerkes came up, the old control was gone. He walked him, and everybody went completely nuts, 'cause it was Speaker's turn.

The Giants crowded round Matty to give him a chance to rest up, and when he begin pitchin' to Speaker, he wasn't wild no more. He slips Spoke one that he had to take a wallop at, but all he done to it was pop it up in the air. The ball was foul and I guess I could of jumped out o' the stand and ran out and catched it. But Merkle thought Meyers was goin' to get it, and Meyers thought Merkle was goin' to get it and finally Matty seen they wasn't neither one goin' to get it, so he started after it, but he was too late. The ball fell about fifteen feet this side o' the coaches' box, and when it come down they wasn't nobody under it.

I could hear Spoke yellin': "Pretty lucky that time, Matty! But I'll crack the next one." Speaker's all right, but he should not ought to of called Matty lucky, not that day. If he was lucky that day, I'd hate to see him when things was breakin' agin him.

This foul ball o' Spoke's was the third out by rights. The game should ought to of been over, and me settlin' with the guy I made the bet with. But the way things had came off, they was one out, and men on second and first and Speaker up, and I don't care who the pitcher is, he can't fool this here Speaker all the time. Spoke done just what he said. He cracked one and before Devore could get it back to the infield, Engel was acrost with the tyin' run, and another base hit would finish it.

I'd like to of knew what Matty was thinkin' about. He could be excused if he said "Golly," even if he don't pitch on Sundays. But if he was sore, he kept it to himself, and he went out there and give Lewis what he had left. He was just as wild as when he was pitchin' to Yerkes; that is, he wasn't exactly wild, but he wasn't given' 'em no good balls to hit and he couldn't bunk 'em into swingin' at bad ones. Lewis stood up there just as patient as Yerkes, and Matty walked him, too.

That's about all they was to it. The bases was choked and Gardner wound it up with a fly ball to Devore, which should ought to of been four out. Yerkes come in with the winnin' run and I guess Devore's throw is just about gettin' to the plate now.

That's how lucky Matty was in that last game in Boston, and that's a fair sample o' the luck he's had in all these World's Seriouses except the first one. If a rotten pitcher got a dose like that, I wouldn't slip him no sympathy. But it sure does give me the colic to have them things happen to a guy that don't have to take off his hat to nobody, and then see the bugs run round hollerin,' "Well, I guess we can beat the great Mathewson!" Yeh, they can beat him with a whole blacksmith's shop full o' horseshoes.

What makes him the pitcher he is? I been tellin' you he's got a lot o' stuff, but so has other pitchers. They's others that's got pretty near as good control, but they ain't nobody that's got the combination like him and knows how to use it like he does, he's a tight-wad with his stuff, and they're spendthrifts. Some pitchers can't see Wagner come up without wantin' to whiff him and hear the crowd cheer. Matty don't want to whiff him. He'd a lot rather have him hit the first ball and pop it up in the air. Cheers won't do them others no good when their souper's gone. They can't live on what the crowd thought about 'em that time they made the big Dutchman take a drink o' water. Then, he's got this fadeaway that none o' the rest has got, not like he's got it.

His curve is somethin' like Joe Wood's, only now he ain't as fast as Woodie; that is, not all the time. Maybe he's got enough real speed left to cut loose a little of it two or three times a day, and he don't never cut it loose till he's got to. But goin' along that way, he'll have his fader and his curve and his speed when I and you is thinkin' about who we'll call on for pallbearers.

But his fadeaway and his curve and his fast one and his control wouldn't none of 'em be worth near what they is worth if he didn't know all they is to know about pitchin.' It's the old bean that makes him what he is. When somebody cracks one off'n him, it ain't because he guessed wrong; it's because the ball come about a inch away from where he was goin' to put it; maybe it slipped or somethin.' When this young Saier has pulled one over the fence on Matty, McGraw don't say:

"Why didn't you keep it outside?" or "Why didn't you do this or that?" He knows Matty was tryin' to do the right thing and knowed what was the right thing to do. He don't have to sit up nights with him, learnin' him. And it ain't nec'sary for Matty to buy one o' these here books on "The Art o' Pitchin.'" He could write a whole sacklapedia on that, and then not tell half he knows.

He's just a little ahead o' the rest o' the gang in them things—stuff, when he wants to use it, and control and noodle. And besides that, he's a ball player. They ain't no danger of him hittin.'400, but at that they's a whole lot worse hitters right on his club. When he goes up there with a bat, it ain't just to kill time or because it's his turn. His intention is to get on, or to push somebody else round, or drive in a run, and he don't swing at everything that's pitched or keep his bat on his shoulder neither, like some o' them pitchers. He's been known to crack one when it counted, and you don't often look in the papers and see "So-and-So batted for Mathewson in the ninth."

He ain't no speed marvel on the bases, yet I've saw him steal a base and slide into it, too, where most pitchers would be a-scared they might soil their pants. As for fieldin' his position, he's just as good as anybody, and to have him in there is just like havin' five men on the infield. He can grab the bunts, and after he's grabbed 'em he knows where to peg 'em. He don't never fail to cover first base when he should ought to, and you'll always find him backin' up plays where some pitchers would be takin' a afternoon nap. Yes, sir, he's a ball player, and that's a whole lot more'n you can say for a lot o' guys that's gettin' by with a pitchin' job.

They tell me Matty is some golf player. I didn't never have no golf bat in my hands, and I don't know nothin' about the game, but I bet all I got that if he plays it at all, he plays it good. Yes, sir, I bet he's a whale of a golf player, and they tell me they ain't no ball player can touch him in a checker game. Well, I've did some checker playin' myself, and I know they ain't no thick skull can get away with it. It's a game that takes brains, and Matty's the boy that's got 'em. But if he was to tackle blind man's buff instead o' checkers or golf, he'd make a go of it. That's the kind o' guy he is. They's nothin' he's tried that he didn't keep tryin' till he could do it and do it good.

It didn't surprise me none when he turned down that trip round the world. I guess none o' the boys that made the trip is any the worse off for it, but it wouldn't of been in line with Matty's dope to go along. It would just of meant spendin' some o' the stuff he's savin' up to keep him in the league. Every game he pitched would of been just one less game he'd of had left in him, and the games wouldn't of got him nothin' neither. And still, he'd of had to let himself out and do some real pitchin,' or else the crowds would of got sore on him. At that, I guess he'd of went if he hadn't of made the first part o' the trip with 'em, the trip from Cincinnati out to the Coast. They tell me that he had to shake hands with two thirds o' the population of every burg they stopped at. The bugs flocked round the train, and the hotels, all yelpin' for Matty, and it was up to him to let 'em see him, or they'd of been a riot. Well, they all had to shake hands with him, and by the time a couple o' million hicks has shooken your hand, you feel like as if your old souper was beginnin' to go back on you. I s'pose that's the way you'd feel; I don't know, 'cause I wasn't never pestered much with people tryin' to slip me the glad hand. Matty prob'ly says to himself: "London and Paris and Egypt and Rome and them other towns on the schedule is all big towns with big populations. If half them populations shakes hands with me, I won't have no more arm left than a angleworm." So he scratched his entry, and you can't blame him. And I bet McGraw didn't coax him much.

When the Giants don't want Matty no longer, he can make a world trip of his own, and go acrost the ocean in his own yackt. But I guess by that time they'll be runnin' trains acrost or maybe the oceans will of went dry.

College man, war hero, Christian Gentleman (one of his actual nicknames), Christy Mathewson may have been the most beloved baseball player of his time. While players like Ty Cobb, Honus Wagner, and Walter Johnson were admired—Lardner, as we will see, did a similarly appreciative article on Cobb for *The American Magazine* in 1915—they were not adored in the manner of Mathewson.

This affection led Lardner to write one of the greatest of all opening paragraphs of a World Series game, after the final game of the 1912 Series, which appears in the following section.

Lardner's hopes that Mathewson's poor start in 1915 was nothing to worry about were not realized. He won only eight games and lost fourteen, a great comedown from his 24–13 record the year before. The following year he was traded to the last-place Cincinnati Reds, which inspired Lardner to write the following, which is sometimes mistaken for an obituary. Mathewson died in 1925 of tuberculosis, which he developed after a chemical gas attack during a World War I training exercise in France.

> My eyes are very misty
> As I pen these lines to Christy;
> Oh, my heart is full of heaviness today.
> May the flowers ne'er wither, Matty
> On your grave in Cincinnati,
> Which you've chosen for your final fadeaway.

Notes

1. An example of the casual racism of the times. African dodger, also called Hit the Coon, was a popular carnival game in the early 20th century in which an African

American man would stick his head through a canvas curtain and attempt to dodge balls thrown at him by customers.

2. Telegram delivery boy.

3. Welsh lightweight boxer who had won the world championship a month earlier.

4. White Sox pitcher Ed Walsh, who was dominant for seven seasons, but whose career was shortened by injuries.

5. Red Sox manager Jake Stahl.

Mordecai Brown

The Reporter's Friend

Chicago Tribune, Dec. 6, 1916

So far as the big leagues are concerned, Mordecai Brown, they say, is through. If the gentleman from Indiana needs consolation he may perhaps find a bit in the knowledge, hereby imparted to him, that there is more genuine regret among the baseball writers of our beautiful city over his departure than over the passing of any other athlete whose work has redounded to the honor and glory of Chicago, etc.

Brownie was not only the most popular ball player among the ball players, but also far and away the most general favorite among the scribes. That he was liked and respected by fellow members of the Cub pitching staff, speaks volumes for his personality. Pitchers, most of them, are human, and being human, not apt to harbor the tenderest feelings toward those indubitably their superiors in skill. Brownie was, in his top form, the best of a great pitching corps. Yet every other member of that corps was sincerely fond of him.

However, we are dealing here with his standing with the newspaper men. He was not a live source of news, owing to his reticence. His modesty prevented his giving us valuable columns about himself for use on rainy days. But he could tell, by looking at you, when you were broke. While you were still wondering from whom to borrow five, he would come up and, without saying a word, hand you ten.

As present day salaries go, he was drawing far less than he was worth. But he was drawing far more than were we reporters, and knowing this, it hurt him to see us spend. So he did most of the spending for us, against our protest, of course.

We (editorially, this time) never fully appreciated Brownie, though he had done us innumerable favors, until one day in the season of 1909. It was the last day in Philadelphia and the next stop was New York. We had a tentative engagement in New York at eight-thirty that evening, an engagement we wanted to keep. In the forenoon, we sought out Charlie Williams, the walking time-table.

"Is there a train out of here for New York round six o'clock?" we asked.

"Why?"

"I want to get there early this evening."

"So does everybody else," said Charley.

(Everybody was young then.)

"There's a train on the Reading at six," continued Charley, "and we can get it at the station near the park if the game's over in time. I asked Shettsline[1] if he'd start early, but he wouldn't. So we'll just have to take chances."

The P.L. tried to help by selecting as pitcher, Orval Overall, one of the fastest workers in the pastime. Big Orrie proved fast, and effective, too, but no more effective than Sparks of the enemy. At the end of the eleventh, we had given up hope of an extra evening on Broadway, for it was a quarter after five and everything pointed to a long tie.

But in their twelfth, the desperate Cubs fell on the Philly pitcher and drove home two runs, the first of the game.

"Now, if he can just hold 'em!" we said, and started making up the box score. But the Phillies weren't quite through. The top of their batting order was up, and whoever was lead-off man singled. Otto Knabe walked and the next gentleman sacrificed. A base hit would tie it again, and two such wretched hitters as Magee and Bransfield were in line.

Out went Orrie and in came Brown; the tying run on second base; the crowd barking at him; one out, and Philadelphia's best batsmen to face.

Six balls Brownie pitched, all curve balls, the curvin'est balls we ever saw. And three times apiece Magee and Bransfield swung, and missed three times apiece.

While the Cubs hurriedly changed their clothes, we as hurriedly wrote our story; a story about one per cent as good as the game warranted.

On the train we shook the three-fingered hand.

"Much obliged, Brownie. I've got a date in New York this evening."

"So Charley said," replied Mr. Brown. "Come on in the next car and I'll buy you dinner."

Mordecai Brown, nicknamed Three Finger because of a farm-machinery accident when he was a child, won 239 Major League games, and his 2.06 lifetime earned-run average remains the sixth lowest in Major League history. Lardner's affection for him was returned as shown in a letter Brown wrote to *The Sporting News* when his "Pullman Pastimes" articles were reprinted in 1941.

"That series should bring back many happy memories for us old-timers," wrote Brown, who was then 65 and operating at a gas station in Terre Haute, Indiana. "Ring is dead, but all of us old Cubs remember his rich humor and the youngsters of today should get a kick out of his yarns, too."

Note

1. Phillies owner Bill Shettsline.

Noisy Johnny Kling

Chicago Tribune, May 16, 1917

The Cubs nicknamed him Noisy because they thought he didn't say anything. But the gentlemen who hit against the Cubs when he was catching, especially the very young gentlemen, will tell you there was never a catcher who could tie him for garrulity.

"His line of chatter was effective, too," says Larry Doyle.[1] "McGraw warned me, when I broke in, that Kling would try to get my goat, but the warning led me to expect that he'd be rough, the way the catchers had been in the Three Eye, when I was a recruit there. They'd called me a busher and criticized my appearance and found fault with my swing. They had me so mad for a while that I couldn't do myself justice, but when I got up nerve enough to give them as good as they sent, I had them stopped.

"Kling was different. His stuff kept my mind off what I was trying to do, and a kid facing pitchers like Brown, Pfiester, Overall, and Reulbach didn't have much chance unless he concentrated.

"First time I met him was at the Polo Grounds. I came up in the first inning.

"'Well, Boyle,' he said, 'I bet you're glad to get away from Davenport.'

"I told him my name was Doyle and that I came from Springfield.

"'Did you always hit left-handed out there?' he asked me, and while I was saying yes, Brownie slipped over a fast ball for a strike.

"'You stand up like a veteran,' said Kling. 'From the way you hold your bat and stand, I'd say a curve ball wouldn't bother you any more than a fast one.'

"I told him I didn't know which I'd rather hit.

"'Well,' he said, 'we'll have to try you on both and find out. This next one's going to be a curve.'

"Then I thought to myself that it would surely be a fast one and I got all set to crack it. It was a curve and I guess I pretty near broke my bat swinging.

"'You thought I was stringing you,' said Kling. 'You don't know me. But you took a mighty nice cut at that ball and now I know you're stuck on the fast ones. So I guess we'll have to slip you another curve.'

"So Brownie pitched another curve and again I was looking for a fast one and I was out on strikes.

"'Don't blame that on me,' said Kling. 'It's your own fault if you don't take a fella's advice.'

"When I got back to the bench, McGraw asked me whether Kling had been riding me. I told him no, that he'd talked all right.

"'You forget that!' said Mac. 'Don't pay any attention to anything he says. He's John Bull.'

"But I made a nice play on the infield before it was my next turn to hit, and when I went up there again he wasn't talking curves and fast balls. It was all about what a beautiful stop that was, and how I looked as if I'd make good whether I could hit or not. And he made me foul out on a bad ball in the pinch.

"I'll bet it was two or three series before I learned not to listen to Kling and I don't know how many base hits I lost by my innocence. But I have one consolation. I know of other players in the National league who didn't get wise to him for years, and they weren't bushers either."

An exceptional defensive catcher, Kling played a key role on the Cubs' world championship teams in the first decade of the twentieth century. He was also an excellent pool player and several times threatened to stay home and play pool if the Cubs didn't meet his contract demands. In 1909, he actually did so and won the world's championship of pool while the Cubs finished second in the National League. He returned the following season and the Cubs won the pennant.

Note

1. The best second baseman in the National League in the 1910s, Doyle famously said "It's good to be young and a Giant."

Casting Stones with Rollie Zeider

Chicago Tribune, May 23, 1917

THE EDITOR HAS JUST RECEIVED A LETTER WHICH BEGINS, "DEAR OWL-eyes." A person who remarks on or calls attention to the physical defects of others is perhaps unworthy of notice, but in this case the writer is so manifestly unfair that we cannot resist brief comment in defense of ourself and in justice to humanity.

In the first place, any one who has seen us will testify that our eyes are probably our most elegant feature. They are large and lustrous, expressive to a remarkable degree and practically irresistible. They compare very favorably with Anna Held's.[1]

In the second place, the person who wrote the letter is not what you could call a Venus D. Milo. If we look like an owl, he certainly is twins with a parrot.

The person who wrote the letter is said to be a ball player, but has never succeeded in proving it. At different times he has occupied every position on the infield, but has failed to make good in any. He cannot field, he cannot run bases, he cannot think; in fact, he cannot do nothing except ridicule the personal appearance of others.

This person was at third base for a time, but the occupants of the third base seats objected to the management, claiming their view of the shortstop was shut off by his profile. He was shifted to second base, but his nose prevented the center fielder from seeing the first baseman. He moved to first base, but the other infielders were so affected by his appearance that they could not throw straight. This person is now trying to play shortstop and making a mess of it.

This person once batted .300 and stole over 100 bases in the Pacific Coast league. It must have been a fine league.

Some enemy of Mr. Comiskey's recommended him to the White Sox and he tried to play the different infield positions on the south side. He made a mess of it. He is now with the Cubs. His limbs look like a wishbone. He came from Auburn, Ind.

Many believe he is a German spy.

A utility infielder who played all four positions, Zeider is one of a handful of players who played for all three Chicago teams—the Cubs, White Sox, and Whales of the short-lived Federal League. One of the fastest players in the game, Zeider's 49 stolen bases for the White Sox in 1910 remained the club record for seventy-six years.

Note

1. A popular stage and film actress who achieved notoriety as a spurned mistress of Florenz Ziegfeld.

Casey in the Field

Chicago Tribune, May 13, 1919

CHARACTERS.

Casey Stengel, Pittsburgh's right fielder.

Bugs, occupants of the right field stand.

Time—Sunday P.M.

Place—Cubs' park.

ACT 1.

[Pittsburgh's first inning is over. Casey, who has flied out, dons glove and sun glasses and takes his position.]

A Bug—Well, Casey, back to Pittsburgh for you.

Casey—O, I get three more raps today yet.

Second Bug—You ought to be wrappin' bundles somewheres.

Casey—That's what you do week days, I guess.

Second Bug—Do you want me to git you a job?

Casey—Not in a cheap dump like where you work at.

Second Bug—Well, we wouldn't have you there.

Casey—Well, don't worry. I ain't lookin' for a job.

Second Bug—Well, you will be lookin' for one if you don't wake up.

Casey—You should worry.

Third Bug—What do you wear them glasses fur, Casey? Can't you see without them glasses?

Fourth Bug—He's gittin' old. His eyes is failin' him.

Casey—You should worry.

ACT 2.

[Pittsburgh's fourth inning is over. Casey has been called out on strikes *and is pretty mad about it.]*

A Bug—Never mind, Casey. You can't hit 'em if you can't see 'em.

Second Bug—Was the sun in your eyes, Casey? You ought to wore them glasses up to the bat.

Casey—Some of them umpires ought to wear them, I guess.

Third Bug—Why, what's the matter with them umpires, Casey?

Casey—O, they's nothin' the matter with them umpires. They're the best in the league except when I'm up there.

Third Bug—You better shet up or they'll tie a can to you.

Casey—You better shut up yourself.

ACT 3.

[Pittsburgh's sixth inning is over. Casey has been left on second base, which he reached on an error by Pick.]

A Bug—Well, Casey, you didn't git fur.

Second Bug—That was some hit, Casey. It pretty near got past the second baseman.

Casey—I should worry as long as I get on there.

Third Bug—Douglas is makin' a monkey out of you.

Casey—Well, you're makin' a monkey out of yourself.

Third Bug—And you're makin' a monkey out of yourself, too.

Casey—Well, I get paid for makin' a monkey out of myself. But you pay to get in here and make a monkey out of yourself. That's the difference between you and I.

Third Bug—You won't be gittin' paid very long if you keep this up.

Casey—You should worry.

ACT 4.

[Pittsburgh's eighth inning is over. Casey has flied out again.]

A Bug—Well, Casey, you've had your four raps. You're some rapper.

Casey—Well, I either get out or I don't get out, so I should worry.

Third Bug—Your team's licked, Casey.

Casey—Yes, we never win when I don't hit.

Third Bug—You must be in last place, then.

Fourth Bug—How'd you like to play on a good team, Casey?

Third Bug—It wouldn't be a good team no more with him on it.

Fifth Bug—Well, good-by, Casey. Don't forgit to write.

Fourth Bug—He can't write.

Casey—Neither can you.

TY COBB MEETS BABE RUTH

In his time, Ty Cobb was widely considered to be the greatest player baseball had ever known.

His time ended in 1920.

That was the year Babe Ruth was sold by the Boston Red Sox to the New York Yankees, abandoned pitching, hit 54 home runs, and changed baseball forever. (No player in the history of the game had previously hit as many as 30 home runs in a season, and a decade earlier, Cobb himself had led the American League in home runs with nine.)

It's hardly a surprise that Lardner was fascinated by Cobb. His competitiveness and intelligence, particularly while running the bases, made him Lardner's kind of player and "Tyrus," his deconstruction of every aspect of Cobb's brilliance, is the longest article he ever wrote about a single player.

Lardner's admiration was so great that in "Ty Cobb's Inside Baseball," he presents a partial history of the Detroit Tiger star's many arguments with players and fans, some of which became physical, and somehow manages to forgive them all. Readers will have to decide for themselves whether he proves his case.

Ruth, on the other hand, represented everything Lardner disliked about the sharp turn baseball took after he single-handedly put an end to the dead ball era. "Baseball hasn't meant much to me since the introduction of the TNT ball that has robbed the game of the features I used to like the best," he wrote.

But Lardner was hardly immune to the national fascination with Ruth, and his charming "How to Pitch to Babe Ruth," which he wrote during the 1920 season, shows Lardner if not leading the parade at least joining it.

By 1929, when Ruth had become the stuff of legend, Lardner surrendered again by making Ruth the subject of one of his fantasies in which he has him strolling the streets of Baltimore with H.L. Mencken and summoning up the ghosts of Edgar Allen Poe, O. Henry, and one of the Karamazov brothers.

Tyrus

The American Magazine, June 1915

Sit down here a while, kid, and I'll give you the dope on this guy. You say you didn't see him do nothin' wonderful? But you only seen him in one serious. Wait till you been in the league more'n a week or two before you go judgin' ball players. He may of been sick when you played agin him. Even when he's sick, though, he's got everybody I ever seen skun, and I've saw all the best of 'em.

Say, he ain't worth nothin' to that club; no, nothin'! I don't know what pay he's gettin,' but whatever it is, it ain't enough. If they'd split the receipts fifty-fifty with that bird, they wouldn't be gettin' none the worst of it. That bunch could get along just as well without him as a train could without no engine.

He's twicet the ball player now that he was when he come up. He didn't seem to have no sense when he broke in; he run bases like a fool and was a mark for a good pitcher or catcher. They used to just lay for him when he got on. Sully[1] used to tell the pitchers to do nothin' but waste balls when he was on first or second base. It was pretty near always good dope, too, because they'd generally nail him off one base or the other, or catch him tryin' to go to the next one. But Sully had to make perfect pegs to get him even when he knowed beforehand that he was goin.' Sully was the boy that could make them perfect pegs, too. Don't forget that.

Cobb seemed to think they was only one rule in the book, and that was a rule providin' that nobody could stay on one base more'n one second. They tell me that before he got into the South Atlantic League he was with a club down there in Georgia called the Royston Rompers. Maybe he thought he had to keep on rompin' up here.

Another thing was that he couldn't hit a left-hander very good. Doc White used to make him look like a sucker. Doc was a fox to begin with, and he always give you just what you wasn't lookin' for. And then, his curve ball was somethin' Ty hadn't never saw before and it certainly did fool him. He'd hand Cobb a couple o' curves and the baby'd miss 'em a foot. Then, when he was expectin' another one, Doc'd shoot his fast one right past his chin and make a monkey out of him.

That was when he first come up here. But Ty ain't the guy that's goin' to stay fooled all the time. When he wises up that somebody's got somethin' on him, he don't sleep nor do nothin' till he figures out a way to get even. It's a good thing Doc had his chancet to laugh when he did, because Cobb did most o' the laughin' after a couple o' seasons of it. He seen he couldn't hit the curve when it was breakin,' so he stood way back in the box and waited till it'd broke. Then he nailed it. When Ty'd learned that trick, Doc got so's he was well pleased when the balls this guy hit off'n him stayed in the park.

It was the same way with every pitcher that had his number when he first busted in. He got to 'em in short order and, before long, nobody was foolin' him so's you could notice it. Right now he's as good agin left-handers as he is agin regular fellas. And if they's any pitcher in baseball that's got him fooled, he's keepin' the fact well concealed.

I was tellin' you what a wild base-runner he was at first. Well, he's still takin' chances that nobody else takes, but he's usin' judgment with it. He don't run no more just for the sake o' runnin.' They was a time when the guy on the base ahead of him was afraid all the time that he'd get spiked in the heels. But no more o' that. They's no more danger of him causin' a rear end collision, providin' the guy ahead don't blockade the right o' way too long.

You may not believe it, but I'll bet most o' these here catchers would rather have somebody on second base when Ty's on first base than to have him on first base alone. They know he ain't goin' to pull no John Anderson[2] and they feel pretty safe when he can't steal without bumpin' into one of his own teammates. But when the track's all clear, look out!

All my life I been hearin' about the slow, easy-goin' Southerner. Well, Ty's easy-goin' all right—like a million-dollar tourin' car. But if Southerners is slow, he must be kiddin' us when he says he was born down South. He must of came from up there where Doc Cook pretty near got to.

You say you've heard ball players talk about how lucky he was. Yes, he is lucky. But it's because he makes his own luck. If he's got horseshoes, he's his own blacksmith. You got to have the ability first, and the luck'll string along with you. Look at Connie Mack and John D. and some o' them fellas.

You know I ain't played no ball for the last few years, but I seen a lot of it played. And I don't overlook no chancet to watch this here Tyrus. I've saw him agin every club in the American League and I've saw him pull more stuff than any other guy ever dreamed of. Lots o' times, after seein' him get away with somethin,' I've said to myself: "Gosh, he's a lucky stiff!" But right afterward, I've thought: "Yes, and why don't nobody else have that luck? Because they don't go out and get it."

I remember one time in Chi, a year or two ago. The Sox was two to the bad and it was the ninth innin.' They was two men down. Bodie was on second base and somebody hits a single to center field. Bodie tries to score. It wasn't good baseball to take the chancet, because that run wasn't goin' to do no good without another one to put with it. Cobb pegs to the plate and the umps calls Bodie out, though it looked to everybody like he was safe. Well, it was a bad play of Bodie's, wasn't it? Yes. Well then, it was a bad play o' Cobb's to make the throw. If Detroit hadn't of got the best o' that decision, the peg home would of let the man that hit the ball go to second and be planted there in position to score the tyin' run on another base hit. Where if Ty had of played it safe, like almost anybody would, the batter'd of been held on first base where it would take two base hits or a good long wallop to score him. It was lucky for Ty that the umps happened to guess wrong. But say, I think that guy's pretty near smart enough to know when a umpire's goin' to make a rotten decision.

O' course you know that Ty gets to first base more'n anybody in the world. In the first place, he always manages to hit better'n anybody. And when he don't hit safe, but just bounds one to some infielder, the bettin's 2 to 1 that the ball will be booted or throwed wild. That's his luck, is it?

No, sir. It's no such a thing. It's his speed. The infielder knows he ain't got no time to spare. He's got to make the play faster'n he would for anybody else, and the result is that he balls it all up. He tries to throw to first base before he's got the pill to throw, or else he hurries the throw so much that he don't have no time to aim. Some o' the ball players round the league says that the scorers favor Ty and give him a base hit on almost anything. Well, I think they ought to. I don't believe in handin' a error to a fella when he's hurried and worried to death. If you tried to make the play like you do for other guys, Ty'd beat the ball to first base and then you'd get a hot call from the bench for loafin.'

If you'd saw him play as much baseball as I have, you wouldn't be claimin' he was overrated. I ain't goin to come right out and say he's the best ever, because they was some old-timers I never seen. (Comiskey, though, who's saw 'em all, slips it to him.) I just want to tell you some o' the things he's did, and if you can show me his equal, lead me to him and I'll take off my hat.

Detroit was playin' the Ath-a-letics oncet. You know they ain't no club that the Tigers looks better agin than the Ath-a-letics, and Cobb's more of a devil in Philly than anywheres else. Well, this was when he was battin' fourth and Jim Delahanty was followin' him. Ty singles and Del slips him the hit and run sign on the first ball. The ball was pitched a little outside, and Del cuts it down past Harry Davis for a single to right field. Do you know what Cobb done? He scored; that's all. And they wasn't no boot made, neither. Danny Murphy picked the ball up clean and pegged it to Davis and Davis relays it straight home to Ira Thomas. Ty was there ahead of it. If I hadn't o' been watchin' close, I'd o' thought he forgot to touch two or three bases. But, no, sir. He didn't miss none of 'em. They may be other guys that could do that if they tried, but the diff'rence between them and Cobb is that he done it and they didn't. Oh, I guess other fellas has scored from first base on a long single in the hit and run, but not when the ball was handled perfectly clean like this one.

Well, here's another one: I forget the exact details, except that the game was between the White Sox and Detroit and that Tannehill was playin' third base at the time, and that the score was tied when Cobb pulled it. It was the eighth innin.' He was on first base. The next guy hits a single to left field. Ty, o' course, rounds second and starts for third. The left fielder makes a rotten peg and the pill comes rollin' in. Ty has the play beat a mile and they ain't no occasion for him to slide. But he slid, and do you know what he done? He took a healthy kick at that rollin' ball and sent it clear over to the grand stand. Then he jumped to his feet and kept on goin.' He was acrost the plate with the winnin' run before nobody'd realized what he'd did. It's agin the rules, o' course, to kick the ball a-purpose, but how could the umps prove that this wasn't a accident? Ty could of told him that he thought the play was goin' to be close and he'd better slide. I might o' thought it was a accident, too, if that had of been the only time I seen him do it. I can't tell you how many times he's pulled it, but it's grew to be a habit with him. When it comes to scorin' on kicks, he's got this here What's-His-Name—Brickley[3]—tied.

I've saw him score from second base on a fly ball, too, a fly ball that was catched. Others has did it, but not as regular as this guy. He come awful near gettin' away with it agin a little while ago, in Chi. They was also somebody on third when the ball was hit. The guy on third started home the minute Bodie catched the ball and Ping seen they was no chancet to get him. So he pegs toward Weaver, who's down near third base. Cobb's at third before the ball gets to the infield. He don't never hesitate. He keeps right on goin' for the plate. Now, if Weaver'd of been able to of intercepted the ball, Ty'd of been out thirty feet. But the throw goes clear through to the third baseman. Then it's relayed home. The gang sittin' with me all thought Ty was safe. I don't know about it, but anyway, he was called out. It just goes to show you what this guy's liable to do. You can't take no afternoon nap when he's around. They's lots of other fast guys, but while they're thinkin' about what they're goin' to do, he's did it. He's figurin' two or three bases ahead all the while. So, as I say, you don't get no sleep with him in the game.

Fielder Jones used to tell us: "When that bird's runnin,' throw the ball somewheres just's soon as you get a-hold of it. I don't care where you throw it, but throw it somewheres. Don't hold onto it."

I seen where the papers says the other day that you outguessed him. I wasn't out to that game. I guess you got away with somethin' all right, but don't feel too good about it. You're worse off now than you was before you done it because he won't never rest till he shows you up. You stopped him oncet, and just for that he'll make you look like a rummy next time he plays agin you. And after he's did it oncet and got even, he'll do it agin. And then he'll do it agin. They's a lot o' fellas round this league that's put over a smart play on Tyrus and most of 'em has since wished they hadn't. It's just like as if I'd go out and lick a policeman. I'd live to regret it.

We had a young fella oncet, a catcher, that nailed him flatfooted off'n first base one day. It was in the first game of a serious. Ty didn't get on no more that day, but he walked the first time up the followin' afternoon. They was two out. He takes a big lead and the young fella pegs for him agin. But Tyrus was off like a streak when the ball was throwed, and about the time the first baseman was catchin' it, he was slidin' into second. Then he gets a big lead off'n second and the young catcher takes a shot for him there. But he throws clear to center field and Ty scores. The next guy whiffs, so they wouldn't of been no run if the young guy hadn't of got so chesty over the precedin' day's work. I'm tellin' you this so's you won't feel too good.

They's times when a guy does try to pull something on this Cobb, and is made to look like a sucker without deservin' it. I guess that's because the Lord is for them that helps themselves and don't like to see nobody try to show 'em up.

I was sittin' up in the stand in Cleveland one day. Ty was on second base when somebody hits a fly ball, way out, to Birmingham. At that time, Joe had the best throwin' arm you ever see. He could shoot like a rifle. Cobb knowed that, o' course, and didn't feel like takin' no chancet, even though Joe was pretty far out there. Ty waits till the ball's catched and then makes a bluff to go to third, thinkin' Birmy'd throw and that the ball might get away. Well, Joe knows that Cobb knows what kind of arm he's got and figures that the start from second is just a bluff, that he ain't really got no intention o' goin.' So, instead o' peggin' to third, he takes a quick shot for second, hopin' to nail Cobb before he can get back. The throw's perfect and Cobb sees where he's trapped. So he hikes for third. And the second sacker—I don't think the big Frenchman was playin' that day—drops the ball. If he'd of held it, he'd of had plenty of time to relay to third and nail Ty by a block. But no. He drops the ball. See? Birmy'd outguessed Ty, but all it done for him was to make him look bad and make Ty look good.

Another time, a long while ago, Detroit needed a run to win from the Sox. Ty gets to first base with one out. Sully was catchin.' Sully signs for a pitch-out and then snaps the ball to first base. Ty wasn't lookin' for it and he was caught clean. He couldn't get back to first base, so he goes for second. Big Anderson was playin' first base and he makes a bum peg. The ball hits Cobb on the shoulder and bounds so far out in left center that he didn't even have to run to get home. You see, Sully'd outguessed Ty and had pulled a play that ought to of saved the game. Instead o' that, it give the game to Detroit. That's what hurts and discourages a fella from tryin' to pull anything on him.

Sometimes I pretty near think they's nothin' he couldn't do if he really set out to do it. Before you joined the club, some o' the boys was kiddin' him over to Detroit. Callahan was tellin' me about it. Cobb hadn't started hittin.' One o' the players clipped the averages out o' the paper and took 'em to the park. He showed the clippin' to Ty.

"You're some battin' champ, Ty," he says. "Goin' at a .225 clip, eh?"

Tyrus just laughed at him. "I been playin' I was one o' you White Sox," he says. "But wait till a week from to-day. It'll be .325 then."

Well, it wasn't. No, sir! It was .326.

One time, in 1912 I think it was, I happened to be goin' East, lookin' for a job of umpirin,' and I rode on the train with the Tigers. I and Cobb et breakfast together. I had a Sunday paper with me and was givin' the averages the oncet over.

"Read 'em to me," says Ty.

"You don't want 'em all, do you?" I says.

"No, no. Just the first three of us," he says. "I know about where I'm at, but not exactly."

So I read it to him:

"Jackson's first with .412. Speaker's second with .400. You're third with .386."

"Well," says Ty, "I reckon the old boy'd better get busy. Watch me this trip!"

I watched him, through the papers. In the next twenty-one times at bat, he gets exactly seventeen hits, and when the next averages was printed, he was out in front. He stayed there, too.

So I don't know, but I believe that if Jackson and Speaker and Collins and Lajoie and Crawford was to go crazy and hit .999, this Cobb would come out on top with 1,000 even.

He's got a pretty good opinion of himself, but he ain't no guy to really brag. He's just full o' the old confidence. He thinks Cobb's a good ball player, and a guy's got to think that way about himself if he wants to get anywheres. I know a lot o' ball players that gets throwed out o' the league because they think the league's too fast for 'em. It's diff'rent with Tyrus. If they was a league just three times as fast as the one he's in and if he was sold up there, he'd go believin' he could lead it in battin.' And he'd lead it too!

Yes, sir, he's full o' that old stuff, and the result is that lots o' people that don't know him think he's a swell-head, and don't like him. But I'm tellin' you that he's a pretty good guy now, and the rest o' the Tigers is strong for him, which is more'n they used to be. He busted in with a chip on his shoulder, and he soon become just as popular as the itch. Everybody played him for a busher and started takin' liberties with him. He was a busher, too, but he was one o' the kind that can't take a joke. You know how they's young fellas that won't stand for nothin.' Then they's them that stands for too much. Then they's the kind that's just about half way. You can go a little ways with 'em, but not too far. That's the kind that's popular.

Cobb wouldn't stand for nothin.' If somebody poured ketchup in his coffee, he was liable to pick up the cup and throw it at the guy nearest to him. If you'd stepped on his shine, he'd of probably took the other foot and aimed it at you like he does now at the ball when it's lyin' loose on the ground. If you'd called him some name on the field, he'd of walloped you with a bat, even if you was his pal. So they was all stuck on him, was they not?

He got trimmed a couple o' times, right on his own club, too. But when they seen what kind of a ball player he was goin' to be, they decided they'd better not kill him. It's just as well for 'em they didn't. I'd like to know where their club would of finished—in 1907 and 1908, for instance—if it hadn't of been for him. It was nobody but him that beat us out in 1908. I'll tell you about it later on.

I says to him one day not long ago, I says:

"You wasn't very strong with the boys when you first come up. What was the trouble?"

"Well," he says, "I didn't understand what was comin' off. I guess they meant it all right, but nobody'd tipped me that a busher's supposed to be picked on. They were hazin' me; that's what they were doin,' hazin' me. I argued with 'em because I didn't know better."

"You learned, though, didn't you?" I says.

"Oh, yes," says Ty, "I learned all right."

"Maybe you paid for your lessons, too," I says.

"Maybe I did," he says.

"Well," I says, "would you act just the same way if you had it to do over again?"

"I reckon so," he says.

And he would, too, because if he was a diff'rent kind o' guy, he wouldn't be the ball player he is.

Say, maybe you think I didn't hate him when I was playin' ball. I didn't know him very well, see? But I hated him on general principles. And I never hated him more'n I did in 1908. That was the year they beat us out o' the big dough the last day o' the season, and it come at a time when I needed that old dough, because I knowed darn well that I wasn't goin' to last no ten years more or nothin' like that.

You look over the records now, and you'll see that the Detroit club and us just about broke even on the year's serious agin each other. I don't know now if it was exactly even or not, or, if it wasn't, which club had the best of it. But I do know one thing, and that is that they beat us five games that we'd ought to of copped from 'em easy and they beat us them games for no other reason than that they had this here Georgia Peach.

The records don't show no stuff like that, but I can remember most o' them games as if they was played yesterday, that is, Cobb's part in 'em. In them days, they had Crawford hittin' third and Cobb fourth and Rossman fifth. Well, one day we had 'em licked by three runs in the seventh innin.' Old Nick was pitchin' for us and Sully was catchin.' Tannehill was at third base and Hahn was switched from right to left field because they was somethin' the matter with Dougherty. Well, this seventh innin' come, as I was sayin,' and we was three runs to the good. Crawford gets on someway and Cobb singles. Jones thought Nick was slippin,' so he hollered for Smitty. Smitty comes in and pitches to big Rossman and the big guy hits one back at him. Smitty had the easiest kind of a double play starin' him in the face—a force play on Crawford at third and then the rest of it on Rossman, who wasn't no speed marvel. But he makes a bad peg to Tannie and the ball gets by him. It didn't look like as if Crawford could score, and I guess he was goin' to stop at third.

But Tyrus didn't pay no attention to Crawford. He'd saw the wild peg and he was bound to keep right on comin.' So Crawford's got to start home to keep from gettin' run over. Hahn had come in to get the ball and when he seen Crawford startin' home, he cut loose a wild peg that went clear to the bench. Crawford and Cobb both scored, o' course, and what does Ty do but yell at Rossman to follow 'em in, though it looked like sure death. Sully has the ball by that time, but it's just our luck that he has to peg wild too. The ball sailed over Smitty, who'd came up to cover the plate. The score's tied and for no reason but that Tyrus had made everybody run. The next three was easy outs, but they went on and licked us in extra innin's.

Well, they was another game, in that same serious I think it was, when Big Ed had 'em stopped dead to rights. They hadn't no more business scorin' off'n him than a rabbit. I don't think they hit two balls hard all day. We wasn't the best hittin' club in the world, but we managed to get one run for the Big Moose in the first innin' and that had ought to of been a-plenty.

Up comes Cobb in the fourth and hits one that goes in two bounds to Davis or whoever was playin' short. If he could of took his time, they'd of been nothin' to it. But he has to hurry the play because it's Cobb runnin,' and he pegs low. Izzy gets the ball off'n the ground all right, but juggles it, and then Ty's safe.

They was nobody out, so Rossman bunts. He's throwed out a mile at first base, but Ty goes all the way to third. Then the next guy hits a fly ball to Hahn that wouldn't of been worth a nickel if Cobb'd of went only to second on the sacrifice, like a human bein.' He's on third, though, and he scores on the fly ball. The next guy takes three swings and the side's out, but we're tied up.

Then we go along to the ninth innin' and it don't look like they'd score agin on Big Ed if they played till Easter. But Cobb's up in the ninth with one out. He gets the one real healthy hit that they'd made all day. He singled to right field. I say he singled, because a single's what anybody else would of been satisfied with on the ball he hit. But Ty didn't stop at first base. He lights out for second and whoever was in right field made a good peg. The ball's there waitin' for Ty, but he slides away from it. Jake thought he had him, but the umps called him safe. Well, Jake gets mad and starts to kick. They ain't no time called or nothin.' The umps turns away and Jake slams the ball on the ground and before anybody could get to it, Cobb's on third. We all hollered murder, but it done us no good. Rossman then hit a fly ball and the game's over.

I remember another two to one game that he win from us. I don't recall who was pitchin'—one o' the left-handers, I guess. Whoever it was had big Rossman on his staff that day. He whiffed him twicet and made him pop out another time. They was one out in the eighth when Cobb beats out a bunt. We was leadin' by one run at the time, so naturally we wanted to keep him on first base. Well, whoever it was pitchin' wasted three balls tryin' to outguess Tyrus, and he still stood there on first base, laughin' at us. Rossman takes one strike and the pitcher put the next one right over and took a chancet, instead o' runnin' the risk o' walkin' him. Rossman has a toe-hold and he meets the ball square and knocks it clear out o' the park. We're shut out in the ninth and they've trimmed us. You'll say, maybe, it was Rossman that beat us. It was his wallop all right, but our pitcher wouldn't of wasted all them balls and got himself in the hole if anybody but Cobb'd of been on first base.

One day we're tied in the ninth, four to four, or somethin' like that. Cobb doubled and Rossman walked after two was out. Jones pulled Smitty out o' the game and put in Big Ed. Now, nobody was lookin' for Ty to steal third with two out. It's a rotten play when anybody else does it. This ain't no double steal, because Rossman never moved off'n first base.

Cobb stole third all right and then, on the next pitch, Rossman starts to steal second. Our catcher oughtn't to of paid no attention to him because Walsh probably could of got the batter and retired the side. It wasn't Sully catchin' or you can bet no play'd of been made. But this catcher couldn't see nobody run without peggin,' so he cut loose. Rossman stopped and started back for first base. The shortstop fired the ball back home, but he was just too late. Cobb was acrost already and it was over. Now in that case, our catcher'd ought to of been killed, but if Tyrus hadn't did that fool stunt o' stealin' third with two out, they'd of been no chancet for the catcher to pull the boner.

How many did I say he beat us out of? Five? Oh, yes, I remember another one. I can make it short because they wasn't much to it. It was another one o' them tied up affairs, and both pitchers was goin' good. It was Smitty for us and, I think, Donovan for them. Cobb gets on with two down in the tenth or 'leventh and steals second while Smitty stands there with the ball in his hand. Then Rossman hits a harmless lookin' ground ball to the shortstop. Cobb runs down the line and stops right in front o' where the ball was comin,' so's to bother him. But Ty pretends that he's afraid the ball's goin' to hit him. It worked all right. The shortstop got worried and juggled the ball till it was too late to make a play for Rossman. But Cobb's been monkeyin' so long that he ain't nowheres near third base and when the shortstop finally picks up the ball and pegs there, Cobb turns back. Well, they'd got him between 'em and they're tryin' to drive him back toward second. Somebody butts in with a muff and he goes to third base. And when Smitty starts to pitch agin, he steals home just as clean as a whistle.

The last game o' the season settled the race, you know. I can't say that Tyrus won that one for 'em. They all was due to hit and they sure did hit. Cobb and Crawford both murdered the ball in the first innin' and won the game right there, because Donovan was so good we didn't have no chancet. But if he hadn't of stole them other games off'n us, this last one wouldn't of did 'em no good. We could of let our young fellas play that one while we rested up for the world's serious.

I don't say our club had a license to be champions that year. We was weak in spots. But we'd of got the big dough if it hadn't of been for Tyrus. You can bet your life on that.

You can easy see why I didn't have no love for him in them days. And I'll bet the fellas that was on the Ath-a-letics in 1907 felt the same toward him, because he was what kept 'em from coppin' that year. I ain't takin' nothin' away from Jennin's and Crawford and Donovan and Bush and Mullin and McIntire and Rossman and the rest of 'em. I ain't tryin' to tell you that them fellas ain't all had somethin' to do with Detroit's winnin' in diff'rent years. Jennin's has kept 'em fightin' right along, and they's few guys more valuable to their club than Crawford. He busted up a lot o' games for 'em in their big years and he's doin' it yet. And I consider Bush one o' the best infielders I ever see. The others was all right, too. They all helped. But this guy I'm tellin' you about knocked us out o' the money by them stunts of his that nobody else can get by with.

It's all foolishness to hate a fella because he's a good ball player, though. I realize that now that I'm out of it. I can go and watch Tyrus and enjoy watchin' him, but in them days it was just like pullin' teeth whenever he come up to the plate or got on the bases. He was reachin' right down in my pocket and takin' my money. So it's no wonder I was sore on him.

If I'd of been on the same club with him, though, I wouldn't never of got sore at him no matter how fresh he was. I'd of been afraid that he might get so sore at me that he'd quit the club. He could of called me anything he wanted to and got away with it or he could have took me acrost his knee and spanked me eighty times a day, just so's he kept on puttin' money in my kick instead o' beatin' me out of it.

As I was sayin,' I enjoy seein' him play now. If the game's rotten or not, it don't make no diff'rence, and it don't make a whole lot even if he's havin' a bad day. They's somethin' fascinatin' in just lookin' at the baby.

I ain't alone in thinkin' that, neither. I don't know how many people he draws to the ball parks in a year, but it's enough to start a big manufacturin' town and a few suburbs. You heard about the crowd that was out to the Sox park the Sunday they was two rival attractions in town? It was in the spring, before you come. Well, it was some crowd. Now, o' course, the Sox draw good at home on any decent Sunday, but I'm tellin' you they was a few thousands out there that'd of been somewheres else if Cobb had of stayed in Georgia.

I was in Boston two or three years ago this summer and the Tigers come along there for a serious o' five games, includin' a double-header. The Detroit club wasn't in the race and neither was the Red Sox. Well, sir, I seen every game and I bet they was seventy thousand others that seen 'em, or better'n fifteen thousand a day for four days. They was some that was there because they liked baseball. They was others that was stuck on the Red Sox. They was still others that was strong for the Detroit club. And they was about twenty-five or thirty thousand that didn't have no reason for comin' except this guy I'm tellin' you about. You can't blame him for holdin' out oncet in awhile for a little more money. You can't blame the club for slippin' it to him, neither.

They's a funny thing I've noticed about him and the crowds. The fans in the diff'rent towns hates him because he's beat their own team out o' so many games. They hiss him when he pulls off somethin' that looks like dirty ball to 'em. Sometimes they get so mad at him that you think they're goin' to tear him to pieces. They holler like a bunch of Indians when some pitcher's good enough or lucky enough to strike him out. And at the same time, right down in their hearts, they're disappointed because he did strike out.

How do I know that? Well, kid, I've felt it myself, even when I was pullin' agin Detroit. I've talked to other people and they've told me they felt the same way. When they come out to see him, they expect to see him do somethin.' They're glad if he does and glad if he don't. They're sore at him if he don't beat their team and they're sore if he does. It's a funny thing and I ain't goin' to sit here all night tryin' to explain it.

But, say, I wisht I was the ball player he is. They could throw pop bottles and these here bumbs at me, and I wouldn't kick. They could call me names from the stand, but I wouldn't care. If the whole population o' the United States hated me like they think they hate him, I wouldn't mind, so long's I could just get back in that old game and play the ball he plays. But if I could, kid, I wouldn't have no time to be talkin' to you.

The other day, I says to Callahan:

"What do you think of him?"

"Think of him!" says Cal. "What could anybody think of him? I think enough of him to wish he'd go and break a leg. And I'm not sore on him personally at that."

"Don't you like to see him play ball?" I says.

"I'd love to watch him," says Cal, "if I could just watch him when he was playin' Philadelphia or Washington or any club but mine."

"I guess you'd like to have him, wouldn't you?" I says.

"Me?" says Cal. "All I'd give for him is my right eye."

"But," I says, "he must keep a manager worried some, in one way and another; you'd always be afraid he was goin' to break his own neck or cut somebody else's legs off or jump to the Fed'rals or somethin.'"

"I'd take my chances," says Cal. "I believe I could even stand the worry for a few days."

I seen in the papers where McGraw says Eddie Collins is the greatest ball player in the world. I ain't goin' to argue with him about it, because I got nothin' but admiration for Collins. He's a bear. But, kid, I wisht McGraw had to play twenty-two games a year agin this Royston Romper. No, I don't, neither. McGraw never done nothin' to me.

Notes

1. White Sox catcher Billy Sullivan, whom Cobb called the "finest ever to wear shoe leather." He is said to be the first catcher to position himself directly behind the batter and invented the inflatable chest protector.

2. In 1903, John Anderson of the St. Louis Browns tried to steal second base when it was already occupied. For years afterward, this was referred to as a "John Anderson play."

3. George Brickley played for the Athletics for a few games in 1913, then went on to play football for Trinity College and a few pre-NFL professional football games for the Cleveland Tigers and the New York Brickley Giants.

Ty Cobb's "Inside" Baseball

He's Always Quarreling, but His Craze to Win Does that, and He's Popular

Boston American, June 18, 1911

He was here last week, not long enough to get very well acquainted with the general public of Boston, but plenty long enough to convince said public that he is not yet prepared to yield the baseball crown to Joe Jackson or any other "upstart from the minors."

It is not strictly accurate to say there is only one Cobb, for he has a brother, also a ball player, and a son, who may be one. But there is only one Ty Cobb, and, as Charles Comiskey says, you have to hand it to him. This same Charles Comiskey had seen "King" Kelly, Bill Lange, Hugh Duffy and all the other great ones perform in their palmy days and he hesitated not a moment when the question was put to him: "Who is the greatest ball player of all time?"

Cobb had beaten Comiskey's team time after time, had taken the pennant from the White Sox in the final game of the 1908 season, and yet the Chicago owner gave him his full meed of praise, instead of calling him "lucky," or "fresh," or "dirty," as many another has done.

Cobb's various accomplishments are ancient history. There is nothing to be said of his mechanical ball playing that the "fans" have not seen for themselves and appreciated. But there is a great deal to Cobb's work that does not appear on the surface or that is overlooked by the public because it is busy watching something else.

The general impression prevails that Cobb is not popular with his teammates and that he has hardly any friends on rival teams. Nothing could be farther from the truth. Ty has an argument with one of the other Tigers almost every time the Detroit club engages in a close game. Other great ball players have their "spats" under similar conditions, but that does not mean that they are disliked. Cobb quarrels more often with his mates simply because victory means more to him than it does to the majority of athletes. He is crazy to win, and he sometimes forgets his manners in the heat of battle.

For the benefit of the "fans" who have been led to believe that Cobb has few friends on his own team or on others, it might be well to call attention to the scene that takes place before every Detroit game. Cobb will usually be found "warming up" with some of the members of the other club. He is "kidding" them and they are handing it back to him, but there is no real hostility between him and the men with whom he happens to be conversing. And the same is true when he is with the rest of the Detroit players. Ty is something of a "kidder" and he likes word battles next to the actual conflicts of the diamond.

In the Spring of 1908, Cobb had a real fight with Catcher Charley Schmidt. It took place in the Southern training camp.[1] It was caused by a disagreement between the two over Ty's treatment of colored people; rather, one colored person. Schmidt and Cobb went behind the stand at the ball park and had it out, and the catcher, who has taken up the fight game professionally, had all the better of it. Cobb admitted that he was licked and then he and Schmidt became fast friends. As for the other Tigers, they were divided about evenly in their partisanship, but none of them held anything against Cobb for his share in the proceedings.

The recent coldness between Cobb and Sam Crawford was brought about by an argument between Ty and Donie Bush over signs. Bush was, and still is, just ahead of Cobb in the batting order. Now Ty has a complicated set of signals for the man on base when he is at bat. He claims that he must use at least five hit and run signs to deceive the opposing batters. Most players have only one. Bush got mixed up two or three times and failed to read Cobb's signs right.

In the middle of one game, in the 1910 season, one of these mix-ups occurred and it resulted disastrously for the Tigers. Whereupon Cobb gave Bush a sharp "call" and Donie, who is some sharp conversationalist himself, came back. But be seemed to be getting the worst of it and Sam Crawford went to his rescue.

It was then that Sam and Tyrus got into a rapid-fire duel of epithets that could scarcely be called complimentary. They said everything they had to say and then didn't speak to each other for a long time. Manager Jennings insisted on a patching up of the quarrel this Spring, and now the two are good friends.

Crawford, who, by the way, is faster this season than he has been for years, seldom gets mixed on signs. Cobb is ahead of him, and Ty does whatever he is told to do by Sam when the latter is at bat. And the plays that the two pull off through their silent understanding are good samples of the real value of "inside baseball."

In the first inning of last Monday's game here two were out and the bases were empty when Cobb came up and beat out a slow hit to Purtell. It was natural to suppose that he would either attempt to steal on the first or second ball, or that Crawford and he would work that hit and run. Two balls were pitched out, but Ty failed to go.

On the next one he started at full speed and Crawford, instead of swinging or letting the strike go over, laid down a bunt and beat it to first. It didn't have to be a perfect bunt because the Red Sox were taken entirely by surprise.

Purtell came in to field the bunt and third base was left unguarded for the moment. Of course, Cobb kept right on going, and, of course, he reached it in safety. The play was a dandy, but it was wasted, for the usually reliable Delahanty fell a victim to Hall and struck out. If it had been in the latter part of the game and if the Tigers had needed a run to win or tie, you can bet that Cobb would have attempted a theft of home, and he would have come close to getting away with it. As it was, he had to play safe and conserve his efforts for later on.

The public gains its impression that Cobb is unpopular through his evidently harsh verbal altercations on the field, with members of his own and rival teams. He does argue with the rest of the Tigers and he does quarrel with his opponents, but it is all in the day's work, and is usually forgotten the moment the game is over. It is Cobb's overwhelming desire to win that is at the root of all his squabbling.

Cobb appears unable to get through a battle at Philadelphia without some sort of unpleasantness. He has quarrels with Frank Baker and Cy Morgan, which appear to be fixtures. Boston "fans" will remember the birth of the Morgan-Cobb disagreement.[2] The controversy with Baker arose over the latter's assertion that Ty had spiked him purposely. There was a great deal of fuss about this case, and the two players have been at each other ever since. The Tigers say that Baker deliberately kicked Cobb when the latter was sliding back to third base in one of the games of Detroit's recent series at Shibe Park. Cobb then attempted to tread on Frank's foot. It is hard to get at the truth of these complaints and cross-complaints because each club backs its own man. But Cobb has friends among the Athletics and that was proved last Fall, when he took part in the All-Star series that helped the American League champions in their preparation for their brush with the Cubs.

Cobb doesn't care whom he "bawls out." Hughey Jennings has been scolded fiercely by the "Georgia Peach." To be sure, Hughey has been there with the back talk but it never served to frighten Cobb into silence.

Cobb stands out there in center field and tells his mates about all the mistakes they make. Then he tells them again on the bench. He informs the pitchers that they worked like high school kids against certain batters, charges the infielders with ignorance and negligence and even "calls" his fellow outfielders when he thinks they have pulled a "bone."

Some of them shoot hot language back at him and swear they will never associate with him again, but they are all his friends after the game, or after they have had two or three days in which to think things over.

Tyrus isn't immune from criticism. When he makes a mistake it never goes unnoticed. But he doesn't make many and so his critics don't have much chance to get back at him.

If Cobb were born to be unpopular, his sharp tongue would surely make him very much so with his fellow players. But to prove to your own satisfaction that the other Tigers are his friends, you have only to "knock" him in their presence, or assert that Jackson, Wagner, Lajoie, Speaker or someone else is his superior as a ball player. If they don't just laugh at you they will show temper and express themselves after the manner following:

"If you'd travel around with us and see him every day you wouldn't talk about other ball players in the same breath. And if you claim that Wagner or Jackson or anyone else is in a class with him you'd better go to the nearest alienist and have your bean examined. We'll pay the fee."

Notes

1. A vicious racist, Cobb was involved in any number of incidents with Black people. This one, which occurred in 1907—Lardner got the year wrong—concerned Cobb's attack on a Black groundskeeper in Augusta, Georgia, who had committed the unpardonable sin of trying to shake Cobb's hand. When the groundskeeper's wife tried to intervene, Cobb began to choke her. The assault ended when Schmidt pulled him off the woman and punched him in the face.

2. Cobb and others have told the story about his battle with Morgan several ways. Cobb's version is that after Morgan had beaned him, he stood at first and "shook my finger at him as much to say he would get his when the first opportunity arose." A batter then hit a long ball to the outfield, and as Cobb reached third, he saw Morgan covering the plate. Though he was only a few steps beyond third base as Morgan received the ball, Cobb kept running and "made a long and vicious slide straight at him." Morgan stepped out of the way and Cobb scored.

How to Pitch to Babe Ruth

Bell Syndicate, Aug. 8, 1920

To the Editor:

This is just a few items of information about a ball player that maybe you haven't never heard of him so I will tell his name in the first paragraph and his name is George Ruth but they call him Babe on acct. of him being over 6 ft. tall and pretty near as wide and he is a great left hand pitcher that don't pitch.

Well 1 day in May I had seen a whole lot of different sporting events that bores you to death and the White Sox from old Chi was playing in New York city so I thought I needed a little more boring and I went out to Polo's grounds and went down on the bench and Mgr. Gleason was setting there and he says hello to me, but I just made a face at him, but he asked me to set down a minute and a boy name Wilkinson was going to pitch and he was out there warming up and finely he got warm and come into the bench and Mgr. Gleason said:

"Come here and set down a minute Wilkie, as I want to talk to you."

So Wilkie set down and Mgr. Gleason said to him:

"Say listen Wilkie. They's a man on this New York club name Ruth and he isn't Cobb and he isn't Speaker or Sisler or Jackson. He's a bird that if you ever throw a ball where he can reach it, that ball won't be available for tomorrow's game and baseballs costs as much money as other commodities now days, so if you don't mind, why when this guy comes up there don't pitch him nothing that he can lay his bat against it, but roll the ball up there on the ground and I will take the consequences." So Wilkie said yes sir.

Well they started this game in the first inning and the White Sox didn't do nothing and it comes the N.Y. club's turn to get their innings and they was 2 out and Pipp got on 1st. base and along come Ruth. The next I seen of that two dollar ball was when it was floating over the right field bleachers. So when Wilkie come in to the bench Mgr. Gleason says what did I tell you and Wilkie said I didn't mean to pitch it where it went.

So the next time Babe come up all as he got was a 3 base hit cause they were pitching more careful to him. Well after a while it come necessary to put in a pinch hitter for Wilkie and little Dickie Kerr was sent in to finish the game. Mgr. Gleason didn't tell Dickie where to pitch to Babe because Dickie's what you might call a old timer, so Dickie pitched one at this bird's Adam apple and he hit it into the right field stand for another homer, as I have nicknamed them.

Now this isn't no reflection on neither of these pitchers which I hope is both friends of mine, but, if I was manageing a ball club in the American League, I would tell them how to pitch to this bird. I would stand on the mound and throw the first ball to first base and the second ball to second base and the third ball to third base, and then I would turn around and heave the fourth one out in right field, because he couldn't be in all those places at once and further and more they's a rule that makes a batter stand in the batter's box and if a person pitches in that direction with this guy up why all you can say about them is that they're a sucker.

For inst. the last time the White Sox was here, a certain prominent Chicago baseball writer was setting next to Col. Huston that owns a chunk of the Yanks and this George Ruth comes up and the Col. says to him how much will you bet that he don't crack one out of the park on this occasion. So the baseball writer says what's the proper odds. So the Col. says well I don't want to cheat you and I will bet a pt. to qt. that he murders one. So the sucker took it and the first ball was a foul that went into Mr. Sucker's ft. and the next was a ball and then the old boy took one right over the middle for another strike and the next one hasn't yet been located, but when last seen was soreing over a cigarette sign in right center.

Another way to make him stop hitting home runs off of you is to refuse to pitch when its your turn.

The most useless thing in the world when this guy's up there to bat is the opposeing catcher, because if you can throw a ball past Mr. Ruth why it don't make no difference if its catched or not whereas if you try and throw one over the plate, it won't never get as far as the catcher.

A couple wks. ago a guy come here with the St. Louis Brown and struck the Babe out 6 times in 1 afternoon and if he is smart he will let that go down into posterity and the next time they tell him its his turn to pitch vs the N.Y. club he will say he has got a sore arm.

Pluck and Luck

Colliers, March 16, 1929

Mr. Ruth was not christened Babe, even in his infancy his parents never referred to him as Babe or Baby either one. You can't go around the house speaking of Baby when the person you mean is six feet two in his rompers and weighs two hundred and twenty pounds. His real given name is James Joseph and only when the war broke out did he acquire the nickname Gene.

The Babe's ankles are the envy of many a Broadway chorus gal. They are too slender to support him, so Colonel Ruppert has to attend to that. It is an open scandal amongst the baseball experts that these ankles are the reason he hits so many balls out of the park; it is less of a strain on them to trot around the bases than to dash full speed.

And I might state at this point that Mr. Ruth favors a very sensible change in the playing rules of the National Pastime; he wants it fixed so that when it becomes evident that a ball hit by him or anybody else is headed into the stands or over the fence, the batsman shall be permitted to return at once to the bench from wherever he is at without going through the ridiculous formality of circling the bases. This would save time as well as wear and tear on the ankles and the bases themselves and decrease the number of divots to be replaced in the base lines by the groundkeeper.

Harry Frazee sold the Babe to Colonels Ruppert and Huston for $137,500. Personally I am like Mr. Frazee and would rather have $137,500 than the Babe, because I have no stadium in which to keep him and besides there are already four Babes in my home and the congestion is something terrible.

One of Mr. Ruth's boyhood pals in Baltimore was Henry L. Mencken; they used to take long walks in the woods together, looking for odd Flora. It was an ideal companionship, for both loved to talk and as neither one could understand the other, no law of ethics was broken by their talking simultaneously. I would repeat some of their conversations, but Mencken's words can't be spelled and the Babe's can't be printed.

When the Babe was twelve years old and Mencken thirty-seven, their strolls together became infrequent; the Ruth boy would telephone Mencken and say, "H.L. I won't be able to accompany you this afternoon; I've got to stay home and mend the highboy." Or some other flimsy excuse.

Mencken was not deceived, but hardly hurt, and decided that some day when his little friend did not have to stay home and mend the highboy, he would ask him pointblank the real cause of the estrangement. Babe, however, confessed before H.L. had mustered courage to put the question.

They had been sitting in one of the lower branches of their favorite tree, a full-grown hickory, idly watching the antics of a couple of elfs, MacDonald and Goldstein. It came time to go home and they dismounted.

"Wait a minute," said the Babe. "I think I'll take this along with me."

And before Mencken realized what he meant, he had picked up the tree, thrown it over his shoulder and started along the path toward town.

"You perhaps wonder," he said to his companion, "what I intend to do with it."

"No," replied Mencken. "But I do wonder whether you have noticed that Nathan has taken a fancy to the word 'presently,' using it to signify 'at the present time, now a definition called obsolete by Webster."

"I thought you would," said the Babe. "Well, I purpose biting off the roots, the branches and the bark and employing it as a bat."

It then dawned upon Mencken that the Babe had gone into baseball and his admiration for the youngster was so great that he, too, became a devotee of the game, and to this day, whenever the Yankees are playing in New York, you will find the famous editor and critic in the Algonquin Hotel, casting sheep's eyes at a blank page of copy paper.

On the afternoon following the above episode, there was a game between Ruth's school team and a team of horses from the Pimlico race track. The Pimlicans were surprised when they saw the Babe come up to bat with his nude tree, and something more than surprised when he swung and missed the first pitch but knocked down the third baseman, shortstop and left fielder.

There was an argument which resulted in a ruling from the umpire that the bat must be shortened so that even when reaching for a ball outside the plate, the Babe could no more than graze the third baseman's chin. Ruth, disgruntled, gnawed the tree apart at the point indicated by the official and with the abbreviated utensil knocked the next pitch through a lavatory window in the Dupont Hotel at Wilmington.

The Babe began his baseball career as a shortstop, but a left-handed shortstop had to turn around twice before throwing to second or first base and this process made Ruth so dizzy and bewildered that he developed into one of the greatest left-hand pitchers in agonized baseball.

His record with the Baltimore club soon attracted the attention of big league scouts. An ivory hunter from the Philadelphia Nationals was the first to reach the scene and advised his employer to lay off as it would take a quarter of a yard of extra material to build the Babe a uniform. And when you stop to think that a ball player had to have a home uniform and a traveling uniform, well, zounds!

The New York Giants were tipped off that Ruth liked malt beverages and Mr. McGraw turned him down, saying, "I have already had too many pitchers full of beer." (Editor's note: This one came from the Old Testament—Deuteronomy 2168. Operator: What office? Editor: Deuteronomy. Operator: Thank you.)

Brooklyn rejected him when Manager Robinson learned that he (the Babe) was a prolific user of such language as is seldom heard outside the theater. "I'll brook no rival on my club," said Robbie.

Gracious! Hey-day! Gemini! God bless me! Lackadaisy! Save the mark!"

The Baltimore owners wired Jim Callahan, manager at Pittsburgh: "What will you give for Ruth?" He wired back: "Don't want her. Am married."

They wired Frank Navin at Detroit. He wired back: "Thanks. Already have a pitcher."

The White Sox experienced a stroke of tough luck. They sent Ted Sullivan to the Maryland metropolis to take a look at the young prodigy. Ted went on to Annapolis through a misunderstanding and witnessed a game between the Navy and Penn State. The Navy, which Ted thought was the Baltimore club, had a terrible left-hander, who Ted thought was Ruth. In four innings, the left-hander was hit for a total of seventy-eight bases and gave twenty-two bases on balls. Ted reported by telegraph to Mr. Comiskey that he did not consider Ruth quite ready for fast company.

On the train leaving Annapolis Ted was told that he had not spent the afternoon in Baltimore, but was now headed thither. When the train pulled into the City of Magnificent Tunnels, Ted sought a hotel and stayed there all night, determined to see Ruth pitch the next day's game.

But next day, at Oriole Park, he discovered that Ruth had pitched the preceding day's game and was now on one of his long walks with Mencken. "The Babe's in the woods," was the way they expressed it. Mr. Sullivan had to hurry home to Chicago to attend a clinic. And a week later Ruth was sold to the Boston Americans for twenty thousand dollars in anonymous checks.

The Babe has been in nearly every world's series since and it may be cheering news to the National League that if the Yankees don't win the pennant next year, they are going to lend Ruth, for the duration of the series, to whatever American League club does.

He used to hate autographing baseballs, and if any of you people think it ain't a job, gather a crowd of fifty thousand lunkheads around you some day and while they are sitting on your shoulders or running up and down your back, try to sign your name on eight thousand globules. Babe grumbled and grumbled till one time Charley O'Leary, who had been seated on the Yankee bench ten years reading a book, said to him: "Shut up, you big ox! Suppose your name was Alyosha Karamazov."

It is estimated that if all the balls autographed by Mr. Ruth were placed one on top of the other, the second one would roll off the first one before you were ready to pile the third one on top of the second one.

There was a season when it was said that the Babe was not taking proper care of himself and that his days as a big-league star were numbered. But he fooled everybody by suddenly cutting out cosmetics, reducing his waistline to three laps to the mile and beginning to run bases like Ty Cobb on roller skates.

"My habits," he explained, "were not affecting my prowess as an athalete, but they were raising h—l with my ability as a writer. You hear that Edgar Allan Poe, O. Henry and other great experts did their best writing while under the influence of balsam or catnip. But, believe me, a man can't consecrate unless their head is void. I am not going to burn out my brains with prophylactics. I don't need brains in baseball, not against our competition anyway. But some day my ankles will realize what they have been standing up under all these years, and then it will be necessary for me to make my living with my pen."

"What will you write?" inquired a bystander. "Short stories, a play, novels, articles?"

The bystander strolled off without waiting for the reply, which was:

"No. Just mash notes to the baseball fans of St. Louis."

BASEBALL POEMS

Lardner began including poems in his baseball coverage as early as 1910, his second season covering the Cubs. They usually appeared in notes at the end of his game stories and were very often "written" by Frank Schulte, the Cubs' right fielder, an excellent player who twice led the National League in home runs and won two World Series with the team.

But beyond his ability as a player, Schulte was a kindred spirit and Lardner was lucky to find him. A clubhouse entertainer who specialized in satire, poetry, and comic depictions of his teammates, Schulte was clearly an influence on Lardner's early depictions of baseball players, both in his journalism and his fiction. Lardner had no qualms about adopting Schulte's verses for his own purposes and then simply taking over the player's voice. He became so protective of Schulte's work, in fact, that he complained about how it was treated by his editors.

"They are making such awful mistakes with Mr. Schulte's poetry up in The Tribune office," he wrote Ellis Abbott, the woman he would marry, "that I am almost discouraged by it, or with it, and will pass it up entirely unless they leave it alone. It is bad enough to start with, without their ruining it."

On March 6, 1910, after injuring a finger in a spring-training game in New Orleans, Schulte wrote:

Right field it is not play,
I proved that very fact today;
Yes, yes, I showed them how today,
The first fly ball that came my way.
I caught it on my finger's end.
It made my finger break or bend.
So just remember this one thing.
Get out there early in the spring.
And stick your finger through the ball,
And then lay off till next fall.

On April 12, after a game was rained out, Schulte wrote:

Rain, rain, go away
Save yourself for some sad day,
When Schulte doesn't want to play.
Now I don't mind a little storm
Quite early in the day.
But when I've donned my uniform
I'd sooner, rather play.

But while Schulte was Lardner's go-to poet, other players were also given a chance to exhibit their literary style. Heine Zimmerman, the Cubs' third baseman, led the league in batting and home runs in 1912, and when he put together a 23-game hitting streak early in the season, Lardner wrote the following on May 23:

Heine Zimmerman's exuberant spirits, resulting from his tremendous batting streak, have overflowed in the form of poetry. "If Schulte can write it, why can't I?" remarked Heine last night, and slipped us this child of his brain:

There is an outfielder named Frankie,
He's homely and ugly and lanky.
A good hitter once,

But now he just bunts,
And daily grows more and more cranky.

There is a third baseman called Heine,
A better third baseman than Steiny;
When, he meets one square,
Each lady bug fair
Says: "Golly, I wish he was meine."

By the time Lardner returned to Chicago after his year in St. Louis and Boston, he was confident enough to use rhymes in his game coverage—or rather in his off-day and rainout coverage—as in the following lead from the Chicago *Examiner* on May 13, 1912:

It didn't rain so awful hard, it didn't rain so much; there wasn't any blizzard that could really be called such; we asked most everybody that we met upon the street and couldn't find a single soul who'd swear that there was sleet; we asked some information from the man who gathered mail, and he said that nowhere on his route had he encountered hail; we ran across a pioneer who'd lived here since a boy, and he vowed he'd seen a stronger wind sometimes in Illinois; but the awful combination of the wind and rain and all, it rendered quite impossible the scheduled game of ball.

And so the Cubs, who play (at times) with so much skill and science, were forced to wait until today to get back at the Giants. . . .

When Lardner noted another rainout in the same fashion on July 12, the *Examiner* copy desk responded with a headline that neatly captured the spirit of the story:

Sox and Athletics Have to Fly
For When One Inning Has Gone By
Water Issues From the Sky

PHILADELPHIA, Pa.—The lightning flashed, the thunder roared, and then suddenly there leaked and poured the wettest rain that ever caused postponement of a game. Now, just one inning had gone by when water issued from the sky. One inning of a game you know will never in the records go. But still, if you would like to hear what happened, listen, reader, dear.

The pitcher for the Sox was Benz, who in the Winter butchers hens. Chief Bender was Mack's pitcher bold. He's pretty good, but pretty old. Well, Rath could find no ball he liked, and, sad to say, right out he striked. But Captain Lord, sometimes called Harry, beat out an infield hit to Barry. Jack Collins, who does lots of things, on this occasion took three swings. Ping Bodie's name was quickly Dennis; he died from Barry to McInnis. . . .

And when he accompanied the White Sox to Boston, the following appeared on Aug. 26, 1912:

BOSTON, Mass.—Dear Reader: Here we are once more in Boston by the ocean's shore. In Massachusetts' famous town, the fish is fresh and bread is brown, where it is sure a royal treat to eat and eat and eat and eat.

Three men are missing from the fold, the rest are lonesome, young and old. Ed Walsh, he stopped in Meridian to see his two kids once again. He'll be here in the morning mail to beat the Red Sox without fail. Jack Collins went to Pittsfield, Mass., to call upon his fair young lass. At least, that's what the boys all said; when we asked Jack, he turned real red.

Well, there's another absentee, the holder of the captaincy. Way amid the pines of Maine to see his family again went our smart captain Harry Lord, for virtue is its own reward. He's going to remain up there till we have had our first affair with Boston's Red sox, then return, his well known salary to earn . . .

There were also were times when Lardner would write a poetic sidebar to his main story as in this one from the *Examiner* on July 22, 1912:

NEW YORK—We interviewed the latest addition to the pitching corps [Eddie Cicotte] on the proper pronunciation of his name. Here, is what he has to say:

This pretty name of mine is not,
As some folks claim, just plain Si-cot;
Nor is it, as some would have it, Sic-ot,
Although I'm sure I don't know why not.
And furthermore, take this from me,
I don't pronounce it Sick-o-tee;
And you can also make a note
That it is surely not Si-cote.
You stand to win some easy cash
By betting it's not succotash,
Nor is it sassafras so cute,
Nor any other kind of fruit.
I do not call it Kokomo,
Though many folks pronounce it so.
I guess you're wise enough to know
That this sweet name's not Cicero.
And now you've learned it's none of those
Why I will just jump back to prose
And tell you plainly, truthfully,
The way you should refer to me

Having muttered all this, he went on to inform us that the proper way is See-cot, with the accent on the first syllable, as in Fogarty, McIntyre, Lord or Rath.

Lardner's use of poems in what were, after all, reports of games, might have seemed out of place to some readers, but once he returned to the *Tribune* in 1913 to write "In the Wake of the News," there could be no complaints. He had a columnist's latitude now and he meant to use it. His very first "Wake" column, which appeared on June 3, gave a sample of what was in store when he celebrated the fact that he would no longer be a traveling baseball writer:

OPENING CHORUS
Good-by, everybody; good-by, Jimmy Cal;

Good-by, William Gleason; good-by, Doc, old pal;
Sully, Matty, Harry, and Morrie, good-by, good-by.
Sure hope you all will feel sorry the same as I.
Good-by, good old Edward; good-by, little Ray;
Good-by, all you White Sox—I quit gadding today.
[Encore]
Good-by, Johnny Evers; good-by, Lurid Lew;
Good-by, Charley Williams; good-by, Lower Two;
Schulte, Heine, Jimmy, and Larry, good-by, good-by.
P'rhaps you'll look me up when you tarry awhile in Chi.
Good-by, clams and swordfish; good-by, Gay White Way;
Good-by, joys of Brooklyn—I quit gadding today.

Just a few weeks later, he took his poetic relationship with Schulte to another level, throwing in Zimmerman for good measure, and inventing a feud between them. It began with a story in the *Tribune* on June 19, saying that a Cubs fan was offering Zimmerman, a notorious baiter of umpires, $100 if he could control his temper and avoid being thrown out of a game for the next two weeks. Half a $100 gold certificate would be presented to him before that day's game and the other half if he stayed on his best behavior.

Amazingly, Major League baseball went along with the gag—the mind reels at the thought of such a thing happening today—and in a ceremony at home plate, umpire Bill Klem gave Zimmerman one half of the bill. The *Tribune* commemorated the event with a picture of Zimmerman in uniform examining his prize, and the following day, Lardner enlisted the aid of Tennyson to sum up the situation in a poem.

A SPLIT CENTURY
Half a C, half a C,
Half a C, sundered,
Cut from the other half.
Half a big hundred.
Forward the Cub Brigade!
"Charge at the umps!" they said,

But Zim in silence stood.
O you big hundred!

Past the Great Zim the pill
Whistled. "Strike three," said Bill,
And the Great Heine knew
William had blundered;
His not to make reply,
His not to query why,
'Though 'twas outside and high.
Silence is golden, Zim.
O you big hundred!

Players to right of him,
Players to left of him,
Players in front of him
Hollered and thundered,
Bellowing like a calf
At the whole umpire staff,
But Heine's jaws are locked.
Earning the other half
Of the big hundred.

The *Tribune* milked the story for the next two weeks, noting every time Zimmerman's patience was tested, and on July 2, one day before the two weeks were up, Lardner wrote another poem, this time enlisting Shakespeare as his muse:

HEINE'S SOLILOQUY
The C or not the C, that is the question—
Whether 'tis nobler for the dough to suffer
Mistakes and errors of outrageous umpires,
Or to cut loose against a band of robbers,
And, by protesting, lose it? To kick—to beef—
To beef! Perchance to scream: "Ah, there, you dub,

You ----- ----- ----- ----- ----- -----!!!"
But that sharp flow of breath, what would it cost,
A sloughing off of these one hundred bucks,
Must give me pause—there's the respect
That makes dumb agony of two long weeks;
For who would bear the crazy work of Klem,
Cy Rigler's slips, the raw mistakes of Quigley,
The guesses wild of Orth and Hank O'Day.
When he himself might his quietus make
With a few cuss words! Who would Brennan bear.
Or shut up under Eason's worst offense,
But for the dread of dropping all that dough,
Of losing all those togs, deprived of which
No guy is really swell!—Yes, I'll keep still.
Thus money does make cowards of us all;
And thus the native Bronix disposition
Is stifled by a bunch of filthy luc;
And ravings of my own fantastic sort
Are all unheard, though my long silence does
Disgrace the name of Heine.

The following day, Zimmerman at last won the other half of the bill. To the surprise of only the most gullible, the *Tribune* revealed that the anonymous "fan" who had put up the money was the newspaper itself. And Lardner, who knew a good thing when he saw one and was not about to let the story end, enlisted Schulte to keep it alive. First, though, he had to be sure of Schulte's bona fides.

"In recent interviews," he wrote on July 6, "Luke McGluke, owner of the Dublin club in the Japanese League, has made vicious attacks on the Wake . . . asserting that the Wake was trying to deceive the public by signing Schulte's name to stuff he did not write and charging that the Schulte poems, than which there is none other, were direct and uncalled for knocks at the Dublin club.

"The Wake stands for clean sport and clean sport reporting and desires to assure the public that it has been deceived if Mr. Schulte is not the author of the things he writes." He would print Schulte's reply, he said, and let his readers decide for themselves.

"In answer to the vicious charge made by President McGluke," Schulte wrote, "I will say that, to all intents and purposes, I write the verses over which my name appears. By this I mean that I read them the day after they are written, or rotten . . . I nearly write them; that is, I sit near the person who do. I will admit that (Cubs infielder) Red Corriden writes some of them, but I give him the inspiration and always approve what is rotten before it appears in print. Hoping I have convinced you that I write what I write. I am, etc."

That was good enough for Lardner, who wrote, "Mr. Schulte's gentlemanly note convinced the Wake that in regard to this here now controversy, to which there is nothing to it. Mr. Schulte does not draw his enormous salary from the Wake for the mere use of his name. . . . "

But on July 18, the plot thickened when Schulte expressed some petulance over the attention, and the money, Zimmerman had received in a poem titled "Life."

For two whole weeks, I've wrote this poem;
But not a cent for mine,
'Though Heine got a hundred bucks
For not saying nothing the same length of time.
I need some money to buy fudge
And lemonade and clothes,
But I'm not getting any,
So I guess I'll have to close.
Note—Nevertheless, Mr Schulte has promised us another
poem entitled "A. Epick," the first installment of which will
appear in an early issue.—Ed.

"A Epick" turned out to be a series of poems that Lardner purported to believe wasn't up to Schulte's usual standard, and he responded on July 28 with a parody of the battles between managers and players that have always been a regular occurrence in baseball.

SCHULTE SUSPENDED

Wake's Great Poet Bawled Out and Punished for Loafing

"Frank Milton Schulte," Lardner wrote, "considered by many the most reliable and consistent hitter on the Wake team, was last night severely reprimanded and then indefinitely suspended for alleged soldiering on the job. The suspension followed a war of words between Schulte and the manager of the Wake, during which Schulte sassed his boss. Regarding the trouble, Manager Lardner gave out the following statement:

"Ever since the start of the Epick series, I have been convinced that Schulte was not trying. I have been in the game long enough to know that he is one of the greatest poets of modern times, but I must say that his work on the Epick has been awful. I knew he was capable and naturally reached the conclusion that he was loafing. I won't stand for anything like that among my men. Hence his suspension. He will be reinstated only when he apologizes to me and promises to try to give me his best services.

"A few details of the quarrel between the manager and his star were gleaned from some of the other players. After Saturday's Epick, Schulte was called on the club house carpet. "You've been laying down on me," the boss is reported to have told him. "You've got to brace up or stand for a fine." "If you don't like my stuff," Schulte retorted, "get somebody else." This made the manager mad and he said: "That remark means a vacation for you."

It is said that Schulte has long been dissatisfied with his berth on the Wake and wants to be traded to Breakfast Food or Day Dreams.[1] But the Wake manager has no intention of letting go a man who is capable of filling so much space."

Two days later, after two Cub players substituted for Schulte, Lardner relented and the story ended. "SCHULTE REINSTATED," the headline read. "Wake's Great Poet Will Be Back in Game Tomorrow."

"It was formally announced at Wake headquarters last night that the differences between Frank Marvelous Schulte and the management had been patched up, and that Schulte would have his regular position in tomorrow's lineup. While Manager Lardner would not admit it, it is said that he was far from satisfied with the work of substitutes, Art Phelan and Red Corriden. Schulte has promised to work harder . . ."

Lardner's baseball poems could be terse, as in one that ran on June 20, 1913:

SHORT STORY
Shotten-walk:
Stovall-bang;
Pratt-Biff, blooie;
Good-by, Lange.

Or sardonic as in one that ran on August 2, 1913:

JUST NOW—
Their game is
Famous
For its
Witless
Blunders;
Those runless,
Wonless,
Catchless,
Matchless,
Stopless,
Copless,
Useless,
Mooseless,
Spitless,
Hitless Wonders[2]

Or mocking as in one that ran on December 15, 1914:

BASEBALL—A SPORT
Players who jump for the dough,
Bandits and crooks, ev'ry one.
Baseball's a pleasure, you know.
Players should play for the fun.
Magnates don't care for the mon.'
They can't be tempted with gold.
They're in the game for the fun—
That's why Collins was sold.[3]

Or his specialty, a play on words, as in one that ran on December 10, 1918:

THE NEW CUB BOSS
Some folks undoubtedly will speak
Of William Veeck[4] as William Veeek,
But those who wish to be correc'
Will speak of him as William Veeck.

As for those readers who preferred sports coverage of a more traditional bent, Lardner had this answer:

"A Sioux City reader says there is too much poetry in the Wake. We haven't noticed any."

Notes

1. Regular features in the *Tribune.*
2. A reference to the original hitless wonders, the 1906 Chicago White Sox, who had the lowest team batting average in the American League but upset the powerful Cubs in the World Series.
3. The best second baseman of his era, Collins led the Philadelphia Athletics to three World Series championships, then was sold to the White Sox for $50,000 in 1914, the highest price ever paid for a player.
4. President of the Chicago Cubs from 1919 to 1933 and the father of Bill Veeck, the maverick owner of several Major League teams.

BETWEEN INNINGS: RING ON RACE

THE BASEBALL PLAYERS LARDNER HAS MENTIONED SO FAR IN THIS book—and it is true of those who will appear in the articles and columns yet to come—have one trait in common.

They are all white.

If Lardner ever mentioned a Black player in any of his writing, I can, with one small exception, find no record of it. Likewise, he never seems to have contemplated organized baseball's original sin—its refusal to admit Black players that lasted for more than half a century.

And then there is this. In an article on the 1920 World Series, Lardner works in this reference to Christmas: "Abe Claus has forgot the boys this year and it don't seem like the merry Yuletide it was a year ago."

And this, in an article on the 1921 World Series, "On the way out I was stopped by a man who looked like his name was Cohen."

As for Lardner's odd reference to the Jewish New Year in that same series, the mind reels.

What are we to make of this?

Lardner's writing on subjects beyond baseball offers some clues of the manner in which he was infected by the casual racism and anti-Semitism that was a part of American society a century ago.

In a column he wrote from the 1916 Republican Convention, for instance, Lardner tells of taking a Black delegate to a hotel bar in Chicago where he is not welcome. It is a heartening story of thumbing his nose at racism that is marred by Lardner's references to the delegate as a "culled gemman."

In other articles, Lardner uses such words and phrases as Jap, greaser, wop, frog, ebony hue, descendants of sunny Africa, partly white American, prune-colored orchestra, and others that make today's reader wince. They also made Ring Lardner, Jr., the two-time Academy Award–winning screenwriter who was a devout champion of social justice, ponder his father's contradictory attitudes toward Blacks and Jews that he had witnessed while growing up.

On the one hand, Lardner offered to resign from a Long Island country club that complained when he brought Ed Wynn, a Jewish comedian, to play golf. On the other hand, Ring Jr., wrote in his memoir, *The Lardners: My Family Remembered*, "I can also remember him speak, in a burst of justified indignation, of 'that damn Jew Ziegfeld,'" who occasionally hired Lardner to write sketches for his famous follies. As for Blacks, Ring, Jr., wrote, "He somehow kept on believing, as he had been brought up to believe, that blacks in general were inferior, even after he had come to admire individuals like (singer and comedian Bert) Williams, Paul Robeson, and the composer J. Rosamond Johnson."

But there is another factor to consider, which is that Lardner's use of hateful language was in accord with what often appeared in American newspapers in the early part of the twentieth century. Even those who heed the historian's warnings about "presentism"—observing events of the past in light of current practices and beliefs—will find themselves astonished and appalled at the gratuitous manner in which prejudice was expressed by writers and cartoonists in newspapers and magazines of that era. Minorities in general and Blacks in particular were consistently ridiculed, marginalized, patronized, and caricatured in ways that would not be tolerated in general circulation media today.

So while Lardner's biases may have been a part of his upbringing, they were also prevalent in the journalistic atmosphere in which he worked. These were the times in which he lived, and he was very much a man of his times. Which is not to say he didn't understand and occasionally comment on the absurdity of some of the customs of his era.

The only reference I can find to a Black player in all of Lardner's work appears in a brief poem he wrote in the *Chicago Tribune* in 1914. It was a reference to the best baseball player in Chicago—and perhaps in all of baseball—in the first two decades of the twentieth century, John Henry "Pop" Lloyd, a hard-hitting shortstop for the Chicago American Giants of the Negro Leagues. As the Cubs were meandering through a mediocre season, Lardner had some advice for the team's manager, Hank O'Day, in a poem titled "Then We'd Cop Sure."

If I were Hank I b'lieve that I
Would go out south some night,
And there corral a certain guy
Named Lloyd and paint him white.

THE WORLD SERIOUS

Exhausted Tigers Extend Series

Chicago Tribune, Oct. 15, 1909

DETROIT, MICH.—THE DETROIT TIGERS WON THE SIXTH GAME OF the world's series this afternoon, 5 to 4, and thus made necessary a seventh contest to decide the title.

But that doesn't tell half of it. Without a doubt it was the most exciting world's series game ever perpetrated. There may have been just as close battles in world's championship wars in the past, but there never was such a nerve racking one when so much depended on the result. Whatever the reputation of the Tigers in the past, it must be admitted that they showed their gameness today and came out on top in a combat which many clubs would have given up as lost at the end of the first half of the first inning.

It cost Detroit something to win the game, but no one is counting the cost, and Tom Jones and Charley Schmidt, both of whom were hurt badly in the tense ninth inning would take the same wounds a thousand times provided they could be received in such a good cause.

The Tigers didn't dash gleefully off the field at the finish. One of their number, Tom Jones, was carried away to the clubhouse by his teammates unconscious. Another one, Charley Schmidt, hobbled painfully to the dressing room, and all but fainted when he reached it. And still another, George Moriarity, dragged his spiked limbs at a snail's pace while the rest of his pals gave him and the other two injured their expressions of sympathy.

While George Mullin will be hailed universally as the real star of the contest, one must not lose sight of the fact that the work of Charley

Schmidt had as much to do with the result as anything else. Never before today did Schmidt catch a world's series game that earned him so much as honorable mention. But he was there this time and no backstopper in the country could have worked more consistently and brilliantly than the stocky Tiger. He didn't figure much in the hitting, but he did catch wonderfully, and he was the chief engineer in two double plays that did much to bring victory Detroitward.

Gathering a bunch of three runs before a soul was out in the opening round, the Pirates looked like winners all over until the home part of the fourth. In this round the Tigers tied up the score and then proceeded to get a little lead for themselves. They reached the ninth inning two runs to the good, and because the weak end of the Pittsburg batting order was coming the game looked as good as won for the American leaguers.

But the Pirates had not quit. Jocko Miller, who had been doing better hitting than at any time in his world's series career, led off with a clean single to right. Bill Abstein, who looked like a joke before Mullin in his previous attempts, followed with a safe wallop to center, and there were men on first and second no one out, and only two tallies needed.

Of course, it was up to Wilson to bunt. He did so, and laid down the ball so perfectly that he probably would have beaten it to first base even if Tom Jones had not dropped Schmidt's throw. Tom made a nice try for Schmidt's peg, but he had to get in front of the runner to do it. Wilson crashed into him with no thought of hurting anybody. The ball sailed out of Jones' hands and the Tiger first sacker toppled over as if shot. Before Delehanty could recover the ball Miller had scored, making the Tigers' margin only one. Abstein raced to third, while the Detroit players rushed to the side of the injured athlete. Wilson stopped at first.

Jones was unconscious. He lay there, dead to the world, until Trainer Tuthill and four other Detroiters lifted him to carry him to the clubhouse. He was awake for a second during his trip, but he relapsed into the Land of Nod and didn't know a thing until it was all over. In the meantime the crowd had forgotten the injured hero and was looking with all its eyes at the two Georges—Gibson and Mullin—on whom everything depended.

Manager Jennings was out in the middle of the diamond giving words of encouragement to Mullin and readjusting his team. Matty

McIntyre was called to left field and Davy Jones moved to center. Sam Crawford, whose reputation as a first sacker is not to be sneezed at, came in to take up the task of the wounded member of the Jones family. Sam had a chance to show his skill immediately,

Mullin cool and slow, shot a curve over for Hackenschmidt. Gibby leaned against it and sent it bounding to Wahoo Sam. The latter picked it up cleanly and shot it home, whither Abstein was hastening to register the run that would tie it and give the Pirates a chance to go home tonight with the title. But Schmidt took Sam's peg, blocked the runner at the plate, and tagged him out while the crowd yelled madly. It was not known at the time that Schmidt was even badly hurt. But the contact with Abstein's spikes tore a huge chunk out of the catcher's thigh and he suffered intense pain when he tried to stoop and sign for the next pitch.

Mullin's troubles were not over by any means. There was only one out. Wilson was on second and Gibson on first and the Pirates still needed one to make it a draw. Of course, Philippe[1] was not given a chance to bat. In his place came Eddie Abbattichio. The Italian fouled off two and then waited for three balls. It was up to Mullin to retire him on his next swing or hand back the advantage for which the Tigers had worked so hard to their rivals. Mullin put all his stuff on what he offered Abby in the pinch. As he raised his arm Wilson started running for third and Gibson for second. Abby missed the ball entirely and Schmidt's hurried but perfect throw to third caught Wilson and wound up the game.

It was in this last play that Moriarity was hurt. He couldn't get out of the way of Wilson's spikes without risking defeat for his team. He stood the gaff and did the tagging part so plainly that there wasn't a murmur about Klem's correct decision.

The noise made by the Detroit bugs at the conclusion of the game surpassed in volume anything that has been heard since the proceedings began last Friday. There was a rush to congratulate the Detroit headliners, but the crowd, seeing the plight of Schmidt and Moriarity, gave up the plan of carrying the athletes off the field and comforted itself by cheering the limping pair all the way to the clubhouse. . . .

Perhaps because the players of both teams were exhausted, the final game of the series two days later was an anticlimax as Pittsburgh won 8–0.

NOTE

1. Pirates pitcher Deacon Phillippe.

The Tears of Christy Mathewson

Chicago Examiner, Oct. 17, 1912

BOSTON—When Steve Yerkes crossed the home plate yesterday it made the Boston Red Sox the world's champions in the tenth inning of the deciding game of the greatest series ever played for the big title. While the thousands, made temporarily crazy by a triumph unexcelled, yelled, stamped their feet, smashed hats and hugged one another, there was seen one of the saddest spectacles in the history of a sport that is a strange and wonderful mixture of joy and gloom. It was the spectacle of an old man, as baseball players are called, on the New York players' bench with bowed head and drooping shoulders, with the tears streaming from his eyes, a man on whom his team's fortune had been staked and lost and a man who would have proven his clear title to trust reposed in him if his mates had stood by him in the supreme test. The man was Christy Mathewson.

Beaten 3 to 2 by a club he would have conquered if he had been given the support deserved by his wonderful pitching, Matty is greater in the eyes of New York's public than ever before. Even the joy-mad population of Boston confesses that his should have been the victory and his the praise. The game was over, the title that probably will be the last one fought for by that king of pitchers was lost, and Mathewson, cool and usually unaffected by adverse fortunes of war, was a broken man. The majority of the thousands present were too busy with their wild celebration to notice him, but there were a few who watched his slow and sad progress to the bench and later to the club house.

Charley Herzog, who certainly cannot be blamed for New York's failure to win, rushed up to Matty as he staggered off the field, threw his arm around the big pitcher's neck and poured forth words of comfort and sympathy. Mathewson did not seem to hear them. He shook Herzy off and had no answer to the condolences offered by Doyle and McGraw, who were eager to impress on him that he was in no way to blame for the defeat.

Matty picked up his sweater and moved on in silence. Soon he had disappeared under the stand to join the other Giants in their dressing room, to hear their bitter arraignment of each other and to be told, time and again, that he deserved better, a truth that none knew more positively than himself. The Red Sox, fearful that they would be hurt in the rioting of the crowd if they loitered on the field, had hastened to their own club house, and the scene there was vastly different from that a couple of doors away.

Boston had come from behind twice, had tied New York's early lead in a brilliant seventh inning rally, had almost despaired when the Giants scored again in the tenth, and then, to cap it all, had not only caught up once more but had counted a third run, just enough to settle the question of supremacy beyond all doubt. What difference did it make to the Red Sox that they had been blanked in their part of the tenth and that the world's title would have belonged in New York, if Matty's backing hadn't crumbled to pieces?

The palm was theirs and they remembered nothing else. They had been accused of quitting and they had seen some of their opponents give up more bare-facedly than they had ever done. The score was down in black and white, 3 to 2, in favor of Boston, and that was enough to drive sympathy for Mathewson from their thoughts.

Well, to begin with, the score was tied up at one to one when the Giants came into their end. The party Snodgrass, more famous than he ever was before, was thrown out on a ground ball to Smoky Joe Wood. Red Murray, who had driven in New York's only previous tally and who was still engaged in the task of making the country forget his falldown against the Athletics, smashed a fierce double into the temporary bleachers between Speaker and Lewis. Merkle immediately came through with what most people considered a title winning hit. It was a sharp single to center, and Murray had no trouble scoring.

Speaker made a hurried play on the ball, for it was his duty to try for a peg to the plate, but he fumbled in his haste and Merkle ran to second. One of the most surprising things in the series followed. Herzog, who has played in the series as if he were super-human, struck out. There was no question about it. He just naturally whiffed and went back to the bench without audible comment. The next occurrence was lucky for Wood in two respects. Chief Meyers' blow might have gone through to center and scored Merkle. Furthermore, it might have killed Smokey Joe. As it was, it hit him in the right side and dropped lifeless in front of him. He had sense enough left to pick it up and toss it to Stahl in plenty of time to get the chief for the last out. Wood was badly hurt by this clout and he had to be assisted to the bench. Fortunately, there was no more work for him to do.

Down in the right field corner Ray Collins had been warming up constantly and it would have been up to Ray to get busy if the Sox had tallied only one run instead of two.

Wood is a pretty fair hitter, but in his helpless condition there was no chance to send him up to bat. So Clyde Engle was the party chosen. It will be remembered that Clyde, in one of the other battles, had delivered a double in a pinch. This time he hit as hard as he could, but he struck slightly under the ball. Snodgrass raced over toward left, waved Murray away and camped under the falling pill. It struck his hands squarely and kept right on to the ground, moved by the law of gravity.[1]

Engle had not run as fast as he could from the plate, but he speeded up enough to get to second before Fred could recover the sphere and hurl it to the infield. The Sox were now playing for one run, so Hooper was sent up to sacrifice. His two attempts went foul. When he had to hit, he sent a long fly to center, and it must be confessed that Snodgrass made a good catch of it. At this juncture, Matty made his only mistake of the inning. He passed Yerkes. We are not saying that the cool youngster wouldn't have hit safely, but it was bad business to walk him and Mathewson didn't mean to.

Then came Merkle's contribution to the cause. Speaker lifted the first pitch for a foul and it struck bottom, although it ought to have been caught easily. As was mentioned before, Merkle, Meyers and Matty started for it, and all of them stopped. It isn't safe to trifle this way with the Speaker person. He picked up his bat, which he had thrown in disgust toward the bench. The next thing Matty served him he cracked on the nose. It traveled to right field a mile a minute and Engle sped home with the tying run Yerkes hustled to third, Tris waited to see what became of Devore's throw, and when he observed that Meyers fumbled it he chased to second. Duffy Lewis came up with the chance of a lifetime staring him in the face. Matty tried to make him swing at two bad ones. He refused. Then Meyers and Mathewson consulted and decided it was better to walk Duff and try for a double play rather than put one over. So Lewis strolled and choked the bases. Matty pitched all he knew to Gardner and was rewarded by getting two strikes on the Boston third sacker. Two balls followed, and then Larry pulled a long fly to right, a fly that Devore had to go back after.

He caught it all right and aimed a throw toward Meyers, for that was his duty. But the throw reached the Indian long after Yerkes had touched the plate. . . .

Note

1. The error, one of the most memorable in World Series history, continued to haunt Giants' center fielder Fred Snodgrass. "Hardly a day in my life," he said in 1940, "hardly an hour, that in some manner or other the dropping of that fly doesn't come up, even after 30 years. On the street, in my store, at my home . . . it's all the same. They might choke up before they ask me and they hesitate—but they always ask."

A Plea for Help

Chicago Tribune, Sept. 29, 1915

FREND HARVEY. I RECD. YOURS OF THE 27 INT. AND WOULD SAY IN A reply that I would jest as leaf go to the worlds serious under certun conditions. In the 1st. place please make Mr. Sanborn[1] keep the score of the diffrunt ball games because I have forgot how to keep the score. All so in in the 2d. place have Mr. Sanborn write in his stuff how the games come out who wins and who looses and so 4th. because I would probly over look miner detales.

In the 3d. place I would expect the paper to pay my exigences to and fro Boston and Phila or where ever it is there going to play the game at. All so my bord bill at the diffrunt hotels and on the bord of the trains accept when I am invited to meals by some sucker. And I will try to fill my self up good when some sucker is paying for the meal so as the paper wont be stuck so hard when I hafe to pay for them my self.

In the 4th. place I wisht you would ask Mr. Sanborn to get a hold of a ticket to all the games for me and see that I get in to the press box and dont half to set on some bodys lap behind the club house or over in the next block. If it was here in Chi I wouldnent have no trubble because people knows me here but its diffrunt in the east and not even the pollicemans knows who I am because when I was trying to get some wheres near the ring side at the Mcfarland Gibbons dance I ast a policeman to help me and I told him my name and where I come from and he says What, the (he used a bad word) do I care who you are or where you come from. And he wouldent act like my escort.

It might be a good idear to leave me set between Mr. Sanborn and 1 of the boys from the other Chi papers and I would pertend like I was busy writeing my own stuff but all the wile I would be lissening to what the man from the other paper was dictateing to his operator and then I would leen over and tell Mr. Sanborn and he could use it like he made it up hisself.

I supose you will want me to pick the winner of the serious like I picked the winner of the brutal prize fight down to Brixton beech. I can pick the winner O.K. if you give me time to think over it. But may be it wouldent be a bad idear if I and Mr. Sanborn was to both of us pick the winner and him pick 1 club and I pick the other and then witch ever club come out on the top you could put a peace in the paper that our man picked the winner.

I want it under stood that I been in both Phila and Boston many a time in fact I lived in Boston for a while so its not no treat for me to vissit ether place and I will expect my expences pade and I dont consider it no vacation.

I wonder if you could give me a little information a bout what should a man ought to take a long on a trip like that in the way of close. I got 1 sute case and I know where I could borry an other 1 but I dont know will it be necessary to take a long 2 peaces of baggage but still I want to be drest jest as good of the rest of the repporters. I was thinking I would take a long my buster Brown sute and my sailor sute and ware my velvet sute on the train going and comeing. And then of course I will need a change of linens and a extra hankercheif and a extra pare of hoses and a night gown and I wont only need 1 night gown because I will spend most of the nights on a train going back and 4th. bet. Boston and Phila if they deside to play the serious in them 2 towns. But you know best a bout these things and give me what ever information you can. And of coarse I will get all cleaned up and shaved beffore I start.

And 1 more thing Harvey do you want my storys sent in by telegram or male? I hope you will find time to give me all this information and all so agree to the conditions named in the above and Im sure you will find them fare to both sides.

Respy. R.

Note

1. The *Tribune*'s I. E. (Sy) Sanborn was one of the top baseball writers of the era.

A Rainy Day in Philadelphia

Chicago Tribune, Oct. 8, 1915

PHILADEPHIA, PA—FREND HARVEY: UNLESS IT RAINS LIKE ITS been doing all day today there going to start the world serious here tomorrow. I and Mr. Sanborn is stoping in the same hotel that the Boston Americans is stoping at and the Boston Americans is 1 of the 2 clubs thats in the serious so if they call off the game tomorrow we will know a bout it right away and will send you word so you wont think there playing a game when they aint playing a game because we will be right here in the hotel and will see for our self weather the boston players gos out to the park or stays here in the hotel and if they stay in the hotel that will mean its raining out doors. But I want to tell you something funny about us picking out this hotel to stop at.

I dident pick it out myself but Mr. Sanborn did. I says to him the other day in Chi where are we going to stop in Phila he says we will stop at the Aldine. I says fine its a good hotel. He says well the reason I picked it out was because it will be quiet and not crowded and they wont be no ball club stoping there so we will have plenty of room and be away from the bugs.

So we come here to the Aldine club and come to fine out the hole Boston eleven is stoping here and all so the Boston news paper men witch is even worse. Of coarse the Boston club's not here today because they been playing a important game over to NY city but they will be here before I get threw writeing this junk and the hotel will be jammed with people that knows the diffrunt players by there 1st names to speak to. So when we found this out I says to Mr. Sanborn your a fine guy and the next time I and you comes to cover the world serious I will do the picking of hotels and I will pick a hotel thats so good that the ballplayers wont never think of it.

And he says he got mixed up because he had been stoping here all summer and evry time he come here they wasent no ball players here accept the Chi white sox and he figgured the Chi white sox wouldent be here this time because they was playing some practise games with the Cubs out in Chi. And he figgured the Boston Americans wouldent be here because they hadent never been here when he was. Fine figgureing hay Harvey because of coarse evry time he was here with the white sox the Boston Americans was on there home grounds playing some other western club and not in Phila a tall.

Well anyway as a result of his figgureing wear in the same hotel where the Boston Americans is comeing and if we half to sleep 4 or 5 in a bed its mr. Sanborns falt. If it doesnt rain tomorrow they will be a big crowd that ever seen a game in Phila on the National league grounds. Every body will be there accept the people that lives in Phila. The latter cant get no tickets. There the people thats supported the Phila ball club ever since 1876 so the owners figgure they saw enough baseball and don't need to see the world serious.

People that lives right here have been a round the hotel all day begging we fellows from out of town to get them some tickets so they can see the ball games. But we havent got no tickets to give them because all the tickets had all ready been gave out to people from Seattle Washn and New Orleans, St. Lose and Boston.

The owners of the Phila club has been very carefull to suply tickets to these royal rooters from Boston that never done nothing for no body includeing there wifes. They had to be fixed up with tickets because 1 of them is the mare of Boston and would make a big holler if he and his friends dident get in to the ball pk. In order to be elected mare of Boston you got to be a base ball bug and all so a royal rooter and a man that will stand up for Boston rights and can sing the river shannon. When a mans running for mare of Boston the only pledge hes got to make is that he will go to all the ball games and act crazy. He don't half to sine no promuss to keep the salloons open on Sunday.

They isent much to write a bout here today. Mr. Sanborn went down to press head quarters this pm and got us both fixed up with a ticket to the games. Besides the ticket we was both gave a red badge to ware on our sutes to show that we was news paper men and entitled to get in and not peeple from Phila. When I seen the color of the badge I was glad I bought a gray sute for fall instead of a pink 1.

Theys a lot of roomers going a round but you cant tell what to beleive and what not to beleive. 1 of the roomers is that Alexander will pitch tommorows game. I wouldent bet a nickle on it because the papers says that Pat Moran told them so and of coarse Pat Morans is to smart to tell the news papers what pitcher hes realy going to use. If he says its going to be Alexander its safe to bet that it will be Baumgardener or somebody may be Kiliifer.

Theys an other roomer that the Phillys isent going to play there 1st inning because they dont think theys any use because Hughey Fullerton says in his dope that there going out in 1 2 3 order, so instead of playing and waisting the time they will just tell the repporters to mark them out in there score books and then they will start-in with the 2d inning and cravath at bat because hughey says that Cravath will get to 1st base. It would simplify matters a hole lot if Hughey would tell what was going to happen evry inning threw the hole serious and then the clubs wouldent half to play and the people and the reporters wouldn't have to watch them but just let Hughey tell how it was comeing out and save all the ware and tare. Of coarse they wouldent be no money tooken in at the gate that way but the club owners could fine there own home town fans so much a peace to pay expenses of the serious and the home town fans would be just as well off because they cant get tickets to the games any way.

They was a big parade on Broad st today and I and Mr. Sanborn and some bum repporters from other towns was watching it and we dident know what it was so finely Mr. Sanborn ast 1 of the by standers what was it and he says it was the Phila firemans celebration. So Mr. Sanborn says what is the Phila firemans celebrateing and the man didnt answer so I horned in and says there celebrating because they put out a fire. Pretty good hay Harvey.

And 1 more thing. I dont want to give no free advertising to no body but Ive got 1 of these here watchs that cost a dollar. Well when I left Chi yest the watch was on Chi time. And when I got to Pittsburgh last night it jumped a head a hour to eastern time with out no body touching it. Hows that Harvey?

Lardner Probes Giants' Scandal; Finds 'Dodgers'

"Wake" Editor Decides Not to Attend Ball Game and Dines with Friends.

Chicago Daily Tribune, October 5, 1916

New York—A man that's got a weak heart and three dependent children would have been a sucker to go over to Ebbets field in the bureau of Brooklyn today and tooken a chance of witnessing another such a kind of a game as the Dodgers and the Giants put up yesterday, and speaking of Dodgers, they tell me that that word just about described the New York infielders yesterday whenever one o the Brooklyn boys hit a ball that the Giants had to move quick to get out of the way of it.

When the New York newspaper men and baseball reporters advised me to stay away from Ebbets field and when I seen in the papers where McGraw was so disgusted that he had gone to the races whenever they are, I made it up in my mind that it must be pretty desperate and why should I risk it?

For instance, McGraw has lived through a whole lot of distressing scenes like the world series of 1913 and the Cubs of 1916 and the Reds and Cardinals of pretty near any year, and if he could not stand it to take another look at his Giants where would I be at.

McGraw figured to himself that if he went to the races, he might probably see a horse hold back and let some other horse win but it would be done artistically and besides he should worry what the horse done because he is not managing horses but Zimmermans and Herzogs and etc.

They was a big lot of talk around here today about the way the Giants acted in the game that cinched the pennant for the Brooklyns. Most of the men I talked with was reporters and they did not seem to have no kick coming.

One of them said: "It means we will be through in four games instead of five or six because Brooklyn has not got no Alexander."

Another one says: "Thank God for the Giants. They kept us out of Philadelphia."

They is also a big lot of talk about the league investigating the game and punishing the men on the New York club that was supposed to be doing the laying down. But I can tell right now what will happen. Nothing will happen.

As far as investigating is concerned, they should ought to be an investigation of why William Klem was not appointed one of the umpires and a worlds series without William Klem umpiring will be like a newspaper that has not got nothing in about Judge Landis.

After I had gave up the idea of going to Brooklyn, I had to hustle round and try and find somebody to buy my meals and the man I tackled for lunch was Clarence Briggs and he said he did not have time. That is a funny line in itself, a cartoonist not having time to do anything.

F.P. Adams finally agreed to buy the lunch and Grantland Rice is going to buy the dinner and Chas. Van Loan is going to buy tomorrows breakfast and after that I don't know, but I am bound to have a miserable time because of the milk famine.

The Brooklyn bunch is going to Boston Friday noon and we will all go along with them and probably go with Mr. Robinson and of course I don't mean in the same seat.

The way it looks like now, Rube Marquard is going to pitch the first part of the first game for Brooklyn and the other men Robbie is depending on is Pfeffer and Coombs, with Sherrod Smith as fourth choice. If all these men shows good form in the game Saturday, Cheney may start Monday.

And may the best team win four straight.

Your Correspondent Sizes Up the Series

Chicago Tribune, Oct. 6, 1916

NEW YORK—Mr. Bud Fisher, who draws the Petey and Gaston cartoons, called up today and asked: "How are you going to Boston?"

"In good shape," was my apt answer.

"But listen," was his startling rejoinder, "I am going to drive up there friday and I will have room for you in my car."

"That sounds fine," says I, and I immediately went out and bought a seat on the train that leaves here at one P.M. and gets to Boston at six oclock. That's what I think of Bud Fisher and his cat and his cartoons. Bud Fisher may be a nice guy and everything, but the day I ride anywhere with him and his car will be the day Brooklyn wins the World's series from Boston.

And speaking of that, the World's Greatest Newspaper has probably been informed by its New York correspondents that there is a great deal of betting and that the odds favor Boston, 8 to 5. Well, listen, as Bud Fisher says, I was up in John Doyles billiard parlors today and John Doyles billiard parlors knows all about the betting on everything, and the betting on the World's series is nothing to nothing. For some reason or other, everybody seems to know that Boston is going to walk in and while the people who live in Brooklyn are, ipsofacto, or whatever it is, crazy, they have not reached the stage where they will back their so-called ball club at odds of anything less than twenty eight to one.

Now, mind you, I am not saying that the Robins will lose, but if they dont lose, I will work the rest of the winter for nothing.

Walter Trumbull, who writes baseball on the New York World, or something, says I ought not to use the capital "I" so much.

"What ought I to say," I asked him, "when I am talking about myself?"

"Use we, or the writer, or your correspondent," he says.

So your correspondent will try to remember that for the rest of this remarkable story.

Your correspondent arose at ten o'clock and answered the telephone and the man at the other end was Jerome Kern, who wrote most of the music to the Follies, and I can't say that fearlessly, but if we said he wrote the libretto, he would sue the paper for a million dollars libel.

"Will you come to lunch?" he said.

So the writer said he would, and at lunch your correspondent met Pelham Grenville Wodehouse, the Britisher, and he acted just as glad to see the writer as if we had been Wilhelm Tell, the Kaiser of Germany.

So they talked and your correspondent tried to listen and finally got bored and thought we had better hustle around and get some baseball news. So your correspondent sought out Harry Hempstead, the owner of the Giants, and asked him whether it was true that John McGraw would be fired for saying that his team laid down to Brooklyn.

"Yes," said Mr. Hempstead. "I am going to fire McGraw and here are some other things I am going to do: I am going to make the price of box seats ten cents a piece, and I am going to play Schupp at third base on account of his left handedness, and I am going to trade Zimmerman back to Chicago for Al Campion, and I am going to take the club to Medicine Hat to train next Spring."

In other words, the stories to the effect that McGraw is going to lose his job are nearly as true as the ones about Brooklyn backing its ball club at odds of eight to five.

John K. Tener,[1] Garry Herrmann,[2] and Ban Johnson[3] were interviewed today on the big scandal, meaning the game New York is said to have thrown to Brooklyn.

"What are you going to do about it?" the Commissioners were asked by your correspondent.

Ban answered first. "I have been asked to take charge of the United States army commissary department," he said.

Garry Herrmann said: "Sweet Adeline. Sweet Adeline, at night, dear heart for you I pine."

Mr. Tener said: "May Old Glory long wave over the National pastime and the home of the free."

Some Brooklyn writer said today that the Robins would probably win because they are not afraid of anything and that just about hits the nail on the head, because if the Robins had been cowards they would have faded in front of the fierce opposition of the Giants tuesday and on the other hand, the Red Sox with the exception of Heine Wagner and Bill Carrigan, will probably be scared to death of catching infantile paralysis during the two games here.

The latest dope on the series itself is that Rube Marquard will pitch the first inning for Brooklyn and Babe Ruth will pitch the first nine for Boston.

Notes

1. President of the National League.
2. President of the National Baseball Commission.
3. President of the American League.

Lardner Story Starts as Verse, Turns to Prose as Fattens Purse

Chicago Tribune, Oct. 7, 1916

BOSTON, Mass.—I thought that this was just the time to write my story all in rhyme. I rose this morn at half past 8 and wondered how it got so late. I shaved and dressed and packed my grip and got all ready for the trip and went downstairs and paid my bill and said "I'm from Chicago ILL."

The cashier said: "Why, I dont care if you're from there or anywhere, so long as you have got the dough; just say good-by and off you go." So off I went and with elation rode to the new Grand Central station and paid the driver forty cents for taking me from there to thence.

In fifteen minutes there I found a train that was Massachusetts bound and got aboard and took a seat and ordered something nice to eat and then the Cleveland boys came in and wanted money for to win and asked me for to play some poker with nothing wild but the joker, Hugh Fullerton, he just came in and ordered both of us some gin so then I whispered: "I suppose I'd better write the rest in prose."

So the details are that I won $7 in the poker game with the Cleveland boys and they play the funniest game you ever saw. Six cards are dealt to you on the draw and the joker is wild and then you draw down to five cards. So I won seven and a quarter in their crazy game and then we were in Boston. So then I went to the hotel and the first person I saw was Hank O'Day and I said to myself "Here's a story." So I bot him a cigar. And I did not get any story that you could print.

"Hank," I said to him, "will you try not to make any mistakes in this series?"

"I never made a mistake in my life," was his reply.

"No," I says, "but it is a matter of record that you signed to manage Cincinnati."

So he did not have any answer to that, so then I left the hotel and went down to where the Brooklyns were stopping. Now you know and I know that I only know five men on the Brooklyn club, namely Larry Cheney and Jimmy Johnston and Jack Coombs and Chief Meyers and Rube Marquard.

So I was going to interview one of them but could not because they were all out at a show. So all the news that I got was that Marquard is going to pitch the first inning for Brooklyn as I told you yesterday and Coombs will pitch the second inning and Pfeffer the third inning and so on and I know a whole lot more of inside stuff, but if I wrote it I might be interfering with Mr. Sanborn and besides the cost of white paper is high. I will try to write a good story tomorrow.

Inning by Inning with the Red Sox and Robins

Bell Syndicate, Oct. 8, 1916

Boston, Mass.—Mr. Sanborn is supposed to be writing the game in detail, but I will send it that way, too, and try to get it different. So here is what happened:

First Inning.

We came out in a taxi, and somebody else paid for it. The umpires pointed around for a quarter of an hour and as there wasn't anybody on the field except the ball players and the Brooklyn club, one could not help from wondering, as they say, what they were pointing about. The announcer said that Mr. Shore and Mr. Marquard would pitch. As regards Mr. Shore, we believed it.

So the first inning started and Mr. Shore pitched a fast ball over the plate and a man named Myers hit it and broke the altitude record, and Mr. Cady catched it and Mr. Myers was mighty glad, because he thought all the time he was going to strike out. So then Jacob Daubert struck out, and there was no question about it, because Jacob had three healthy swings.

Then Jake Stengel, or whatever his first name is, rolled out, and then the Bostons came to bat according to the rules, and Hooper and Janvrin struck out and everybody said what a great pitcher Marquard is. But Tillie Walker hit one on the beak for 3 bases and then Marquard was not such a great pitcher. But Richard Hoblitzell grounded out.

Second Inning.
For the life of me I can't remember what the Brooklyn did, but it wasn't worth mentioning. Duffy Lewis came up for Boston and walked or something. It was Gardner's intention to sacrifice, but he did not figure on who was catching for the Dodgers. He bunted and Chief Meyers gummed it all up. Scott did sacrifice and Cady was passed a-purpose and Shore struck out and Hooper hit one in the eye, but Myers caught it.

Third Inning.
In Brooklyn's half, Daubert struck out only once because they would not let him bat twice. In Boston's half, two guys struck out, and then Hoblitzel, who cannot possibly hit a left-handed pitcher, tripled to right, and George E. Lewis, who cannot hit anything except in the regular season and during the world's series, doubled to left and scored a run, and then they caught him off second base and nothing else happened.

Fourth Inning.
Believe me, Shore looked almost good enough to pitch for the Niles high school team in this round. Stengel hit one somewhere and Wheat kissed one in the eye and it went over Hooper's bean, and Stengel scored and Wheat was on third, and then this here George Cutshaw hit a single to right field, only it wasn't a single, because Hooper catched it prone on his back and Wheat tried to take an unfair advantage and score while an outfielder was sitting down with the ball, but Hooper, remaining seated, threw him out as far as from here to the city hall. The Bostons done nothing.

Fifth Inning.
I was out getting a sandwich.

Sixth Inning.
From where we are sitting we could see the Charles river and a man went by in a rowboat and Mr. Sanborn said: "Do you see that man?" and I said "Yes," so he said, "That man is a sculler." "Yes," was my reply. "What is the difference between he and a world's series ball player?"

asked Mr. Sanborn. "I don't know," was my reply. "What is the difference between a sculler and a ball player?" "Well," said Mr. Sanborn, "a ball player has only one skull." No runs.

Seventh Inning.
Olson and Cutshaw played up to form and Boston scored three runs.

Eighth Inning.
Pfeffer pitched for Brooklyn and held Boston to one run.

Ninth Inning.
Shore left his fast ball on the bench and Brooklyn was just about to tie the score when Carrigan cheated and changed pitchers. Boston refused to play the last half.

Nothing Happened

Chicago Tribune, Oct. 10, 1916

BOSTON, Mass—Friend Harvey, this is just a few lines to leave you know how we are getting along. We are getting along good now Harvey and it looks like we would be all through Wednesday night and back home some time Friday.

A man named Hi Myers came pretty close to being killed today and this was how it happened. He hit a ball in the first inning and touched all the bases and the Brooklyns had one run. Then the Bostons tied it up and acted like they were through for the day till a man named Del Gainer hit one in the fourteenth inning and then it was all over. But if the home run Myers made had of win the game for Brooklyn and prolonged the series to five games instead of four or if it had of wound up in a tie, I would of borrowed a gun and shot Hi Myers. That is how I feel about the series.

Well Harvey I got up at nine o'clock in the morning and dressed in an hour and a half like usual and had some breakfast and a man from St. Paul paid for it. Then I packed up my typewriter and Bozeman Bulger had a taxicab hired and took us out to Braves Field and I forget who paid for it, but I know who did not. So pretty soon we wended on our way up to the press stand and the royal rooters band was playing "Tessie" and I did not have no gun on my person and besides I could not see them but could only hear them and that is bad enough.

So somebody asked me who I thought was going to pitch, so I picked up a copy of the Boston paper that I used to work on till they threw me out and the paper said the pitchers would be Leonard and Cheney, so then I knew it would be Ruth and Smith.

Well nothing happened till the first inning and then they was two out and this here Hi Myers kissed one in the eye and it was a home run and I dont know why they call him Hi because the ball he hit never went more than three feet above terra and firma and everything.

So then nothing happened till the third and it was Scotts turn to bat first for the Red Sox and it is a notorious fact that he never hit a ball in his life. So he hit for three bases and then he staid on third base while Thomas was getting himself threw out and then Ruth hit to Cutshaw and you could not expect a Brooklyn infielder to make two perfect plays in succession so Cutshaw fumbled long enough to let Scott romp in from third and the game was tied up.

So then nothing happened till the fifth and then they was two out and Thomas cracked one down the third base line and Wheat played it like an old washer-woman and instead of it being a single like it ought to been it got through Wheat and Thomas was going to make three bases. But Ivan Olson conceived the brilliant idea of tripping him up and he did so and nobody was looking except all the umpires, so after Thomas picked his self off of the ground they told him to romp along to third base. Then Mr. Olson and Heine Wagner, who was coaching at third, had some bitter words and it looked like one of them would kill the other and make a good story, but no such luck and when I say that I dont mean that either one of them deserves to die because they are both nice fellows, but it would of made a good story.

So then nothing happened till the seventh inning when Myers hit a ball to Janvrin and the young dancing master kicked it round awhile and finally picked it up and threw it to first base and Mr. Quigley said Mr. Myers was out though nobody knew why until somebody explained that Mr. Quigley was graduated from the University of Kansas.

So nothing happened until the last half of the ninth until Janvrin hit a left ball to left field and Wheat could not reach it so Janvrin was safe at second base. So then Tillie Walker was sent up to bunt and Mr. Carrigan knew he could not bunt and never could bunt but gave him one more chance to prove it so Tillie staid up there till he fouled one and then Jimmy Walsh came up instead of him and bunted one straight at Smith and Smith threw it to Mowrey and Janvrin ought to of been out as far as from here to Amsterdam, but Mowrey dropped the ball. This looked like the end of a perfect day, but Hobby sent a short fly to Myers and Janvrin was a dead baby at the plate. So somebody told Smith about Duffy Lewis and they walked him a purpose and Gardner fouled out and we had to sit there awhile longer.

So then nothing happened till the tenth this here Hitless Scott hit another single and Thomas sacrificed and Ruth came up and if he had of hit as far as he wanted to the horsehide as they call it would of died an early death in the Charles River, but Babe did not touch it so far as the naked eyeball could judge and William Dinneen said he was out.

So then Hooper hit one about as hard as last summers ice cream and it was a single and Mowrey picked it up and made a smart play, whether you believe it or not. He seen he had no chance to get Hooper at first, so he bluffed to throw there and Scott overran third and set out for home, but Mowrey still had the pill and tagged him.

So then nothing: really happened till the fourteenth and the Robins done nothing, so Bill Carrigan decided this would be the last inning and if nobody scored they would call it a tie and it took smart management to figure that out because nobody could of possibly known it without looking at the atmospherical conditions. So Hobby walked and Lewis sacrificed and Carrigan told Lawrence Gardner to seek the shower bath, so Gainer went up to hit and got one strike and then Hobby was invited to share Gardners bath and McNally went on to run for Hobby and the next thing you knew, Gainer hit one to left field and McNally kept on going till he got home and Wheat made a throw that might of caught Larry McLean or Larry Lajoie but it did not catch McNally, who all he can do is run. So the game was over, but the official scorers said Gainer made a two base hit and insisted on it till we all booed at them. Nothing happened after that and nothing will happen.

Report from Behind Enemy Lines

Chicago Tribune, Oct. 5, 1917

To Commander in Chief Rowland, General Headquarters, White Sox Armies, Comiskey Park.

I have the honor to report that I have just completed a trip here from Philadelphia with the enemy's expeditionary forces. Disguised as a neutral observer, I was able to gather much information which I trust will be of value.

The army is made up of about twenty active units and is charge of Major General McGraw, or some such name. Accompanying it are nine or ten enemy correspondents, some of them apparently intelligent. I talked with them and with several of the soldiers, including one commissioned officer, Captain Herzog. The latter advised me that he had never tried to raise honey dew melons in Maryland, but might plant some next year.

I had a highly unprofitable session with one Zimmerman, said to be a brother of the man who wrote the famous Mexican note.[1] He is from the Bronx and claims to be one of the heavy artillery.

"Hello, Heine," I said to him. "Why, hello, Lahdi," was his reply. "Gimme a cigarette."

And a moment later—

"Gimme a match."

Some of his comrades called him Zimme, but Gimme would be more appropriate.

I got a rise from one Private Rariden by asserting that only one railroad went through Bedford, Indiana. He flared up and retorted that there were actually two regular passenger and freight lines and two coal roads. This was exactly the information I was after and I have no doubt you will find it useful. I feel quite proud of the strategy that brought it out.

Private Holke showed me a letter he had received from a friend in Texas, asking for three tickets to each game played in New York.

"I hear the tickets are three dollars apiece per game," said the writer, "but I feel that we cannot afford to pay more than two-fifty. See whether it is possible to get them at this price." Mr. Holke is unable to figure out why people who can pay their expenses from Texas to New York and back for the sake of a few ball games, should feel it beyond their means to come through with the regular price for seats.

By careful questioning, I learned that in the initial battle, the enemy's defense against our possible counter attacks would be hand grenades thrown by one of four experts—Schupp, Sallee, Porritt or Anderson. Schupp and Sallee throw their bombs with the left hand, which should be contrary to international law. Sallee, in addition to being a left-hander, is thin to the point of invisibility, another violation of the spirit of the rules of warfare. His camouflage is very effective, as he is frequently mistaken for one of the pickets on the fence. This is also true of Porritt, but he has sufficient sense of honor to bomb right-handed.

Enemy correspondents are evidently convinced that the eastern invaders are stronger and better prepared than your own men and a few express the opinion that you will surrender in five days. I have pretended to agree with them in their arrogant views, so as to foster in them, and indirectly in their army, a chestiness which may result in disaster.

On our transport train was a heavy set genial young man whom I instantly recognized as another spy, Germany Schaefer.

"Hello, Germany," I whispered to him when no one was looking.

"S-s-s-h," he shushed. "Call me Schaef. I got through with that other name the sixth of April."

Well, sir, I trust that your armies will fight with that indomitable courage and aggressiveness which has made them conquerors in Autumn wars of the past, wars forced on them by barbarous West and North Siders moved to hatred through jealousy of the South Side's superiority in culture and invention, and that with Gott's help, you may gain an early and decisive military victory so that our people may return to their homes and live in the peace and comfort to which they are accustomed and of which these eastern vandals would rob us.

Respectfully

L.

Note

1. The Zimmerman Telegram was a secret proposal sent by Germany in 1917 asking Mexico to join it if the United States entered World War I. Intercepted by British intelligence, it inflamed U.S. public opinion and generated support for sending American troops to Europe.

The Modern Voltaire

Chicago Tribune, Oct. 8, 1917

AT THE FRENCH FRONT—[Special to Le Petit Journal, Paris.]—Les Bas Blanc made it deux out of deux from Les Géants hier après midi, winning the second game of the serie, sept to deux. Le jeu was un battle royale up to the fourth inning, when the Sox lit into Monsieur Anderson all spraddled out.

M. Anderson was taken hors de combat before the inning was over and M. Perritt got his. The round netted the Sox cinq runs et settled le jeu.

Directeur McGraw crossed everybody by starting another lefthander, Herr Ferdinand Schupp. This Boche was a world beater for un inning, but in the deuxiéme he looked like un franc cinquante.

Opposed to the Hun at the start was M. Rouge Faber of Cascade, Iowa. Rouge was hit hard in the deuxiéme inning, then settled down et pitched très bien. Rouge also gave un grande exhibition of base running, stealing third in the cinquiéme inning avec that base already occupé. Plays like that make the enemy look like a sucker.

M. Burns, avec trois ball et deux strikes, singled to droit. Herr Herzog forced him at deuxiéme, M. Gandil to M. Weaver. Herr Kauff lifted une mouche to right et Jacques Collins dropped it, but recovered in temps to force Herr Herzog at deuxiéme. Foreign Secretaire Zimmerman was hors at first, Eduoard Collins to M. Gandil.

Herr Schupp fanned M. McMullin et M.E. Collins in the Bas demi.

Le deuxiéme inning was plein of excitation. Avec une out, M, Robertson beat out an infield coup. Herr Holke singled à concentrer.

M. McCarty singled to gauche, scoring M. Robertson, Herr Holke following him in when Herr Schalk messed M. Jackson's throw to lieu natal. Herr Schupp et M. Burns wore très facile outs.

In le Chicago demi, M. Jackson led off avec un single. Herr Felsch singled a droit et M. Jackson took troisiéme. M. Gandil hit sauf over Herr Schupp's kopf, scoring M. Jackson. Herr Schalk tried to sacrifice, but bunted into Herr Schupp's mains et forced Herr Felsch at troisiéme. Then Herr Schupp gave M. Faber une basse on balle, filling la bases. That was bien suffisant pour M. McGraw et he yanked Herr Schupp et substituted Anderson. Directeur Rowland took M. Jacques Collins out and substituted Herr Leibold, un gauche-handed hitter. Herr Leibold whiffed et M. McMullin forced Rouge Faber at deuxiéme. La taille was now un tie.

Anderson went très bien until the quart. M. Weaver opened le Chicago demi of that round by beating out a balancoire bunt. Schalk singled à droit. Rouge Faber popped hors trying to sacrifice. Mais Herr Leibold et M. McMullin both hit sauf, scoring deau runs. Anderson was taken hors and in came Poll Perroquet. M.E. Collins et M. Generale Jackson greeted this oiseau with hits et le totale pour le round was cinq runs before Herr Felsch lined into un double play.

Le feature of the troisiéme inning was Rouge Faber's base-running. Avec un hors, M. Weaver reached premier on une botte par M. Fletcher. He advanced to deuxiéme on Herr Schalk's hors et to troisiéme on un single par Faber. Le dernier took second on M. Robertson's useless throw a lieu natal. M. Rouge then stole third and was très surprendre to find M. Weaver there. Le New York catcher threw a troisiéme et Herr Zimmerman, exhibiting grande presence de la intelligence, tagged Rouge. Il est un wonder Herr Heine didn't throw the ball à le champ droit.

Les scorers officieles went noix in the sixiéme et gave M.E. Collins un hit on a play un M. Collins was called hors par le umpire until le dernier saw that M. Perroquct had dropped Herr Holke's throw at first base.

Otherwise, there was not beaucoup more to le jeu. Directeur McGraw proved his generosity of spirit by letting us see quatre of his pitchers. M. Tesreau butting in pour le final Chicago inning and retiring le coté runless.

Le New York neuvieme brought up Herren Kauff et Zimmerman and M. Fletcher. Le first two named kept their records pure et M. Fletcher grounded out to the world's greatest series player, M. Weaver.

Il est the unanimous verdict autour de here that les Giants are the most consistent world's series team in le monde.

The following day, under the headline "The Modern Balzac," Lardner wrote another column in fractured French. We can only wonder if he recalled his jovial suggestion to Eddie Cicotte after the 1919 World Series two years later.

NEW YORK—Je came East today avec les bas blanc et we had un unremarkable trip. You know there is a difference between the White Sox et les Giants. The ball players on the former don't speak to the reporters, but the manager is friendly. On the Giants team, le Managere don't speak to reporters, but the ball players are cordial.

This is what I was told. But je saw some of the Chicago ball players I know and I couldn't resist talking to them. The first was Eddie Cicotte, who happened to be setting at the same petit dejeuner table. No sooner had we got settled when a telegraph guy came in and said:

"The next stop is Syracuse. You can file there."

So we said, "we have nothing to file there." So the telegraph guy says "haven't you nothing to file?" So I and Mr. Crusinberry said, "No." But Eddie Cicotte said, "wait a minute. I'll get off and file my spikes." That a right-handed pitcher's idea of wit.

Mr. Crusinberry and I made all kinds of offers to Mr. Cicotte to throw the next game he pitches, but the poor boob would give us no respectable answer. . . .

Lardner missed the conclusion of the 1917 Series, perhaps because he had been away from home so long and was just as happy not to go back to New York. Of course, he couldn't pass up the chance to make light of his defection.

"The boss has just informed me that I won't have to go back to New York with the other Rats," he wrote.

"Why not?" I asked him. "Don't you like my stuff?"

"Yes, indeed," he replied. "But you can write it just as well from here."

So he wrote about the game, which clinched the Series for the White Sox, from home, noting that "You get all the thrills of writing, if any, without enduring the pains of looking at the so-called athletes on the field of play."

18 Holes

Chicago Tribune, Sept. 7, 1918

FRIEND HARVEY:

Well, Harvey. It was the first time Geo. Tyler ever pitched at Comiskey Pk. and of course he hadn't no idear where they kept home plate, though it was right in plain sight, but anyway he couldn't seem to see it, and when he borrowed a handkerchief off Umpire Hildebrand in the 2d. innings to get something out of Bill Killifer's eye, I felt like hollering at him to pluck the bean out of his own eye before he went after the molt in his catcher's, but they was all ready enough hollering in the press coop with Bill Phelon and Rube Cook and Sam Hall in full bloom, and Sam's the bird that was tipped off in advance that the govt. was going to make all the seniles either work or fight and he's a sporting editor, so he fell down and broke a leg and I only wished it had of been his larnyx.

But when it come the Cubs' second innings, Tyler had a turn at bat and found out where the plate was and after that his control kept getting better and it got so good in the 9th. innings that he hit Strunk's and Whiteman's bats right in the middle and all that saved us was Jean Dubuc striking out in the pinch and Jean was with Detroit long enough so as the ballyhoo boy ought to know the way to pronounce him which is the same as in Iowa, but instead of that, the boy called him Debuck like he was a cartoonist, but he couldn't even draw a base on balls. Jean hit .340 or something out in the Coast League this yr., but it seems Tyler was pitching in the National League all summer.

Well, everybody was crabbing about the 1st. game and how dull and stupid it was, but they couldn't nobody fall asleep watching this one, not even the Deans that had been out on one of Tiny Maxwell's personally conducted slumming tours to the public library. I suppose you heard about the two Irishmen, Otto Knabe and Heinie Wagner, and all of a sudden Col. Barrow looked over the top and seen Heinie inside the Cubs' barbed wire and he shouted "Boys, who will volunteer to bring back my star lieutenant?"[1] and several responded, but by the time they was half way across nobody's land, Otto and Heinie was yelling kamerad at each other. It seems Otto called Heinie something that got him mad and Heinie is one of the best tempered birds in baseball and it takes a mean lexicon to rile him, so Otto was the logical choice.

Well, Sam Agnew caught Bush for 7 innings, but he caught cold when the band played the S.S.B. and made him take off his cap, so Schang went up to hit for him in the 8th. and he hit all right, but they nailed him trying to romp to third base on a single by Hooper and I couldn't see where he wouldn't of been as well off on 2d. base with his club 3 behind, but I can't manage the Boston club very good from the press coop, though Bill Phelon directed the Cubs O.K. from up there, because I heard him yelling "pitiful fools" and I thought at first he was referring to those who had paid to get in, but it was the Cubs he meant and he hadn't said it more than five or six times when they went out and grabbed themself a three run lead. But as I say, I couldn't stop Schang at second base and he probably cost Boston a tally and when he was throwed out, poor Joe Bush was so desperate that he took off his shoe to see if they was any runs in his stocking.

Well, Harvey, in regards to the morning game, we played out to Jim Crusinberry's club, Lincoln Pk., and I and him beat the eastern cracks, Nick Matley of Boston and Harry Cross of the Times Square A.C. and at that I didn't play my best game because it says on the score cards out there that players must start from the first tee and besides when you live in a loop hotel and step out of the elevator in the A.M. with your suitcase and bat bag, you half to fight 3 or 4 bellhops that wants to caddy for you over to the desk and the management thinks you're trying to jump your bill and make you wait till somebody has run up to your rm. and seen that you left your toothbrush and all and it kind of throws a man off, and besides the dressing room out there is a bench back of the first tee and it's a co-ed club so I played in my civies, but I did change a tire on Shields Ave. right after the afternoon battle.

Just as we was going to tee off, a young man that Nick said was the managing editor of the course come up and asked me if I had a button and I said no I hadn't been home for a week, so he said if I didn't have a button I must pay a quarter and he charged all of us a quarter apiece, but we played the match for the lunches and I and Jim didn't mind the quarter when we seen we had them beat, but where do you think they took us to lunch, Harvey? Out to the bards room at the ball pk., where it's free.

Well, Harvey, they won't be no morning game tomorrow though Chas. Weeghman invited us out to Edgewater, but I have got to hustle around all morning and find out how I am going to register here when I'm not, and besides the Dr. says he wants to take a look at my throat and he's been so good to me that I can't hardly refuse him a good time once in a wile.

But they's another ball game tomorrow and I hope those aviators[2] stays away so as I won't half to carry a stiff neck on my vacation, and they call them aces, Harvey, but I would say they was deuces wild, but if they must see the game, why can't they loosen up and pay to get in instead of wanting everything free like a reporter.

R.W.L.

Notes

1. Wagner had played for the Red Sox earlier in the season.

2. Some sixty Army Air Force planes appeared over Comiskey Park as part of the opening ceremonies, becoming the first flyover at a sporting event. These were also the first games to feature the playing of "The Star Spangled Banner," which was done during the seventh-inning stretch. With the United States at war, the regular season was shortened and the Series was played in September.

A Hot Tip from the Umpire

Bell Syndicate, Oct. 1, 1919

CINCINNATI, O—GENTS: THE WORLD SERIOUS STARTS TODAY WITH a big surprise. A great many people figured that the White Sox would be scared out, and would never appear. But sure enough when we woke up this morning and come down to breakfast, here was the White Sox as big as life and willing to play. The first bird I seen amist them was Ray Schalk, the second catcher.

"Well, Cracker," I said, "I never expected to see you down here as I had been told that you would quit and would never appear." "Well, Biscuit," was his reply, "here we are and that's the best answer."

So after all that is said and done the White Sox is down here and trying to win the first 2 games on their merits so it looks like the serious would not be forfeited after all.

Most of the experts went to the 2 different managers to try and learn who was going to pitch the opening game. So to be different from the rest of them as usual, I passed up the two managers and went to the umpires. The first one I seen was Cy Rigler and I have known him all my life. "Who is going to win, Cy?" I asked. "I don't know," was his ample reply. You can take that tip or leave it. Personally I am betting on his word. He will give them the best of it if possible.

The next umpire I seen was Quigley. "My system," he said, "is to call everybody out."

The 2 American league umpires could not be seen as they was both up writing their stuff, but you can be sure that neither of them will give anybody the best of it. So all and all, it looks like a even break in the umpireing.

That brings us to the hotel accommodations. A large Chicago newspaper has got the prize rm. of the lot, namely, the smoking rm. off the ball rm. in the Gibson. This means that if any body wakes up at 3 in the morning and wants to smoke why they can do so without moving out of their rm. And if they want to dance why all as they have to do is go in the next rm. And look for a partner.

A great many people has written in to this hotel to ask how I am going to bet so they can do the opposite and make big money.

Well, gents, I might as well tell you where I stand. I dont believe either club can win as neither 1 of them has got a manager. But I do know both of the so-called managers personally and I have asked them who is going to pitch the opening game and they both say everybody on the staff so it looks like a free hitting game with Gerner and Mayer in there at the start and Mitchell and Lowdermilk to relieve them, but neither has made any provisions in regards to who is going to relieve us newspapers guys.

The other day as you may remember, I tried to make a comparison of the 2 clubs man for man and when I come to the shortstops why I said the logical thing, which is that no shortstops can win the serious as nobody ever hits to the shortstops in a big event like this. But thousands of birds wrote in personal letters to know what I thought of the 2 shortstops any way so I suppose I have got to tell them.

Well of the 2 shortstops mentioned Risberg and Kopf will be in there at the start of the serious but they will both be took out before the serious is 9 games old.

Compareing the both of them, Risberg is a Swede, but on the other hand Kopf hits from both sides of the plate. Both of them is tricky and is libel to throw a ball to a different base than expected. Kopf is the better looking but Risberg is the tallest and if they ever try to drive a high line drive over his head they will get fooled.

The 2 stars of the comeing serious has both been overlooked by the experts and I refer to Sherwood Magee and John Collins whom a lot of you think wont be in there. Even if they are not they are both good fellows.

Another question the public keeps asking we experts is who gets the advantage of having the serious 9 games in the stead of 7. Well gents all as I can say is it isnt the newspaper men. Further and more I wouldnt be surprised if neither ball club liked the new regime as I have nicknamed it as it looks to me like both mgrs. would use up all the pitchers they have got tomorrow and wouldn't know what to do next.

All together it looks like a long serious, and whoever made it nine games had it in for us.

Kid's Strategy Goes Amuck as Jake Doesn't Die

Bell Syndicate, Oct. 2, 1919

CINCINNATI, OHIO—GENTS: UP TO THE EIGHTH INNING THIS PM, we was all setting there wondering what to write about and I happened to be looking at Jake Daubert's picture on the souvenir program and all of a sudden Jake fell over and I thought he was dead so I said to the boys:

"Here is your story. Jacob E. Daubert was born in Shamokin, Pa., on the 17 of April, 1886, and lives in Schuykill Pa. and began playing with the Kane, Pa., club in 1907. With Cleveland in 1908 and Toledo for two years. Joined the Brooklyn club in 1910 and remained there until this season. Then joined the Cincinnati Reds and fell dead in the 8th inning of the 1st. game of the World Serious."

So everybody got up and cheered me and said that was a very funny story but all of a sudden again Jake stood up and looked at the different pts. of the compass and walked to 1st. base and wasn't dead at all and everybody turned around and hissed me for not giving them a good story.

Well Gents I am not to blame because when a man has got a fast ball like Grover Lowdermilk and hits a man like Jake in the temple, I generally always figure they are dead and the fact that Jake got up and walked to 1st. base is certainly not my fault and I hope nobody will hold it vs me.

That was only one case where Mr. Gleason's strategy went amuck. His idear there was to kill the regular 1st. baseman and then all Mr. Moran would have left to do would be to either stick Dutch Reuther on 1st. base where he couldn't pitch or else stick Sherwood Magee over there where he couldn't coach at third base. But Jake gummed all up by not dying.

Well another part of Mr. Gleason's strategy was dressing the White Sox in their home uniforms so as they would think they was playing on the home grounds in front of a friendly crowd but the trouble with that was that the Reds was all dressed in their home uniforms so as you couldn't tell which club was at home and which wasn't and it made both of them nervous. Then to cap off the climax Mr. Gleason goes and starts a pitcher that everybody thought he was going to start which took away the element of surprise and made a joker out of the ball game.

If he had of only started Erskine Mayer or Bill James or any of the other boys that I recommended why the Reds breath would have been took away and even if they had of hit they couldn't of ran out their hits.

The trouble with the White Sox today was that they was in there trying to back up a nervous young pitcher that never faced a big crowd in a crux before and when he got scared and blowed why it was natural for the rest of them to also blow up. But just give these young Chicago boys a chance to get use to playing before a big crowd with money depending on it and you will be surprised at how they get on their ft. and come back at them.

Nobody should ought to find fault with Mr. Gleason, however, for what happened today. As soon as it was decided that they would have 9 games in this serious why the Kid set down and figured that the rules called for 9 men on a side and if 1 Red was killed per day and the serious run the full 9 games why they would only be 1 man left to play the final game and 1 man cant very well win a ball game even vs. the White Sox the way they looked. But Daubert didn't die as expected and they will know better next time then to hit a left handed 1st. baseman in the egg. As for the game itself they has probably never been a thriller game in a big serious. The big thrill come in the 4th. innings when everybody was wondering if the Sox would ever get the 3rd. man out. They finely did and several occupants of the press box was overcome. The White Sox only chance at that pt. was to keep the Reds in there hitting till darkness fell and make it a illegal game but Heinie Groh finely hit a ball that Felsch could not help from catching and gummed up another piece of stratagem.

Before the game a band led by John Philip Sousa played a catchy air called the Stars and Stripes Forever and it looks to me like everybody would be whistling it before the serious runs a dozen more games.

It now looks like the present serious would be 1 big surprise after another and tomorrow's shock will occur when the batterys is announced which will be Rube Bressler for the Reds and Lefty Sullivan for the Sox. This will be the biggest upset of the entire fiasco.

I seen both managers right after today's holy cost and Moran said hello old pal, and Gleason said hello you big bum so I am picking the Reds from now on.

The Other Member of Ring Family Got Breaks Today, Gents, So the Reds Copped

"There is a Strong Resemblance Between Us," Writes Lardner, "Jim Pitches Better Than I write and I Pitch Better Than He Writes; We're Both a Trifle Wild."

Bell Syndicate, Oct. 4, 1919

CHICAGO, ILL—GENTS: THERE IS A STRONG FAMILY RESEMBLANCE between the Rings. Both of them is handsome and has beautiful curves. Both of them is inclined to be a trifle wild. Jim[1] has a bit more speed. Neither of them has much luck, at least they told me down in Cincy that Jim was the Jinx bird of the National League all summer as the Reds never batted much behind him, as for me, the boys has been batting me around only a trifle.

Jim pitches better than I write and I pitch better than he writes. Jim is a decided blonde while I am a kind of dapple gray since the serious opened up. On account of Jim's complexion he don't look so bad when he don't have a chance to shave.

Jim got a lot of praise today while all I got was insults. For instants, I was down in the hotel before the game and a Chicago man a man from Cincy was trying to bet but they couldn't find no one to put it up with and finally the Chicago man spots me and introduces me to the Red bird and the latter said he wouldn't bet under such conditions.

As for today's game they was a scribe down town this a. m. that 2 men asked him who was going to pitch today and the scribe said Cicotte and 1 of the men said you are as crazy as Cicotte has such a sore arm that he can't wash the back of his neck.

So when we come out to the Park this scribe told me about it and I said they wasn't nothing in the rules of today's game that required Cicotte to wash the back of his neck or any of the newspaper men neither.

"Well," said the other expert, "the man was just speaking figuratively and ment that Eddie had a sore arm." "Well," I said, "if he has only got 1 sore arm he can wash the back of his neck as I only use 1 when I am going to a party." "The back of your neck looks like it," said the other expert. "Yes," I said. "But what is the difference or not about Cicotte only having 1 sore arm as he only pitches with 1 arm." "Yes, you bum but that is the arm the man said was sore." That is the kind of clever repartee that goes on between experts and no hard feelings on neither side.

But of course the 2 of us looked Cicotte over carefully when he got out there to pitch and we came to the conclusion that it must have been his left arm that was sore after all and if he practices hard he can learn to wash the back of his neck with his right a specially if he was born right handed like a man should ought to be.

No, gents, it wasn't no sore arm that beat Eddie today but just the other member of the Ring family finally getting some of the breaks and the way I seen the game you couldn't believe that either of the 2 birds had any impediment in the old souper as I have nicknamed it. Eddie had a sore heart when it was all over but theys other seasons coming and maybe another game in this serious which don't look like it would end or a month as I took for another 1 of them 40-day rains to begin early tomorrow a. m.

Gents, do you remember when they decided to have the serious go 9 games instead of the conventional 7 and a whole lot of people said that was soup for the Reds as Mr. Gleason didn't have the pitchers to go 9 games. Well, now it looks like the disadvantage was vs. Pat Moran as if the serious had of only been skedooled to go 7 games why by now he would of only had 1 more to win by now whereas on the other hand Mr. Gleason has still got the same pitchers he had to begin with. The only people therefore that gets the advantage is the athletes themselves as they get paid for 5 games instead of 4 and beg to assure the public that the newspaper men wishes they had kept it 4 games as we don't even get the privilege of talking back to the umpire.

Tomorrow's game will be postponed till the 4th day of November and I hope before that time they will give me a room with bath.

Note

1. Jim Ring, the starting pitcher for Cincinnati in the fourth game of the World Series, shut out the White Sox, 2–0, on three hits. Eddie Cicotte, one of the Black Sox who was later banned from baseball for his role in throwing the Series, pitched well himself, giving up two runs on five hits.

Rain, Gents, Puts Me on Par With Guy Who Told Caesar About the Idears of March

And Now, Looking Over Situation Caused by Downpour, and After Careful Study of Pitchers, I Find it Will Have Absolutely No Effect, Writes Lardner.

Bell Syndicate, Oct. 6, 1919

CHICAGO—WELL, GENTS, I GUESS THEM EXPERTS WHO HAVE BEEN sniggering in their sleeve at me because maybe once in a while I make a little mistake about who is going to win a ball game or something will do their laughing on the other ft. After the little trick I showed them Saturday when I come right out is print and said yesterday's game would be postponed on account of rain.

The prediction is all the more wonderful when you set down and figure out that this is the first Sunday it ever rained in old Chi when they was a ball game skedooled at Comiskey pk. So me coming out and saying it would rain today puts me on a par with that old guy in Rome that told Caesar he was going to croke on the idears of March, and sure enough he did, and it was first time in his life that he ever done it in that month or any other month in the calendar, you might say.

The first thing I done when I woke up yesterday was look outside of the window, and the instant I looked out I seen it was drooling, so I ordered up the morning paper and layed down and turned to the humorous column called "Today's weather." Well, whoever writes it said: "Probably showers, with lower temperature and versatile winds." But he didn't mention nothing about postponing no ball game, so if he comes forward with the claim that he is in the same class as myself and that old Rome guy, why he will himself laughed out of the league.

Now the next thing is to predict what effect will the rain be on the remains of the world serious. Well, they's several ways of looking at it and a man that jumps into conclusions and says this and that and the other thing without setting down and giving the matter thoughts is libel to become the Philadelphia of predictors.

So during the sermon yesterday morning I leaned back and kind of half closed the old eyes and studied the matter from all angles, and here is some of the conclusions I reached, and I will give the way I arrived at them so you fans will have some idea on how a great man's mind works.

Well, then to begin with, there is the effect on the railroad companies which had their trains all fixed to start for Cincinnati last night, and either they had to go empty or else call up all the porters and say, "George, you don't need to show up tonight." This problem is out of my line and up to the R. R. Administration.

Question No. 2 is, which club gets the benefits out of the rain? To answer this a man has got to know how rain affects the different pitchers. For inst, Grover Lowdermilk always gets taller after a heavy rain. Dick Kerr usually gets cross and mean. Lefty Wms. just kind of half smiles and makes the best of it. Eddie Cicotte plays a lot of practical jokes on the rest of the boys.

Bill James simply lets things take their course, and waits for the clouds to roll by. I have not yet become acquainted with Mr. Wilkinson, but as they tell me he runs a farm down East, I suppose he hasn't no objection to a little rain provided it don't have no heavy wind with it.

Now, take the Cincinnati staff, and a man stumbles onto some startling facts. On a rainy day in the regular season Slim Salice generally most always goes to the races, and the way he feels the next day depends on who win. Well, they wasn't no races here yesterday or race riots neither one, so I haven't no idear if Sal will be sunny and gay or morose.

As for Dutch Reuther they was 1 day last summer when the Reds was supposed to play hero but they was a regt of Chi soldiers going to be welcomed home that same day so of course it poured rain and I was wadeing along Clark st. and met Dutch and he was wearing a raincoat so the Red fans needn't have no fear that he will come down with a heavy cold.

I never seen Jimmy Ring after a rainstorm but if he is like the rest of the Rings he will probably look like he ought to get his clothes pressed. Personally I never carry a bumbershoot and always look worse than usual when I come in out of the wet and when I look bad I get mad and bark like a dog.

The one who is libel to be the most surprised is Luque[1] as they tell me it never rains in Cuba. Eller, Fisher, Mitchell and Gerner is all good natured boys that don't allow a little think like a rain to ruffle them up.

So all in all it looks like the rainy day would have absolutely no effect on either club and it only remains to be seen how the umpires will take it. It will probably make them all the more anxious to get the serious over in a hurry and they will begin calling everybody out.

The game was called off about 11 bells yesterday a. m., after a consultation between Mgrs. Gleason and Moran, which run something like as follows:

> Moran—"Hello, is this you, Bill? They tell me the grounds are too wet to play on them."
>
> Gleason—"Well, the outfield is pretty wet, but we had the infield covered and we could play the game on that."
>
> Moran—"Oh, no, we won't, for Happy and Lucky Felsch might get an extra base hit."
>
> Gleason—"Well, good by, old pal."
>
> Moran—"Good luck, old chum."

Note

1. Dolf Luque, the first Latino pitcher in Major League Baseball. He was also the first to win a World Series game and the first to lead both leagues in wins and shutouts.

Gents, You Can't Expect a Southpaw With Oil Stock to Respect Other Folks' Leases

Happy Go Lucky Felsch Finely Got One and Pat Said to Himself if a Man is Unlucky Enough to Let That Guy Hit He Is Better in the Club House, Writes Lardner.

Bell Syndicate, Oct. 8, 1919

CINCINNATI—GENTS—INSTEAD OF GOING TO LATONIA YESTERDAY I sent my jack over by a messenger and told him to throw it through the gate and, in the meanwhile, I went out to the so-called National Pastime. My first experience was trying to get into the park without showing a ticket and the guy stopped me and says, "Where is your ticket, Brother?"

Well, I never seen this bird before in all my born days, but I have got three perfectly good brothers, so I gave him a keen glance to see if maybe he was one of them, but if he was he had changed a whole lot, so I said, "Which of my brothers is you?" And he kind of fumbled and stalled and couldn't answer nothing back, so I simply passed it up by showing him my ticket and going into the ball park.

Upon the runway I met a lady from Philadelphia who says, "Well, the series will be all over," and I asked her how did she know and she said because Cincinnati is a one-night stand and all they have got to see is Fountain Square and the Ohio and Garfield's statue. So I quit talking to her as I have seen more than that and I know for a fact that they's a whole lot more to seen here than is visible to the nude eye if you stick around here awhile, which it looks like we would do so now.

After leaving the lady from Philadelphia, much to her regrets, I went to the banquet hall and who should I run into but the president of the other league. "Well, Ban," I said, "are you going to suspend Cracker Schalk for what he done Monday?" I call Schalk Cracker because he calls me Biscuit. "What did he do?" says Ban. "Why," says I, "he hit an umpire and didn't kill him." "I didn't see it," says Ban, and I asked if he was out to the game and he said he was, so that makes two people that go to the game and not watch them, not including the umpires.

A great many of you Gents may wonder why I keep ragging the umpires like this. Well, I really don't mean it and the real purpose is kind of subtle, but I would just as leaf tell you birds what it is. The other day I met Bill Evans and he said, "Keep putting my name in the paper," so I have to sort of pan them or how could I do it; but at that I was kind of wandering around amist the bugs in the ninth inning this p. m. and Bill called a strike on whoever was up to the bat and a lot of maudlins around me began to pan Bill, so I stepped up and said, "Do you know why they have the umpires down there on the field?" and one bird says "No." So I said, "It's because they can see the plays much better than if they was up in the grand stand." That silenced them.

But to get back to Ban, I says, "If you aren't going to suspend Cracker why don't you suspend Carl Mays,[1] as you ought to live up to your reputation as a suspender." It's a wonder he didn't give me a belt in the jaw.

After banqueting on a special brand of ham recommended by Garry Hermann, but I won't mention its name in pure reading matter why I went up in the press coop and looked down on the field and some birds from Texas was just presenting Dickie Kerr with a bunch of oil stock. The difference between a bunch of oil stock and a bunch of flowers which they usually wish on a pitcher is that a bunch of oil stock waits two days instead of one before it withers and dies.

When in the fifth they was a man on third and second and first and very few out and Cocky Collins hit one of his lined drives which don't never seem to go safe and somebody caught it and whoever was on third scored and Waffles Schalk stuck on second base but Dickey was still thinking about this here oil yet and he run down to second and found that somebody else had a lease on that property and along comes Sheriff

Groh and tagged him and said, "You are it." You can't expect a left-hander with oil stock to respect other people's leases on second base.

Between that inning and the subsequent inning Dickey took off his shoe to rest his dogs and it took him such a long while that I was going to walk out and leave the ball game flat as I thought the series was over anyway and I got down on the next floor and first thing you know Dutch Ruether wasn't in there pitching no more as Happy Go Lucky Flesh had finely got one and Pat said to himself if a man is unlucky enough to let Felsch get a base hit he is better in the clubhouse than here anyway I looked out there to see who was pitching and it was the other member of the Ring family.

So that is why I stayed through the ball game, and pretty soon I was parked right beside Dutch Ruether himself, and he said: "Well, it ought to be over by now, but I lost my stuff." So I said let's go to the races today, and he said that was my intentions, but now I have got to come back here again, he acted kind of disappointed over not winning, but great heavens when he gets to be my age he will be glad to be alive, let alone mourning over one ball game.

Note

1. Carl Mays gained infamy while pitching for the Yankees a year after Lardner wrote this column when he hit Cleveland Indians batter Ray Chapman in the head with a high fastball, fracturing his skull. Chapman died in a hospital the following day and remains the only player in Major League Baseball history to die as the result of an injury on the field.

A Dirty Finger on the Ball

Bell Syndicate, Oct. 9, 1919

CINCINNATI—GENTS: THIS IS THE MOST SCANDALOUS AND DEATH dealing story ever wrote about a world serious ball game. They have been a whole lot of talk in this serious about one thing and another and it finely remained for me to get at the facts.

Well, those of you who was out at todays game dont have to be explained to that in the fifth inning Eddie Cicotte pitched a baseball to Larry Kopf and Larry missed it and turned around to Mr. Quigley who was supposed to be umpiring behind the plate and asked this bird to let him (Kopf) see the ball.

Well, Mr. Quigley give Mr. Kopf the ball and he looked at it and Mr. Quigley said "Larry do you want the ball," and Larry said "No I dont want it." So Mr. Quigley said "All right throw the ball back to the pitcher. I cant stop this ball game all day to let an infielder look at a ball." Then I stepped in and said "Give me the ball" so they did.

Well, they give me the ball and here it is laying in front of me and I want to say to all infielders who of course never keep a ball long enough to look at it just what a baseball looks like and if I was an infielder I would catch a ball some time and hold on to it till after the game was lost and then I would study the ball.

Well, here is the ball right in front of me as I try to write. I will describe to you guys as I see it. Well, this ball looks to me like a National League ball. That is what probably deceived them.

Well you see the reason that an infielder dont know what a baseball looks like is because the minute he gets it he has to throw it somewhere.

Well as I said before here is what the baseball looks like. The National League baseball is nearly round.

This baseball which I am going to keep and give to my oldest child is a baseball that needs further description. It is the same baseball that Larry Kopf looked at and I only wished I was as nice looking as him and I wouldn't be writing this horrible stuff or working at baseball.

Well, then, here is about that baseball. It is nearly round and looks nearly like an American League baseball except it has more seams and to be exact it has got 126 seams and if you take an American League ball why it has got 140 seams so why shouldnt you hit them. But at that you take any ball and start counting seams on it and you can count all night and get innumerable seams. Well to distinguish this ball from its brothers it says John A. Heydler on it which makes it a cinch that it is a National League ball as it is a certainty—that John wouldnt sign a ball that belonged to the other league.

Well as for the rest of the ball it looks soiled on the northwest side and I will worry my life away wondering who put a dirty finger on that ball which I have got and my children will still have it after me.

Now we have wrote almost a whole story about a ball. Now let us take a different angle about the game and start in on Morris Rath. At one stage of the game Morris hit a ball and broke his bat and the man setting next to me said that is the only time Morris ever broke a bat in a world's serious.

Another funny thing I heard was as follows.

A man named Wingo come up to the bat and the bird setting next to me said come on Wingo get a bingo.

Ring Sees New Way to Clean Bases

Bell Syndicate, Oct. 11, 1920

CLEVELAND, OHIO—YOUR CORRESPONDENT WALKED OUT ON THIS alleged ball game in the seventh innings and you will half to ask some of the other boys how many hits they got all told off of Mr. Bagby without it doing them no good. Mr. Bagby is said to be a pitcher that his success depends on his knowledge of the opp. batsman. That was the reason he got trimmed the other day in Brooklyn because he hadnt never had no chance to study the Brookin's. Personally it has seemed to us like it would take a Dr in a physcopathical hospital to study some of them birds right. But Mr. Bagby proved today that his one days experience vs them had showed him how they could be beat. The secret is to leave them hit safe and run themselves ragged on the bases.

This game was a conflict between Bagby's brains and Brooklyn's brains. In fact it was a duel of master minds.

The Robins being using their noodle in the last ½ of the first innings. Jamieson and Wambsganss hit singles and theys was mens on 1st and 2nd with nobody out. It looked like this was a situation that hadnt never came up before the Brooklyn nine before. Any way a meeting was called in the midst of the diamond with Olson, Sheehan, Grimes, Koney and Miller in attendants. It was decided that when Mgr. Speaker bunted, Grimes was to sit down on the grass and take a good rest. This piece of strategy worked like a charm. But the Robins then faced another new situation. Namely the bases drunk and nobody out. Another conference was called to decide witch was the quickest way to clear the bases and get a fresh start. The decision was to get Elmer Smith in the hole with 2 strikes and then pitch him a ball that he could hit over the fence.

In the 2nd and 3rd innings the Robins give their brains a well earned vacation and they was fresh and ready for more action when the Indians come in for their 4th turn at bat. This time Doc Johnston got on 3rd base with 1 out and the league of nations decided to walk Steve O'Neill and make a monkey out of Bagby. Three runs, 3 hits, no luck.

In the next innings Kilduff and Miller got base hits off Bagby's master mind and Mitchell cleaned the bases with a line drive to Wambsganss. A expert cuckoo setting in the press box told me that it was the first time in worlds serious history that a man named Wambsganss had ever made a triple play assisted by consonants.[1]

Mgr. Speaker got even with Mr. Robinson in the other ½ of this same innings. Jimmy Johnston had cracked his voice at church in the morning singing in a mixed up quartette with his 3 brothers. A boy named Sheehan from South Chicago was the only 3rd baseman Robbie had and he wasnt eligible. Well neither is Sewell, but Robbie had give Spoke permission to use him in this serious and Sewell is partly responsible for Brooklyn winning two games. So Spoke says sure go ahead and use Sheehan and in this here Cleveland 5th this here Speaker hit a ball to this here Sheehan and he throwed it home to south Chicago for the souvenir of the classic event.

A gal with a cute mouth that works here in the Telegraph says just now that Brooklyn scored a run in the 9th and got 13 hits so Bagby didnt break no records after all as he allowed the White Sox 16 hits one day and they didnt score and probably didnt try to.

As predicted above I came out of the ball game in the 7th and clumb into a car in witch they was 6 other occupants including Mr. Mains, the President of the Michigan Ontario league, but when we got down town, he ast the driver how much it was and the driver says 75 cents a piece so Mr. Mains give him $5.00 and says it is for the whole crowd, though as I say 5 of the passenger was perfect strangers and probably never heard of the Michigan-Ontario League and never will. Being president of a baseball league has drove many another man cuckoo. Mr. Mains has a suite of rms reserved in every hotel in Cleveland and moves from one suite to another suite every morning so as the chamber horse wont half to make up his bed.

It comes to light today that theys been a attempt to frame the serious after all. When Leslie Nunamaker was about to retire the last night in NY city he noticed that his pillow kind of bulged like Mgr. Robinson and he looked under it found $16.00. This was evidently a bribe of $1 a piece for the guys that Mgr. Speaker messes up the order with pretty near every day Nunie hasn't never lived in one big league city long enough to buy property and contract a mortgage so he left the filthy money under the ditto pillow and came back to Cleveland as clean as he left it.

Rube Marquard was out to the pk in a Brooklyn uniform and not stripes. You know Rube was arrested here for alleged ticket scalloping.

It seems Rube had just about cleared himself on the grounds that he wasnt in earnest. His testimony is that he bought $275.00 worth of seats and ast somebody jokingly if they would give him $350 for them. Rube has been in vaudeville and knows a joke when he sees same.

That's about all the news except that the same nines will battle tomorrow and the game may give Robbie a chance to try out Miljus and Mobert, both of which is beginning to feel like they was being overlooked, and they will be a meeting of baseball writers to decide whether or not they will fall off the water wagon.

Personly I am about to romp back to the hotel and jokingly order something to eat and see if the waiter thinks I mean it.

Note

1. Bill Wambsganss' legendary play remains the only triple play, unassisted or not, in Major League Baseball's post-season history.

No Need to Bribe Brooklyn

Bell Syndicate, Oct. 4, 1920

LONG ISLAND—Well, Brooklyn winning the Natl. League penance gives the comeing world serious a international odor, but it is hoped the flavor don't last as long as the sweet perfume witch is still exhaleing out of the 1919 classic. In the early days of the world serious they was a theory that the boys on the winning eleven made more jack than the loosers, but last yr. the Reds only drug down $5,200.00 apiece, witch some people inclusive of the Cook County grand jury say was just pin money along side of what a few of the victims grabbed off.

All joking to 1 side, I wouldn't be surprised if this serious was win and lose on its merits. I will promise the fans that if either club is boughten off it won't be the Robins. The gamblers seen them perform in the serious of 1916, and feel like it would be a waist of money to bribe them to not play their best. They can do that without no bonus. Besides witch the boys on the Brooklyn nine is as nice a bunch as you would want to meet, and I would trust them with anything I got at 6 per cent though several of them has often double-crossed the men they was working for. For inst., they led Stallings and Chance and McGraw and etc. to believe that they wasn't no good so as they could get to Brooklyn, and as soon as they got there—look at them.

Experts is divided amongst themself as to who should ought to cop this set to. The Robins is doped to win by some of them. Others say they would half to be. The latter point to what happened in 1916, but they want to remember that Brooklyn 4 yrs. ago and Brooklyn now is two different boroughs. Some of the Robins witch was in their early forties when they played the Red Sox has had time to mellow without getting over ripe or rancid, as Robbie has kept them in a cool place near the cellar most of the while. And, with a few exceptions, they are mostly all birds that has had too much experience to get scared in a pinch.

To Rube Marquard, for inst., a world serious is just like a bathtub. He has been in more of them than anybody in the Natl League outside of Bill Klem. World serious, I mean.

Personally I don't like neither club's chances, and won't recommend neither of them because even a man like myself can't know everything. Last yr., for example. I told my friends that the White Sox was a cinch and go bet on them, but that was because I didn't have no idear how many good ball players was playing for the Reds that never had their names in a Cincinnati box score. I wish I had my money back. My advice to the fan this time is to watch the umpires close, and if one of them pulls a close one that looks raw write him a abusive letter.

The genl. custom for a expert at this stage, is to take the 2 opposing teams and compare them man for man and in that way the readers will get a pretty good idear of nothing. Look at last fall for inst. All the nuts that writes base ball agreed before the serious that when it comes to the rival 2d basemans, why Morris Rath wouldn't never be on speaking terms with Eddie Collins. But in the games themself Morris was on the bases so much that he got to be a pest, while Columbia's favorite alumnae never found out where 1st base was only by hearsay.

So I am under the delusion that they's other ways of waisting the readers' time and my way is to write a few vital statistics in regards to Robbie's boys witch is not so well known to base ball dumb in genl. as their great American league oppts.

Well then, Konetchy, Kilduff and Kreuger all starts their last name with K. Mamauz, McCabe, can outsing anybody in the American league and the Robins boasts of the best quartet that has been in agonized base ball since the Red Sox left go of Buck O'Brien, Hugh Bradley, Marty McHale and who ever was the 4th thrust in that bird's nest. Robbie's pitching aces is expected to be Smith, Grimes, and Cadoro and we defys any American league mgr. to produce 3 good pitchers with as pretty a 1st name as Sherrod, Burleigh and Leon. The Olson that plays shortstop is the only Olson that his 1st name ain't Ole and the Griffith that plays the outfield is a great grandson of Clark Griffith of the Washington club.

In 1916 President Ebbets of the Brooklyn club was so pleased with his boys winning the penance that he treated them with a ride to Boston in a day coach for the 1st game of the serious. So this yr. the Robins was kind of pulling for the Yankees to win in the other league as they wanted to experience the delights of a trip from Brooklyn to the Polo Grounds in a wheel barrow. However the fates ruled otherwise and it is announced that when the National league champs leaves for the west it will be in a smoker equipped with seats that you can turn over and park your dogs on the top seat and plenty of floor space to throw ashes and get rid of used up eating tobacco.

Ring's in Cleveland and How He Dreads It

Bell Syndicate, Oct 9, 1920

CLEVELAND, O—Cleveland time is one hour behind New York city and Brooklyn, but the train we come on wasn't satisfied with that and throwed in a couple hours more. At that, all hands reached the so-called forest city in plenty time to play a ball game if a ball game had been scheduled, but this was a off day by mutual agreement between Ban Johnson. No squawk was made by President Ebbets, as he figured his athletes would need a extra night rest anyway as they are not use to riding in a sleeper during a world series. The only world serious they was ever in before was a day coach jump between New York and Boston,

To satisfy a nation wide curiosity I will say that 1 and Hughey Fullerton left the Grand Central station Thursday night on the 8:00 o'clock train, witch leaves at 9 o'clock. Mr. Ebbets and Mr. Robinson and the Brooklyn ball players was in the last 2 pullmans. I and Hughey was escorted way up to the front of the train to car 94. A blackface comedian ast what our space was and Hughey says "We got the drawing room." "Witch drawing room?" says George. "It don't make no difference," says Hughey. "I and my friend here is at home in any drawing room." So George seen what class of people we was and stuck us in A.

I been troubled lately with unsomnia, but pretty soon Hughey began telling me how Thursday's game was win and losed and I dozed off and didn't wake up till this AM in a town name Buffalo where the train stopped and couldn't get started again. The conductor was pretty mad and claimed that somebody must be dragging their feet but he couldn't find nobody that their foot wasn't parked inside the cars. Finely he got to the tail-end Pullman and seen Manager Robinson and the mystery was solved. He put it up to Mr. Ebbets to either get another manager or catch another train and the master mind decided to keep Robbie, so the conductor paged a couple of 10 Wheelers to help the switch engine cut off the extra growth and without the 2 cars containing the man-o'-war of baseball we got along pretty good,

I and Hughey went in the dining car where Hughey ordered 2 eggs boiled four minutes railroad time and I had a breakfast that a person wouldn't even dast to hint at in the heavily mortgaged home. Our companion at the table was the Brooklyn delegation of fans and his interpreter,

At Westfield we bought a Cleveland paper that had a picture of George Burns and it said under it "the man that made the feature catch of the serious when he raced to the 1st base stand in Brooklyn Thursday and reached over into the crowd and grabbed a foul ball with one fin." The picture was a picture of George Burns left fielder for the Giants, Some catch Geo.

The paper and the other Cleveland papers is full of stuff about the team witch they call tribe witch is a nickname for the Indians. We ain't been able to find out what the tribe these Indians belongs to but in the last 2 games they looked like one of the Lost tribes.

However nobody is discouraged with the way the serious has went so far, especially the Brooklyn club. Heap Big Chief Speaker of the Tribe expects his warriors to start hitting again tomorrow on the grounds where they piles up most of their .302 batting average this summer and when the Cleveland boys is hitting they generally always scores more runs than vice versa. The Cleveland club's trainer is the only one in the bunch that looks down in the mouth. He is sore because he went to the trouble of having the bats sent clear to Brooklyn where they wasn't used.

It is 7 years since I was to Cleveland before and the last time I left I kissed the Union Station goodby, with a tear in my eye expecting to not never see her no more, but outside of being a little grayer and a few more wrinkles she is still the same old Union Station always ready and willing to give the incoming traveler a hearty laugh.

Our taxi man ast us where the Brooklyn ball club was and we told him they was on the other section and the man says he hoped they would have sense enough not to take a non-union taxi or they was liable to get hurt. Well, I and Hughey took a union taxi and we was liable to get hurt all the way to the hotel and the next time I go riding it will in a taxi scab. And it looks like we would be called out often as the umpire is stopping at this hotel. Ollie Chill witch makes Cleveland his home was on hand to give them a royal reception. You thought 1 was going to say chill reception but I crossed you like I was an umpire myself,

The fact that Ollie and Billy Evans both makes this their home solves the mystery of what umpires do in the winter time. They live in Cleveland or Yonkers or Chicago or Syracuse.

The papers predicts that both Robbie and Spoke will use their pitching aces in tomorrow's game, but that don't mean nothing to me. Aces is getting as common in the public prints as master minds and if they keep on cheapening aces, why pretty soon, a man that holds 3 of them before the draw will throw his cards in in the ash can and say "did you ever see anybody hold such rotten hands?"

Nothing in Players' Sox But Holes

Even With Visiting Brooklynites to Swell Numbers at Dunn's Park, Winner's Share Will About Equal Last Year's Losers.

Bell Syndicate, October 10, 1920

CLEVELAND—THIS WAS A SAD 'XMAS IN CLEVELAND. THE BALLPLAYERS and umpires and reporters woke up with the break of dawn and some of them with a headache and their first thought was of the wife and kiddies and the heavily mortgaged home. But when they looked under their pillow they wasnt nothing in their stockings only a toe hole. Abe Claus has forgot the boys this year and it don't seem like the merry yuletide it was a year ago.

Even with the high school of fish that swum into Jim Dunn ball park today it looks like the winners share of the players in this serious wont be as much as some of the losers got in 1919, not even ½ as much as some of the losers got. A Master mind is needed to peep this serious up and the days is getting shorter.

Incoming trains from the east brought a few Brooklyn nuts that was confident that the Robins had the serious sewed up, but they had left their money sown up in their overalls, these here trains drug in a couple of my old pals that had to stay in New York city a day to get their noses put back in place after Wednesday nights Olympic games where the main event was the china discuss throw.

Mr. Arthur Donnelly showed up on a train from St. Louis. Mr. Donnelly is said to be the biggest undertaker in St. Louis and you know they call it the mound city. Mr. Donnelly runs a ad in the St Louis national league score card witch says "Arthur Donnelly, professional boxer." Mr. Donnelly does such a business that several members of the cardinals witch has long been ready for his expert services is still standing in line.

When we came down in the lobby of the sumptuous hotel this forenoon the joint was a hot bed of umpires. It looks like this was one reason why the Indians was all set to win the pennant. Cy Rigler and Bill Evans and Ollie Chill, all local and tender residents of this peculiar city, are ready and more than ready to take their places. The city of Cleveland seems to be ran by a mayor and a board of alderman and an umpire at each corner to see that the gals is safe when they're out.

Well, we thought that they would have plenty of taxi cabs in a city with such a perfect government, you might say, but the ones that I seen was full as well as their fares and the best I could do was clime into a private owned vehicle that the bird that owned it said he would fetch me out to the ball park for $2.00. It was one of these here machines that they says that theys no place they cant go and my chaufer started out to prove it. Euclid avenue was dirty with traffic and we tried to turn of into a slide street. The traffic cop says, "Why and the hell don't you stick your hand out when you want to turn?" "I did stick my hand out," says my Jehu. "What do you mean why didn't I stick my hand out?" "Well" say that flat foot, "You must have a small hand." "If ain't no smaller than your head" says my Yahoo, and away we went much refreshed by the exchange of Cleveland repartee. The street we went into says street closed, but my man couldn't read very good so went along it pretty near to the ball park and when we got there most of what it left of my hirsute adornments was sticking to the one man top, but it was $2.00 just the same, nothing off for the hair.

Well, I got in too late to tell you who warmed up for the 2 rival nines, but Robbie seemed to have plenty of his aces ready but when they got in there the most of them looked like them other little cards that lives at the other end of the deck. It would have been alright if Robbies deuces had been wild but they wasn't even that.

Amidst those present in the stands today was Warren and Clifton Johnson, brother brothers of Jimmy and Doe Johnson. Warren and

Clifton is here looking at the serious and don't dast says witch way they are pulling. The 4 Johnstons is going to put on a quartette number at a Cleveland church tomorrow am and the regular congregation is urged to come early before their pews is jammed with visiting newspaper men.

Ring Splits Double-Header

Bell Syndicate, Oct. 12, 1920

CLEVELAND, OHIO—They was a double header in Cleveland today. The 1st game was played this morning at the Mayfield Country club between the Bell Syndicate vs. Nick Flatley of Boston and Rube Goldberg of Brooklyn. It came out a tie. I and Rube played for a dollar a hole on the side and I got two dollars of the poor hick's money and he can't afford to loose that kind of money either. The medal score refused to be give out for the fear of incriminating itself. Leave me tell the world that Mayfield coarse makes the engineers club on long island look like a billiard table and Alexa Stirling[1] must be a pretty good female golfer to make it in eighty even if one of the Clevelanders does call her Alex A Stirling.

The other game was what I have nicknamed a duel between two rival south paws or left handers. The Robbins has now had sixteen innings of "Duster" Mails[2] and they hope they won't get any more of him. They will probably get what they hope. Sherry Smith and the rest of the Robbins acted kind of grouchy towards Tommy Connolly all afternoon. They was a little matter of $1,600.00 a piece involved in some of Tommy's decisions and as the Brooklyn players is both older and there are more of them than the Cleveland players why naturally they have got more wives and kiddies and more mortgages on the heavily mortgaged farm. So they thought maybe Tommy would give them a little the best of it on ball and strike.

To an impartial and very ignorant observer like the handsome writer it looked like Tommy was as fair to one side as the other and that aint saying much. His right arm seemed to have suffered a stroke of paresis during the night and he didnt like to call strikes unless the ball was either somewhere near the plate or the batter swang at it, either one. But all and all I have watched the work of the umpires pretty close during this series and none of them has been any better than the rest of them and most of them not one half as good as the other three.

Bill Dineen is the only one who you might say has distinguished himself so far. Bill was due to umpire behind the plate in Saturday's game and his colleagues is very particular about their personal appearances on account of umpires being unpopular enough without looking like a rummy, so they noticed that Bills umpiring pants had run out of creases and they was no chance to get them pressed as it is still Yom Kippur in Ohio, so they signed a petition asking him to wear another pair.

So Bill happened to have a pair of street pants which is same cerulean blue that agonized baseball requires the umpires to wear when they are pretending to work, so he decided to put them on but when Bill walks around the street in his trousers he dont wear shin guards under them, as never in his whole life has man or beast came up and deliberately kicked him in the shins wile he was merely walking up and down the st. so the seamstress that made Bill's trousers didnt allow for shin guards and the result was that when the shin guards was stuck under them, the trousers all worked up.

During the last ½ of the Saturday game Bill was wearing involuntary knickerbockers and the fans and fanettes was so busy admiring his charms that they could not look at the ball game.

Amongst those seen today's pastime was Denton Cy Young, the old pitcher that Hughey Fullerton claims to of discovered and Secretary of War Baker. Newt set up in the upper deck and said it was one of the best battles he ever saw closer than from 3,000 miles away. Willie Wambsganss and Elmer Smith was called up to the plate before the game and presented with a couple of watches for what they done in Sunday's game.[3] Elmer's alleged timepiece had his name engraved on it but when the generous jeweler wanted the same thing done for Wamby, the engraver busted him in the jaw and quit.

A kite flew over the field during the battle with Harding and Davis wrote on. It didn't say what business they was in. That is about all that happened today except George Burns' double in the 6th, witch isn't the same Geo. Bums that plays left field for the Giants and lives in a funny town named Little Falls in the off seasons.

Tomorrow is the last day of our enjoyable stay in the 5th city of the grand old U.S. and president Jim Dunn of the Indians better get a hump on himself or Charlie Ebbets of Brooklyn will finish one up on him. It will be remembered by those that was still able to see the last day in Brooklyn that Charley not only showed us a ball game but also throwed in a vaudeville skitch for one and the same admission. This skitch was a race around the bases between Brooklyn ball players and a heel and toe pedestrian almost in the nude. The man in the nether garments was supposed to walk around once before the other bird run around twice. He done it and it looked to him like somebody had put something under the ball player's pillow, but the crowd would of went nuts over the exciting event if they hadnt already been that way before they come in the park.

Anyway, it looks now like it was up Jim to put on a skitch before tomorrow's game, and may I not suggest that he got hold of the gal that plays "Aphrodite," witch is in Cleveland this week and have her come out and practice sliding to bases in her stage costume, witch is put on with a brush.

The boys from Brooklyn is feeling pretty chipper as we go to press because although the Indians has now won 4 games to the Robbins 2, why it looks like Mgr. Speaker with his inferior pitching staff is now up against a tough proposition and may be forced tomorrow to depend on an unreliable young cuckoo named Covaleski.

Notes

1. Alexa Stirling, a childhood friend and golfing companion of Bobby Jones, won three straight U.S. Women's Amateur championships, including the 1920 Open at Mayfield.

2. After winning seven games without a loss in the final two months of the regular season, Mails pitched 6 2/3 scoreless innings in relief in Game 1 of the Series and a complete-game 1–0 shutout in Game 6.

3. The watches were in celebration of Wambsganss' unassisted triple play and Smith's grand slam home run, both World Series firsts.

Lardner Tips Off Giant, Yank Fan "Symptoms"; Marvels at McGraw's Title Attempt in 5862[1]

Bell Syndicate, Oct. 3, 1921

New York—Well, friends, the big series starts Wednesday and I am in readiness for same except that I can't get my pants pressed on account of it being New Years in New York. And besides that I ain't got no ticket yet but I have at least got a chance to get one which is more than can be said for thousands of the boys that have been infesting the pologrounds all season.

Most people is going to see this series than ever seen a series before, but the number of people that is going to see it is a mere drop in the bucket along side of the number of people that ain't going to see it and my one and only prediction in regards to the series is that it will start a squawk that will be heard around the world.

It is fitting that the big town should do big things in a big way and it's my bet that we are going to enjoy a ticket scandal that will stand as a record for ticket scandals for all time and in behalf of the gents that owns the yanks and giants it is only fair to add that it ain't going to be all their fault.

If you have got to blame somebody, pick on Tris Speaker and his ball players who could of saved the whole situation by throwing up the sponge two or three weeks ago and saying we are licked. Instead of that the two New York clubs hasn't had time to read proof on the tickets let alone look up the thumb prints of the boys they been selling to.

Well, anyway, we are going to have a series and by this time the other experts has no doubt told you how the players of the opp. teams compares to they's no comparison left for me to make, unlest it is to compare the yankees fans with the giant fans and I have made a personal study of the both kinds and will write down a few of the symptoms by which you can tell them apart.

A yankee fan is like a man that owns his first automobile or has just had his tonsils took out, he can only talk on one subject. He can repeat rhymes, tell what different colors are and imitate the acts of others. He can maybe count up as high as 20 and make a sentence with three or four given words in it, but he can't stick to no one piece of work or study and he don't show no resistance to temptation. He is libel to be under size and have a funny shape head. His ears is generally always large and hardly ever the same size. He often complains of dizziness and black specks in front of the eyes. He is careless about his clothing though he may be able to dress himself.

The giant fan is generally kind of helpless looking and libel to be paralytic. He can't protect himself from harm and injury. He is liable to have heavy features with a broad nose and thick lips, dry skin and wiry hair. His hands is short and pudgy. His eyes is on the bias and he don't see things right. He is generally always the last one born in a family. They half to dress him and feed him, but he can pass a higher test of intellect than the Yankee fan for inst he can learn to tell time and the day of the month and give the days of the week in order and make simple change, like returning 20 cents from a quarter and etc.

About 3 per cent of giant fans is total abstainers as compared with 1 ½ per cent of Yankee fans but the last named has had the reason for their excesses. On the other hand, they's a much bigger proportion of divorces amongst giant fans and more of them beats their wife.

Giant fans lives for the most part on figs, tubors and grass, while the staples of the yankee fan's diet is insects, nuts, fruits and seeds. Both fans is noted for their harsh and discordant voices.

Another kind of fan who we may see in small quantities at the series is the Brooklyn fan who is like the giant and yankee fan in general aspects and as a rule has the same harsh cry. Some of them, however, utter low and sweet twittering notes. Many can imitate other sounds of human speech and can be learned to say words if given patient training. Some people have got the idear that this process may be aided by slitting the tongue, a practice as useles and foolish as it is barbarous. It is not certain that the tongue has anything to do with a Brooklyn fan's speech, no more than in other birds.

Well, anyway, friends Happy New Year and who would of thought John McGraw would still be trying for the world's championship in 5862.

Note

1. What on earth?! For reasons best known to himself, Lardner is making a reference to Rosh Hashanah, the Jewish New Year, which began the day before he wrote this column. And what could have possessed the headline writer to put this obscure fact in large print? Here is one case where Lardner could have used an editor. The Hebrew calendar says the year was 5682, not 5862.

No Need To Bribe Either Nine, Bettors Decide—Ring

Absorbing Mystery Is How Both Clubs Won. Picks Giants When Talking to George Kelly's Uncle.

Bell Syndicate, October 5, 1921

New York—Well, the eve of the big series is here and by this time everybody has formed some opinion in regards to same, but mine ain't printable. However, Judge Landis is amongst us and has made the positive statement that he don't care which nine wins, but hopes that it will win on its merits.

President Harding himself couldn't of put the matter more clear, and yet they keep the judge on the bench.

The judge don't need to worry about this series being decided on its merits as information has reached the writer that they was a big meeting of the New York gamblers the other night to decide which team to bribe but they come to the conclusion that it wasn't necessary in either case.

A big baseball game like the one scheduled for tomorrow is a sporting event that gives most people all the thrill they are looking for but with all due respect to the national pastime, it seems to me like it lacks the mystery that makes a big fight or a football match so exciting.

For one thing, baseball don't have no secret practice which is one of the main things that rouses interest in a football game or a fight.

Like for instance, you take a football and for two or three weeks before the Yale-Harvard game the sons of Eli and George is shut up behind locked gates and they's nobody allowed to see what they are doing and you don't never find out till the game is on and then you don't know for sure, though you kind of suspect that they was manicuring themselves all that time.

Or you take a fight like the late battle of the century. Carpentier[1] was kept under cover and the newspaper men was, only permitted to look at him twice a week and then only in spooning matches with a couple of parlytics. So it wasn't till the afternoon of the fight that press and public learned what he had been doing in secret, namely, getting fitted for a new silk bath robe.

But baseball is open and above the boards. The two rival clubs knows all about each other. Generally always they have seen each other play in games so important that they was no chance to conceal their full strength. The Yankees knows that Nehf does most of his best pitching with his left hand and the Giants know that Ruth's weakness is a ball throwed toward second base.

So, as I say, while today's game is a big game as big games goes, and while they's plenty of rivalry between the two teams, still they's no mystery about neither one of them unless it's how did they win the pennant. So while I will go to the polo grounds with the expectations of staying awake all p.m. still and all I would be looking forward to a better time if they was any chance that either of the two managers would spring a big surprise, like McGraw leaving his ball players in the club house and showing up on the field with a herd of zebras, or Huggins insisting on the members of both nines wearing skirts to their knees.

But I suppose we will half to be satisfied with the usual ceremonies that goes with a game like this kind, which on this occasion will include special honors being inflicted on Casey Stengel, the left sided utility outfielder of the Giants. Casey's brother, Horace Stengel, and 200 others of fans from Casey's, Gibraltar, are on hand, having made the entire trip by boat.

They will present Mr. Stengel with a diamond studded roller coaster. Brother Horace and the Gibraltar fans planned to attend the Brooklyn-Boston series in 1916, when Casey was a member of the Brooklyn club, but the boat tipped over ½ way acrost and they had to go back.

Amongst the other celebrities hero for the series is Bill Lange, Uncle of the George Kelly of the Giants.

Bill used to be known as the most sensational outfielder in baseball because he misjudged all the fly balls and finely had to grab them with one hand. They asked me who I liked in the series and of course I knew he was George Kelly's uncle, so I says I liked the Giants. "So did I," says Bill, "till I seen them play."

Note

1. George Carpentier, whose heavyweight championship fight against Jack Dempsey three months earlier produced boxing's first million-dollar gate. Lardner, who often covered boxing, was fascinated by Carpentier, a Frenchman whose intelligence and good looks made him popular with men, and women, who had no interest in boxing. Even George Bernard Shaw, who had been a boxer in his youth, was caught up in the frenzy that preceded the fight, writing, "I stake on Carpentier's victory over Dempsey my reputation for knowing what I write about." Dempsey knocked Carpentier out in the fourth round.

Everybody but Umpires Bats in Seventh Inning

Against the Rules to Hit a Pitcher in the Shower Bath, So Quinn Escapes a More Pronounced Beating.

Bell Syndicate, October 8, 1921

New York—I walked out of this one in the 7th innings. Mr. Huggins had just begin calling on some of his anonymous pitchers and it looked like they might get the side out before it was time to start tomorrow's game. The fans who were betting last night that the Giants wouldn't get a run during the series are now offering even money that they wont get more than 100. After the first two games, McGraw's batters claimed that the reason they couldn't hit was on acct. of the back ground in the center field. The scenery was just the same today, but the boys aint squalking no more.

When the game started the pitchers was Fred Toney and Bob Shawkey. Toney begun his big league career with the Cubs and we stopped at Evansville, Ind., on the spring trip and outside the Elks temple they was an iron hitching post built into the cement walk.

One morning Fred picked up the hitching post and hit Heine Zimmerman over the head with it. This was just a prank on Fred's part and of course nobody was hurt. But playing with iron hitching posts and pitching world series ball games is two different things. When Fred has been there a little over two innings, McGraw decided that he had had enough. The Yanks had four runs, but that wasn't enough.

Bob Shawkey was in the navy during the war and seems to be still at sea.

Burns started the Giants' part of the third with a base hit. Burns flied out and Bancroft singled. Shawkey then passed Frisch to get Young and Young to get Kelly. Then he passed Kelly to get Meusel, but just when his strategy might of begun to show results, Huggins took him out.

With an even start of four runs each, Jess Barnes and Jack Quinn set out to have a pitchers' battle or as some call it, a duel of slab artists. This lasted till the Giants' half of the 7th innings when everybody went to bat but President Stoneham and Judge McQuade.[1] Frisch opened up with his seventh hit of the series. Ross Young, whose batting record up to this time was eight times up and two fouls, come to the plate with the intentions of laying down a sacrifice but Quinn pitched two balls and Ross thought the next one was bad, too, and left it go past, but Mr. Quigley called it a strike. This upset Ross and he slapped the next one to the right field for a double.

Up come Bill Lange's grandson,[2] who you can always count on to walk, either to first base or the bench. This time he picked out first base. The next five gents made five base hits, but only two of them was made off Quinn. You can't hit a man in the shower bath. Rip Collins and Rogers was trotted in the rapid succession and as I was leaving the field, Mgr. Huggins sent to the office for the payroll to find out who else had been signed up on the theory that they should pitch.

When a man has set through two hours and twenty minutes of those kind of baseball you naturally feel weak and imagine my delight when I run into Harry Stevens, the genial outdoor caterer, and he insisted on me coming in the press room for a little lunch. A waiter asked me what would I have and I asked him what was they and he recited the bill of fare from memory, which as I recall it was Lobster Salad, Pork and Beans, and your choice of coffee or some of Jake Ruppert's product.

Well, when I don't get no exercise I half to be careful what I put inside of me, so I told him not to bring me no ham. Mr. Stevens lay out reminds the newspaper boys of last year's spread in Brooklyn, only that the lobster, salmon, beef, turkey, tongue, chicken, and bones wasn't seasoned across the bridge.

On the way out I was stopped by a man who looked like his name was Cohen and he asked me didn't I want to buy the official 1921 world series song and it was only a dime so I bought it and the name of it is "O You Babe Ruth" and they have got a picture of Babe on the cover that he could have them arrested for it. Here is the words to the song:

"Out on the polo grounds they're playing,
To see who the champion will be,
The Yankees and Giants are there to do their best or die,
With McGraw and Miller Huggins standing by,
Chorus—
"O you Babe Ruth,
We're betting on you. Wont you come through
Then there is George Kelly he can hit, too, made twenty-two.
Art Nehf pitches them slow. But we don't care, Bambino, so
long as you come through."

That is the words and I haven't tried the tune yet, but it looks just as good as the words, and it will surprise me if the writers aint heard of when they get out.

Notes

1. Charles Stoneham owned the New York Giants and later sold part of the team to Judge Francis Xavier McQuade. The fact that McQuade ruled in favor of Sunday games from the bench in defiance of New York State blue laws might have had something to do with their partnership.

2. Lardner is talking about George "Highpockets" Kelly, who was the nephew, not the grandson, of Bill Lange, a great player in the 1890s who stole 400 bases in seven years. Lange retired in the prime of his career when his prospective father-in-law forbid his daughter to marry someone as disreputable as a baseball player. The marriage quickly ended, but Lange refused all offers to return to the game.

Lardner Hitting 1.000, Peeved at Weatherman

Bell Syndicate, Oct. 9, 1921

NEW YORK—This was one of the stormy days exclusively predicted by the undersigned and now all I need to make my world series prophecy 1000 per cent perfect is another p.m. of rain and a couple of tie games. The boys will still be playing this series a week from today and by that time some of the visiting firemen will be asking their nurse how the game came out. The spirits is plentiful but the flesh is weak.

When news come that it was raining many out of town fans who had been asleep under the grand stand got up and sought vantage points from which to enjoy the novelty as it was their first glimpse of water since reaching New York.

The opinion amongst the experts seemed to be that the postponement helped the Yankees, It gives Huggins pitchers a chance to rest up. though I wouldn't be surprised if some of them had from now till spring to do that. It also was good for Babe Ruth's arm which is said to be infected so that he can't hardly write,[1] but who ever it benefitted the most, I know who it didn't benefit the most and that is the visiting Elks and scribes. It means ruin and the breaking up of homes for some of we boys, thats what it means.

The storm caused a rush of brains to Harry Stevens cafe under the stand, down there I run into Judge Landis to say nothing about George B. Christian, secretary to President Harding, and Bill Pipp, who is Wally Pipps old man. Mr. Pipp introduced us all to Mrs. Pipp and a couple of pippins. Mr. Christian wouldn't say what was the object of his visit to New York, but; he made the remark that the President would like another golf game with I and Grantland Rice, so that may of been it.[2]

They was a large policeman in the runway between the press box and the lunch room and he challenged everybody that tried to go to and fro, including not only Judge Landis but his secretary Mr. O'Connor. As these two gents is really the two who are running the series, its a wonder the officer didn't bean them with his billie, a policemans place is on the third base coaching line.

Well, friends, that is all I am going to write about a game that wasn't played, this is going to be a long series and us experts will need all the words we got without wasting none on a rainy day.

Notes

1. With the help of a ghostwriter, Ruth was reporting on the World Series for a syndicate run by Christy Walsh, who was baseball's first players' agent.

2. Lardner's celebrity, and that of his friend and equally prominent sportswriter Grantland Rice, led to them having lunch at the White House in May of 1921 and playing a round of golf with President Harding.

Scribes Saved from Overflow of Brains

Bell Syndicate, Oct. 10, 1921

THE FANS MAYBE DON'T REALIZE HOW CLOSE WE WAS TO HAVING A holocaust at this pastime. In the second innings, Shufflin' Phil pitched a sour one that just missed cracking Ward square on the egg. An inch lower and the athlete's brains would of come hurtling into the press coop which was already overcrowded with same. You can imagine what the congestion would of did to the scribes in their weakened condition.

As it was, the only casualty of the day was Carl Mays, who the Giants finally got to in the eighth inning and when they got to him they done a man size job of it. Before the game Carl was a good bet to shut them out again like he done the other day as the first 100 times you bat against him is supposed to be the hardest and this was only the Giants' second chance.

And for seven innings today he held them to two clean hits and a scratch single by Snyder which I call a scratch because the official scorers scratched it off the records. But before they was a man out in the eighth the tail end of McGraw's batting order had earned the run that tied the count and had two men in position to score on George Burns' double. Carl was socked for three hard wallops and a safe bunt in this frame and in the ninth his defeat was turned into a disgrace, for three more guys plastered him and one of these three was George Kelly.

Instead of taking his place in the world's series hall of fame along with Ed Walsh, Christy Mathewson, Chief Bender and Red Faber, Carl's name will now go down in history as the pitcher who Bill Lange's grandson got a base hit off of in the series of 5862, New York time. Saturday's rain was supposed to be soup for Carl as it give him an unexpected day of rest. He looks now like he ought to of took another one.

The real heroes of this battle was Emil Meusel, who the Yankee nuts speak of as that brother of Bob Meusel's, and Johnny Rawlings, the weak sister of the series, according to the boys that play the games a few days ahead of the athletes. An explanation of Emil's conduct may be found in the fact that he was with the Phillies up to two months ago and never knew they was one big league, let alone that Carl Mays was the star pitcher of the other one.

Rawlings has been a busher, too, but you'd think he had been around long enough to hear of Carl. Rawlings' work so far can't be explained in no legitimate way and it seems to me like they ought to keep men like he out of an important series. All he does is make a sucker out of the law and prophets.

People that thronged the Polo grounds this time went there without no expectations of seeing Babe Ruth as the Babe was alleged to be out of it for this game at least and maybe for the whole series on account of a poisoned arm. But the Babe fooled everybody and got in the game after telling his Dr. to go to a place which is said to be already overcrowded with the medical profession.

Babe played with his souper all bound round and it seemed to bother him in throwing. But he grabbed himself off another single and made a new world's record by hitting the most useless home run in the history of organized baseball.

The Giant infield played for Ruth pretty near the same way that National league infields play for Cy Williams of the Phillies. Bancroft moved over to the right field side of second base. Rawlings camped in short right field and Kelly hugged the foul line. The whole left side of the infield was left to Frankie Frisch. Babe's first effort was a roller that went right where Kelly was playing. His second was a single to right field which, by the way, George Burns, the centerfielder, was set just right to stop. When he came up the third time he whiffed and as luck would have it, Snyder was playing right where he could catch the third strike. And if Ross Young had only been setting up in the right field seats he could of catched the one Babe hit in the ninth, and took it home to the wife and kiddies, if any. In this infield arrangement Bancroft is the one that is taking the chance, as he stands right where Babe pickles his line drives. One of these days George Burns will see two balls coming at him at once and one of them will be Bancroft's head.

For some reason or another, the Yankees has quit stealing home. Two of them made efforts to steal second today, but they will go down in history as efforts. Roger Peckinpaugh's attempt was a delayed steal in thc sixth inning. They was so much delay that Roger ain't there yet.

One thing I would like to call attention to and have Judge Landis do something about it before the next series is namely the practice of having the band play the "Star Spangled Banner" just before every game. Gents like myself and George Moriarty and Fred Toney is as patriotic as everybody else, but the exposure is terrible. If we have got to keep doing it, at least make the women do it, too. They ought not to be barred when they have already won the right to smoke cigarets, drink gin and pick their teeth.

That is about all I have got to say except that I was woke up this morning to receive a seventy-five word telegram from Nick Altrock, the main idear of which was that I hadn't mentioned him and his partner, Al Schacht,[1] in none of these articles. So here is your name, Nick, and don't send me no more telegrams and I would of give you a write-up, only if a man starts mentioning the names of different comedians in this series they's no place to draw the line. I might even half to include the box score.

Note

1. Former major leaguers, Altrock and Schacht performed comedy routines before the games and with Lardner's help, later took their act to vaudeville.

Lardner Wants Series Transferred to Great Neck

Bell Syndicate, Oct. 12, 1921

NEW YORK—Tomorrow may wind it up, but if it don't the question will arise as to where to play the ninth and deciding game. The Giant and Yankee owners are planning to play it on the Polo Grounds, but the rules say, or at least they used to say, that the odd contest must be played on a neutral field.

In behalf of the Chamber of Commerce, I wish to point out some of the advantages of Great Neck. We can furnish you a vacant lot right across the street from the country home of Tad, the cartoonist. They's no diamond marked out on the lot, but they's a couple of goal posts and the opposing teams has proved that they can kick the ball around if necessary.

Great Neck can be reached both by land and water. It has good drug stories and groceries, a dentist, five or six doctors, a moving-picture theatre, with matinees Saturday and Sunday, good taxi service, an 18-hole golf course and plenty of churches. They's a couple of restaurants, but we would be glad to have you come and lunch with us if you don't mind taking what I have nicknamed pot-luck. But the main advantage of having this game at Great Neck is that it would do away with the mad scramble for tickets which is bound to come off if the owners persist in stageing the battle at the Polo Grounds.

The lot I refer to ain't fenced in and they ain't no seats. So all the difficulties that attends a ticket sale would be did away. If the owners wants to pick up a little loose change to pay R.R. fares and etc., they could pass a hat and have the fans give what they thought it was worth. They's plenty of money in Great Neck, gents, and most of it is there permanently.

Other towns that has put in a bid for the game is Philadelphia, South Bend, Indiana, and San Francisco. Philadelphia is said to be crazy to see a big league ball club in action. South Bend offers a ball park that is right next to a amusement park, where Bob Shawkey, Harry Harper and Fred Toney could enjoy themselves rideing on roller coasters. But Miller Huggins as quoted as favoring San Francisco, as the trip would give his pitchers four days to rest. He would prefer Melbourne, but the world's cricket series is being played there this month and November.

The big problem around New York is who will Huggins choose to pitch tomorrow's game. One of the experts asked him tonight and he just looked at him. Personally, I figure that he will stick a lot of names in a hat and draw them out, nod if Hoyt's name is the fifth one drawed out, and that ends the drawing. Manager McGraw will probably start Art Neff, which will leave him Fred Toney for the first inning Friday.

Today's game was quite a contrast to the game Tuesday. The pitchers were both so good that you would of thought they belonged to some other club. The Yanks earned their run in the second inning on Pipp's double, Ward's sacrifice and McNally's poke to right. The Giants tied it up in the fourth, when Mays tried a slow hall on Irish Meusel with Ross Young on second base. The slow ball was keeping Yom Kippur and didn't work.

For the first time in the series it was a boot that decided the game. Ward, who otherwise has played sweet ball around second base, messed up Rawlings' grounder with two out in the seventh. Then Snyder gave the ball a long ride to left-center, where it was manhandled, and Rawlings had plenty of time to score. It was a tough game for Mays to lose, but it would of been just as tough for Douglas. The both of them pitched better than they know how. It looks like all there two boys needs to make them great pitchers in no rest and rotten weather.

The weather was so bad that a big majority of the fans and experts wore overcoats. I didn't wear none and I would just as leaf you didn't ask me why not. I am poor but proud.

Well, friends, whether you're a Giant fan or a Yank fan, they's one thing this series learns you, or at least it has leaned me one thing, namely, that a guy named Babe Ruth is some importance to his ball club. We been reading all summer long about the Yankee wrecking crew, which was supposed to mean the whole top side of the batting order. But when you take the Babe out of there the crew looks kind of wreckless.

If the Giants wins this series I wouldn't be surprised if the doctor that ordered the Babe to cease firing would wake up some morning and find something under his pillow for the wife and kiddies. It was a great day for Mr. McGraw when Babe decided to devote all his time to literature.

Bill Klem was amongst those present at this battle and he visited the scribes' dining room after the game. They gave him a hot roast-beef sandwich and he dusted off the plate.

Fans Must Come Early to See Toney

Bell Syndicate, Oct. 12, 1921

NEW YORK—THIS WAS THE SIXTH GAME OF THE WORLD'S SERIES AND the ball players didn't get no money for playing it. Otherwise they would of been overpaid. Miller Huggins was in a desperate situation for pitchers, and nobody can blame him for taking a chance with Harry Harper. Harper had a red undershirt, but that was all. Huggins left him in there till two guys had socked him for homers and one for a single. Then he changed pitchers and it is here that his judgment might be criticized. He picked another guy with a red undershirt. Further and more it hardly seems like Harper was given a fair chance. The Giants only had three hits off him, and none of them was for five bases. At the beginning of the game, Harper's opponent was Fred Toney. I say this for the benefit of the late arrivals. If you want to see Toney pitch you half to get there at 2 o'clock.

Babe Ruth was out of the game with his different injuries and Fewster was in his place. But Toney hadn't heard the announcement made, so when Fewster come up to bat, he thought it was Ruth and passed him. Peckinpaugh fouled out and Miller slapped one at Bancroft that might of been a double play, but it was a little too tough for the Giant captain and went for a single.

Bob Meusel cracked another single which scored Miller. Pipp went out, but Toney tried to fool Ward with a slow ball. The ball only stayed slow till it hit Ward's bat.

McGraw then decided to have Toney for the opening game against Brooklyn, though if I was Mac I would start Fred right back tomorrow, as he ain't never in there long enough to do much harm and having him start games gives Jess Barnes a chance to finish him.

Well the Yanks had three runs to show for their first inning, but three runs ain't nothing. As soon as the Giants got started in their second inning, everybody knew what the red undershirt meant. It meant danger for the people sitting in the right and left field seats. Kelly walked and Irish Meusel socked one into the first base stand. Rawlings flied out for reasons best known to himself. Then Snyder socked one into the left stand, Barnes singled and Huggins changed undershirts.

Well, the score was tied and the Yanks come up for their second round. Schang struck out, which nine other guys also did, before Barnes was through with them. But Shawkey made a base hit and Fewster socked a homer and the Yanks was to runs ahead,

A two-run lead these days looks as big as my share of the gate receipts. The Giants picked out the fourth inning and made it their own. Snyder and Barnes both hit safe and McNally messed up his throw on Burns with the bases full. Capt. Bancroft, who previously had done more writing than anything else in this series, cracked a single to left scoring the Giant battery, and sending Burns to third. Frisch forced Bancroft, but Burns scored on the play. Frisch stole second and Kelly brought him home with a single, This man Kelly has turned out to be nobody's sucker. He drove in the Giants' last run in the sixth and his record for the day was three blows and a walk in five times up.

Now then, boys, we have got this far and everybody is satisfied and I am in favor of calling it off before any one's feelings is hurt. But the plan is to play it out and that means four more games including a tie, to say nothing about another rainy day. So about the best we can hope for is golf next Monday when the caddies is all in school.

The pitchers for tomorrow is another problem. Pretty near everybody knows that Douglas and Mays will start, but heaven only knows who will finish. It is Columbus day, and maybe old Christopher will come back to earth and discover somebody for Huggins.

Amongst the spectators at today's game was John Ringling. He seemed to be studying the athletes carefully and I wouldn't be surprised if a few of them was missing from baseball next season. I might add that

Altrock denies sending me that seventy-six word telegram the other night and he and I have about made up our minds that it was the work of some man or men who had found a place to get a drink in New York in spite of the Volstead law.

That is about all I know of to write except a little experience I had with a couple of tickets. I drove in from Great Neck with Tad, the cartoonist, and I told him I had a couple of extra tickets for the game and he says why not give them to a couple of poor little kiddies. Tad, has a big heart, especially when the tickets is mine. So anyway we picked out two kids about 10 years old outside the Polo grounds and I gave them the tickets and they acted tickled to death. So when 1 finally got in the press coop, I looked up to the seats which my tickets called for. The kids was 35 years older than the last time I saw them.

The Most Important World Series in History

Bell Syndicate, Oct. 3, 1922

NEW YORK—ALL THOUGH THEY HAVE BEEN WORLD SERIOUS PRACtally every yr. for the last 20 yrs. this next world serious which is supposed to open up Wed. p.m. at the Polo grounds is the most important world serious in history as far as I and my family are conserned and even more important to us than the famous world serious of 1919 which was win by the Cincinnati Reds greatly to their surprise.

Maybe I would better exclaim myself before going any further. Well, a few days previous to the serious of 1919 I was approached by a young lady who I soon recognized as my wife and any way this woman says would I buy her a fur coat as the winter was comeing on and we was going to spend it in Connecticut which is not genally considered one of the tropics.

"But don't do it," she says, "unless you have got the money to spare because of course I can get along without it. In fact," she added bursting into tears, "I am so used to getting along without this, that and the other thing that maybe it would be best for you not to buy me that coat after all as the sight of a luxury of any kind might prove my undoing."

"Listen," was my reply, "as far as I am concerned you don't half to prove your undoing. But listen you are in a position to know that I can't spare the money to buy you one stoat leave alone enough of the little codgers skins to make a coat for a growed up girl like you. But if I can get a hold of any body that is sucker enough to bet on Cincinnati in this world serious, why I will borrow from some good pal and cover their bet and will try and make the bet big enough so as the winnings will buy you the handsomest muleskin coat in New England."

Well friends I found the sucker and got a hold of enough money to cover his bet and not only that but give him odds of 6 to 5 and that is why we did not go out much in Greenwich that winter and not for lack of invitations as certain smart Alex has let fall.

I might also mention at this junction that they was a similar agreement at that serious between Eddie Collins the capt. of the White Sox and his Mrs. only of course Eddie did not make no bet, but if his team win, why he should buy the madam a personal sedan whereas if his team lost, why she would half to walk all winter. Luckily the Collinses live in Lansdowne, Pa., where you can't walk far.

Well friends I do not know what is the automobile situation in the Collins family at the present writeing as have not saw them of late but the fur coat situation in my family is practically the same like it was in 1919 only as I hinted in the opening paragraph of this intimate article, it is a d-am sight worse.

Because this yr. they won't be no chance for the little woman to offset her paucity of outdoor raps by spending the winter in the house. She is going to need furs even there.

Therefore as I say this comeing serious is the most important of all as far as we are conserned for Mother ain't the same gal when she is cold and after all is said and done what is home with mother in her tantrums?

So I and my little ones is hopeing and praying that the boys on who I have staked my winters happiness this yr. will not have no meetings in no hotel rooms between now and Wednesday but will go into this serious determined to do their best which I once said was the best anybody could do and the man who heard me say it said "You are dead right Lardner" and if these boys do their best, why it looks to me like as if the serious should ought to be well over by Sunday night and the little woman's new fur coat delivered to our little home some time Monday and maybe we will get invited out somewheres that night and they will be a blizzard.

The Fur Coat Is Already Bought

Bell Syndicate, Oct. 4, 1922

NEW YORK—In the last 24 hrs. the telegraph office at Great Neck has been swamped you might say with telegrams from baseball fans all over the country wanting to know who I have bet on in the world serious in order to win the little woman the price of a costly fur coat.

Well friends as I have not got no broad casting station in our little home, why I guess the easiest way to satisfy the nation wide curiosity in regards to my choice is to make my announcement through the press and I realize that this announcement is going to come like a big surprise as a great many people thinks I am crazy.

Well friends I have bet on the Yankees.

Further and more I would not be throwed into fever of excitement was the Yankees to win in 4 straight games though I have not bet no fur coat on that kind of a proposition.

I hope they won't be no National league fans in N.Y. or elsewhere who will take offense at these here statements and I want to assure one and all that my attitude ain't been influenced in no way by personal animals as some of my best friends is in the National league and my favorite athlete from a stand point of good cheer is young Mr. Stengel.

Not only that but I win a very small wager on the Giants last fall and therefore feel sympathetic towards same. But a man can't let their sentiments run away with them when their Mrs. is hollering for a flee skin coat.

Now I suppose my readers who is reading this article will no sooner read which team I have picked when they will want to know the reason why. Well friends I will exclaim in a nutshell.

The serious last yr. was a triumph of mind over matter but this yr. they ain't nothing the matter.

The Yankees went into the serious last yr. with the Babe crippled and only 2 guys that could pitch. Bob Shawkey who is one of the best pitchers in the league looked like the game of baseball was to him a new toy. Well at this writeing they aint nothing the matter with the Babe and Shawkey is his old self and for the rest of the pitching corpse, you can realize the difference between last fall's and this fall's if you stop to think that Carl Mays, who everything depended on him last year, may not even half to warm up.

Further and more the weak spot of the 1921 defense which was the left side of the infield is now being took care of by the best pair since Weaver and Risberg on the other side. Pipp and Ward are at least as good as ever and Whitey Witt is a pillow of strength to the outfield, as Lou Ritchie used to say and all and all you can't find no weakness out side of the lack of a good left hand pitcher which of course is Harry Frazee's' fault not mine.

Now then how does this season's Giants compare with the champs of 1921? Well, they have got Heine Groh, who is good enough to help anybody's ball club, and they don't miss Geo. Burns on acct. of the way young Stengel is going.

But when old Shufflin Phil[1] wrote that mash note to his dear friend Les, he not only wrote goodbye to his own big league career but also a fond farewell to the Giants hopes of repeating. Under good management you can stagger along and win a pennant without pitchers a specially if the competition is weak. But a world serious is something else.

These is some of the things which has caused me to rely on the Yanks for the madam's eel skin coat and while I am predicting will also state:

1. That the Babe will hit at least 3 out of the park.
2. That Joe Bush will pitch at least one shut out.
3. That people who never seen Shawkey pitch except last fall will be surprised.

This is how I feel about it brother and of course I may be wrong which won't be the 1st. time. But if I am wrong it won't be necessary for Giant fans to write and call my attention to same. The Mrs. will let me know in her own way.

Note

1. Giants pitcher Phil Douglas, one of baseball's better pitchers during this period, had an 11–4 record and a league-leading 2.63 ERA in mid-August. But while feuding with Giants manager John McGraw, Douglas wrote to St. Louis Cardinals outfielder Les Mann offering to desert the team if another one made him an offer and commissioner Landis banned him from baseball for life. Lardner was wrong about Douglas's absence hurting the Giants' chances. They easily beat the Yankees in the Series. Poor Mrs. Lardner.

Mr. Lardner Corrects a Wrong Impression

Bell Syndicate, Oct. 5, 1922

NEW YORK—Well, friends you can imagine my surprise and horror when I found out last night that the impression had got around some way another that as soon as this serious was over I was planning to buy a expensive fur coat for my Mrs. and put a lot of money into same and buy a coat that would probably run up into hundreds and hundreds of dollars.

Well I did not mean to give no such kind of a impression and I certainly hope that my little article was not read that way by everybody a specially around my little home because in the first place I am not a sucker enough to invest hundreds and hundreds of dollars in a garment which the chances are that the Mrs. will not wear it more than a couple times all winter as the way it looks now we are libel to have the most openest winter in history and if women folks should walk along the st. in expensive fur coats in the kind of weather which it looks like we are going to have why they would only be laughed at and any way I believe a couple can have a whole lot better time in winter staying home and reading a good book or maybe have a few friends to play bridge.

Further and more I met a man at supper last night that has been in the fur business all his life and aint did nothing you might say only deal in furs and this man says that they are a great many furs in this world which is reasonable priced that has got as much warmth in them as high price furs and looks a great deal better. For inst. he says that a man is a sucker to invest thousands and thousands of dollars in expensive furs like ermine, muleskin, squirrel skin and kerensky when for a hundred dollars or not even that much, why a man can buy a owl skin or horse skin or weasel skin garment that looks like big dough and practically prostrates people with the heat when they wear them.

So I hope my readers will put a quietus on the silly rumor that I am planning to plunge in the fur market. I will see that my Mrs. is dressed in as warm a style as she has been accustomed to but neither her or I is the kind that likes to make a big show and go up and down 5th ave. sweltering in a $700 hogskin garment in order so as people will turn around and gap at us. Live and let live is my slocum.

So much for the fur coat episode and let us hear no more about it and will now go on with my article which I must apologize for it not being very good and the reason is on account of being very nervous after our little ride from the polo grounds to park row. It was my intentions to make this trip in the subway but while walking across the field after the game I run into Izzy Kaplan the photographer and he says would I like to ride down in a car which him and his friends had hired so I and Grantland Rice got in and we hadn't no sooner than started when one of our fellow passengers says that we ought to been with them coming up.

"We made the trip from Park Row in 24 minutes," he says, "and our driver said he was going to beat that record on the return trip."

So we asked what had held them back comeing up and one of them said that the driver had kept peeling and eating bananas all the way and that he did not drive so good when both his hands was off the wheel. Besides that, they had ran into a guy and had to wait till the ambulance come and picked him up.

Well friends I will not try and describe our flight only to say that we did not beat the record but tied it and the lack of bananas didn't prevent our hero from driving with his hands off the wheel as he used the last named to shake his fists at pedestrians and other riff raff that don't know enough to keep off the public highways during the rush hour.

Most of the things I was going to mention in this article was scared out of me during our little jaunt. One of them however was the man from Toronto that stood in line with his wife from 8 pm Tuesday night till the gates opened Wednesday morning so as to be sure of good seats. According to officials of the club, they could of got the same seats if they had not showed up till a couple hours before the game, but if they had of done that, why the lady would not of had no chance to brag when she got back home. The way it is, why she can say to her friends, "Charley may not be much for looks, but he certainly showed me the night life of New York."

Dividing interest with this couple was a couple of heel and toe pedestrians that done their base circling stunt just before the start of the game. One of them was the same guy that done it before the first game last fall, but this time he was accompanied by a lady hoofer and it is not too much to say that the lady was dressed practically as though for her bath. Casey Stengel expressed the general sentiment in the following words, "If that is just her walking costume I would hate to see her made up for tennis."

Lardner Feels His Way from Park by Candle

Bell Syndicate, Oct. 6, 1922

NEW YORK—No doubt my readers has been tipped off by this time that the 2d game of the big serious was called on acct. of darkness but a great many of them may not know that the umpires and club owners was called a lot of different names which I will not repeat here but suffice it to say that none of them was honey, dearie and etc.

The boys that had paid $5.50 and up to see a ball game did not seem to think it was dark enough for the umps to step in and stop it. Personly I will not express no opinion as some of my best friends is umpires, but will merely state that I started out of the press box the instant it was over and by the aid of a powerful candle which I generally always carry to world serious games when Shawkey and Barnes is scheduled to pitch, why I was able to find my way down to the field where I run plum into A.D. Lasker who had forgot to light his headlights. Will further state that nobody who I passed on the way out to 8th avenue had yet put on their pajamas or made any other preparations that would indicate the fall of night and even when I got down to park's row, pretty near a hr. after the game's untimely end, I was still able to grope my way to the office by feeling along the sides of buildings and was seated right here at my typewriter writing this article before the hoot owls and nightingales begun to emit their nocturnal squawk.

However, one of our fellow passengers on the bus down town was Billy Evans, an umpire himself, and while he admitted that he had not saw none of the outfielders signalling to each other with flares, still and all he says the polo grounds is a terrible hard place for the athletes, and a specially the batters, to see a ball when they's the slightest twinge of darkness. As far as that is concerned there is 2 or 3 of the boys on each of the contending clubs that dont seem able to see the ball any too good even at high noon.

Anyway it means we are going to have a extra ball game to play over and some of we boys who predicted a short serious is being made to look like a monkey. Personly I was never so ashamed of myself since I picked Willard.[1]

The general opinion amongst the writing boys tonight was that the game being a tie is a big help to one of the two teams but I forget which. It certainly aint no help to me and the only thing I liked about the day was the weather, which it would make a person sick to even talk about a fur coat in such weather, and it goes to show what a sucker a man would be to squander thousands and thousands of dollars in a costly fur garment and then may be have a whole winter of just such days like yesterday.

Personly I seen a girlie on the street last night wearing a linen duster and you have no idear how good they look on some people and keep you plenty warm too if you move around and dont stand still.

Well friends, I prophesied in these columns earlier in the week that Bob Shawkey would be a whole lot better this fall than he was last fall and that prophecy certainly come true, but the boy has still got the habit of pitching bad in the first innings and if I was running the Yank ball club here is what I would do. When it was Bob's turn to pitch, why just before the game started I would call Bob to one side and I would say, "well Bob it's the second innings all ready." If he believed it, why they would be nothing to prevent him from stepping right in and pitching his best from the start.

Jess Barnes pitched better than Bob at the start and not so good at finish. The way Jess pitched to Ruth did not seem to rouse unanimous enthusiasm amongst the bugs in the grandstand. Slow balls is what Jess feeds the Babe and the reason for same is because Babe dont hit slow balls out of the ball park. If Jess did not feed the Babe slow balls when he knows he cant hit slow balls so good, why that would make Jess a ½ wit and when he does feed the Babe slow balls, why it shows he is thinking. That is why the crowd hoots him for pitching slow balls, because the average baseball bug hates to see anybody think. It makes them jealous.

Well friends today is another day and may the best team win as I often say to Mother which is what I call the little woman when I am in a hurry and cant think of her name.

Note

1. In the first fight Lardner covered for the Bell Syndicate in 1919, Lardner predicted 37-year-old champion Jess Willard would beat his 24-year-old challenger Jack Dempsey. Willard left the ring after the third round with a broken jaw, cheekbone, and ribs as well as the loss of several teeth. Dempsey held the championship for the next seven years.

It Looks Bad for the Three Little Lardner Kittens

Bell Syndicate, Oct. 7, 1922

NEW YORK—AMONGST THE INMATES OF OUR HEAVILY MORTGAGED home in Great Neck is 3 members of what is sometimes referred to as the feline tribe born the 11th day of last April and christened respectfully Barney, Blackie and Ringer. These 3 little ones is motherless, as the lady cat who bore them, aptly named Robin Hood, took sick one June day and was give away by Fred to a friend to whom he kindly refrained from mentioning her illness.

These 3 little members of the feline tribe is the cutest and best behaved kitties in all catdom, their conduct having always been above reproaches outside of a tendency on the part of Ringer to bite strangers' knuckles. Nowhere on Long Island is a more loveable trio of grimalkins and how it pierces my old heart to think that some day next week these 3 little fellows must be shot down like a dog so as their fur can be fashioned into a warm Winter coat for she who their antics has so often caused to screek with laughter. Yes boys the 3 little kittens is practically doomed you might say and all because today's game at the polo grounds was not called on account of darkness long before it started though they was no time during the afternoon when the Yanks could see.

I probably never would of heard of a cat skin coat was it not for an accidental introduction last night to a man who has did nothing all his life but sell and wear fur coats and who told me that no finer or more warmer garment can be fashioned than is made from the skin of a milk fed kitty.

"Listen," was the way he put it. "You would be a even worse sucker than you are if you was to squander thousands on thousands of dollars on the fur of a muskrat or a mule when you have right in your own asylum the makings of the most satisfactory and handsome coat that money can buy."

"Yes," was my reply, "but the fur of 3 kittens would make a mighty small coat."

"Small coats is the rage," was his reply, "and I personally seen some of the best dressed women in New York strolling up and down 10th avenue during the last cold snap with cat skin garments no bigger than a guest towel."

So while I said a few paragraphs back that the result of this ball game spelled the doom of our little kitties, why as a matter of fact I have just about made up my mind to not buy no costly furs even if the Yankees does come through and bring me out on the right side of the public ledger. Whatever I win in bets on this serious I will freely give to charity.

I would try and describe the game to you in intimate detail was it not played in such darkness that I was only able to see a few incidences. One of these occured in the 3rd innings and consisted of Whitey Witt getting caught asleep off of first base by a snap throw from one of the Smith brothers. Henry Edwards, the dean of Cleveland baseball experts, explained this incidence by saying that Whitey thought he was still with the Athletics. It is more likely however that Whitey was deceived by the darkness into believing it was his bedtime.

The next incidence come in the innings when the Babe tried to go from first to third on a wallop by Bob Meusel that got away from Frisch. Frankie pegged the ball to Heine Groh who stood in Babe's path to third but it was so dark that Babe crashed right smack into him and secured a rolling fall. For a minute it looked like they would be fisticuffs between the 2 famous athletes but Heine suddenly remembered the advice given him by his first school teacher, "Never be a bully," and the fight was over before it begun.

Fifteen minutes before the start of the game the official announcer come up to the press box and said that McQuillan was going to pitch for the Giants. A minute later he come around again and said to make it Scott instead of McQuillan. McQuillan thus broke Fred Toney's record for the length of time spent in a world series ball game.

I will close this article by making a apology to the boys to who I have give tickets for games no 1 and 3 and whose seats is in section 24 which is as far north as you can get without falling out of the grandstand. The gents who sold me these seats thought I was a close friend of the Meusel boys and might want to set out there myself and kid with them.

Yanks Lose, But Lardner Kittens Spared

Bell Syndicate, Oct. 9, 1922

NEW YORK—WELL, BOYS IT LOOKS LIKE IT WAS ALL OVER AND THE only complaint I have got to make is that the traffic regulations was not handled right. The next time the Yankees takes part in a world serious they should ought to have a traffic policeman stationed between 1st and 2nd base and another traffic policeman stationed between home and 1st.

The former should tell the boys when it is o.k. to run to 2nd. And the latter must inform them that when a ground ball is hit to the infield in a world serious the general theory which has never been disapproved is to run on high speed to 1st base which is the base towards the right field from the home plate.

The lack of a adequate stop and go system is what lost this serious on the part of the Yanks. The final game of the serious was marked by the only incedence of brains exhibited by the Yanks during the whole serious. In the 2nd innings with two boys on the bases and one out Joe Bush passed Arthur Nehf to 1st base so as to get the head of the batting order up and not confuse the official scorers. This bit of thinking probably was responsible for nothing.

I will not try and dilate on the rest of the serious only to say that Charles A. Hughes and Eddie Batchelor of Detroit spent this a.m. at the Bronx zoo to try and see more animals. It is hard to satisfy the boys from Detroit.

All as I know what to write about on a occasion like this kind is little incedence that come off. The 1st incedence that calls to mine is in regards to Tommy Rice of the Brooklyn Eagle. Tommy wrote 7,000 words in regards to the 1st game of the serious and page by page it blew out of the window in the costly apartment building in which Brooklyn experts lives. There is no telling what the loss to the world is on account of not being able to read Tommy's story to say nothing about the readers of the Eagle.

Now boys I suppose they is a few interested in whether the little woman is going to get a costly fur coat. The other day I wrote a story to the general effects that we was going to kill our cats and use their fur to make the costly garment. This story was not appreciated in the heavily mortgaged home. After a long argument the master of the house compromised and decided to not doom the little members of the finny tribe to death. Instead of that we are going to use a idea furnished by the same Eddie Batchelor of Detroit mentioned a few thousands words ago.

Eddie's idears is to start a chain letter to all our friends and readers asking them to look around the old homestead and find their family albums and take the plush off of the covers and send it to the undersigned and make a plush coat which everybody tells me is the most fashionable fur on the green footstool. The little woman can wear plush and a specially the red pigment but black and tan plush covers will be welcomed and this man tells me theys nothing more attractive than a black and red and tan blocked coat made out of plush albums.

I was going to say further in regards to the plush albums but Harry Frazee has just butted in with the story of his life. It seems like when Harry was a young man in Peoria his father said to him if you don't be wild and go into the theatrical business and stay around Peoria you will be as big a man as your uncle. So Harry looked at his uncle who was getting $125 per month staring at books.

"Well," says Harry, "I can get more than that catching runaway horses." So he is now catching runaway horses and selling them to the New York club.

As I now sit here and write I am surrounded by a corpse of experts just as ignorant as me and they don't seem to be none of them able to tell who is going to pitch tomorrow. Personally I think it will be Col. Ruppert and Huston.

Fans Agrog as Series Opens

Bell Syndicate, Oct. 10, 1923

NEW YORK—NATIONWIDE BASEBALL FANS IS ALL A GROG TONIGHT over the threatened opening tomorrow of a world serious which after a careful study of who is to be the two opening teams, I have no hesitants in nicknaming it a novelty.

It is possible that the same two clubs has met a couple of times previous in the last few yrs. for baseball's highest horrors, but according to Sam Crane, a veteran expert, this will be their first clash at the Yankee Stadium, This is itself enough to give a person the creeps but to add to the confusion, the opening game will be preceded by a interesting program of track and field events as follows:

1 P.M.—Base-running contest between Casey Stengel and Papyrus.[1] The pair will start from the home plate at the same time and circle the bases in opposite directions. Papyrus going to third base first as horses always run backwards in England. In this connection it may be news to horse lovers, if any, that the big match race at Belmont a wk. from next Saturday will be ran under the same auspices, namely Papyrus will go the wrong way of the track, and those intending to bet on the contest should be warned that the other way round is longer. Conditions will be just the reverse in the brush between Mr. Stengel and Mr. Horse, as first base at the Yankee park is easier to get to than third. The winner will be the one that meets each other and the contest will be judged incognito by the man that refereed the Dempsey-Firpo fight. Donoghue will ride Papyrus and the crowd will ride Casey.

1:12 P.M.—Long distance throwing contest between Geo. Kelly of the Giants, Bob Meusel of the Yanks and Bud Fisher's recent race horse, Hyperion. Geo. and Bob will throw baseballs and Hyperion will throw a jockey.

1:26 P.M.—Radio lecture on "Thrift" by prominent bankers from Shelby, Montana.

1:35 P.M.—Optical test for the umpires to see if they can tell dark from light.

1:55 P.M.—Rendition of the "Star Spangled Banner" by Brooklyn Tree Surgeons military band to allow I and Judge Landis to show our hair.

Before the serious last yr. I come right out in print and told who I was betting on and a good many people took advantage of same. This yr. who I am backing will remain a secret till the 15th of November, when you can find out by inquiring at some of the dept. stores. My winnings last yr. was to of been spent on a fur coat for the Mrs. and it may be of interest to fans that I bought her the coat irregardless rather than see both of us freeze.[2] No matter which way I come out this yr. I am at liberty to spend the winnings on something for myself as I have got the little woman so browbeaten by this time that she will wear the same coat two winters. Personly I ain't made up my mind what to buy, but it will a be dozen new blades or a hot dog depending on results.

Jokes to the side for a moment, it seems to me like the first inning of this first game will give us all a hunch one way or the other in regards to what to expect. If the Babe busts one, the Yankees still has a chance to lose. If he don't do nothing, the Giants still has a chance to lose.

The umpires for the serious was closeted for ½ hour last night with Judge Landis and instructed that daylights savings went out of operation in New York ten days ago. These instructions is hoped to prevent a reputation of last fall's special extra surprise when the umpires saved so much daylight one day that a fan living in East Orange, N.J., got off his train 2 hours after the game was called and died of sunstroke.

Fans who may be a bit timid about attending these games may rest assured that they will be able to enter both parks and showed to their proper seats without no danger of getting hit over the head by a group of bold policemen as baseball is not ran under the influence of the N.Y. state boxing commission.[3]

As the two teams is straining at the leash, all eagerness to get out there on the field and count the house, a old time baseball expert can't resist calling attention to the sad plight of Ernie Johnson, utility infielder on the Yankee team. Ernie started the season as shortstop with the Chicago White Sox, but along in June or some time Chicago ast for wafers and the Yankees refused to wafe. Manager Huggins figured that if they was one thing he needed it was a substitute shortstop, as at that time the regular shortstop, Everett Scott, had only been able to play 1000 consecutive games and might get sick again any day. So Ernie is now a full fledge member of the Yanks, who, according to Hughie Fullerton, finished in first place. And he can't prevent a slight cough when he thinks of the White Sox, who finished in Cleveland.

Notes

1. A British racehorse, Papyrus, won the 1923 Epsom Derby and was sent to the United States for a match race with Kentucky Derby winner Zev on October 20. In front of 70,000 people at Belmont Park, Zev won by five lengths.
2. And thus ends the saga of the fur coat.
3. A month earlier, Lardner and other writers had been denied entrance to Jack Dempsey's heavyweight championship fight against Luis Angel Firpo at the Polo Grounds, their press passes not withstanding. Lardner went around to a pay entrance and walked right in. It was worth the trouble, as Dempsey won perhaps the most thrilling fight ever. Dempsey knocked down Firpo seven times in the first round, but Firpo then knocked him out of the ring—into Grantland Rice's lap, according to Lardner. Dempsey knocked Firpo down two more times in the second round, and the fight mercifully ended.

Only One Team Could Lose that Game—the Yanks

Bell Syndicate, Oct. 11, 1923

NEW YORK—Well, boys, they have started again, and it looks maybe we would be out of the trenches by Saturday night. At the conclusion of this battle the general concensus of opinion among us halfwitted newspaper men that it was a game that could of been lost by only one team in the world, namely the Yankees.

It takes real genius to get beat in a ball game like this one, and it don't seem hardly possible that the Giants can lose any of the rest of them no matter how hard they try.

The only thing that might save the American league champs would be to have last year's umpires re-engaged so that some game might be called wile it is still a tie. However, it might help a little if Manager Huggins would change his tactics and every time one of his boys get a base and send in somebody to run for him. The Yankees made a whole lot of runs this season and in order to make runs they must of visited different bases but today they acted like it was their first trip away from home. This aint knocking the Giants, who played their regular world serious ball and deserved to win. And personally I am glad it was Casey, mighty Casey, that busted it up though I don't suppose he cares whether I like him or not. Well, to begin with the beginning.

On the way from the subway to the press gate the writer must of passed 50 policemens but was neither recognized nor hit over the head. Outside the gate I run into the high commissioner of baseball who asked the newspaper boys the other day to kindly keep his name out of the paper on the grounds that the people was not interested. The judge helped me get away with a couple of Harry Stevens hot roast beef sandwiches which was so good that I took some of the juice home on my coat to show the wife and kiddies.

At 1 o'clock Judge L—s went out on the field and decided it was light enough to play. The clients was then entertained by a novelty in the way of batting and fielding practice, which is usually held in secret before a big game. Messrs. Altrock and Schacht staged their imitation of the misunderstanding between our champion and the wild bull[1] and it was voted the best stunt baseball's star comics has over put on. The gent that announced the batteries in the press box said that Hurt would pitch for the Yankees. This is what they call him in Brooklyn.

Amongst the prominent experts present was Jack Hendricks and Clarence Rowland. Jack is covering the series for Jim Jam Jems and Clarence for the Enclopedia. When Mr. Watson was named as the Giant pitcher, Nick Flatley of Boston said that McGraw was probably sending him in as punishment for not obeying the training rules. He was released on parole after two nervous innings. Mr. Hurt got bumped off in the next innings and I practically decided to nickname the game a airtight pitchers battle. It took one hour and five minutes to get the first three innings over and Judge L—s gave the gathering gloom couple of dirty looks.

During the long and tedious progress of the third innings I sought an interview with Mrs. Caroline Dorsey, of Traverse City, Mich. Mrs. Dorsey is the lady who had stood in line in front of the general admission ticket window since the 14th of May hoping against hope that she would get a ticket. At ten o'clock this morning she received the coveted pasteboard and picked out a choice seat under the scoreboard.

"Mrs. Dorsey," I said to her, "What do you think of the game?" She did not hear me the first time on account of being so far away so I had to put the query once more. "Mrs. Dorsey," I said, "what do you think of the game?"

She did not hear me this time either, and when the game was over I talked to several people who had sat near her if they had heard her say what she had thought of the game, but I could get no information that sounded reliable.

The pastime speeded up after Bush and Ryan took what is called the helm. With the sun under cover the Giants was unable to see Mr. Bush's fast ball until he got in the hole to Mr. Stengel in the ninth when Casey ran an exhibition circuit of the bases.[2] He had been scheduled to run this race against Papyrus before the game but the horse failed to leave his stall. Plenty of Yanks got on base but once there they seemed to be overcome by nausea.

The disease was contagious and Yankee fans all had it leaving the park.

Notes

1. Dempsey's knockout of Firpo had taken place three months earlier.
2. Lardner was writing so little about the games at this point that he all but ignored one of the most famous moments in World Series history, Casey Stengel's inside-the-park homer in the ninth inning. With one of his shoes falling apart, Stengel limped erratically around the bases, and it was left to Lardner's friend Damon Runyon to write the most celebrated description of the event: "This is the way old 'Casey' Stengel ran yesterday afternoon, running his home run home."

Lardner Told 'em Ruth Would be Hero of the "World Serious"

Bell Syndicate, October 12, 1923

Polo Grounds, New York—This article may sound kind of embarrassed as I am writing it in the press box and they's a large crowd of beauty lovers standing in front of the screen giving we newspaper boys a long admiring look and this in spite of the fact that a little ways off is seated two other movie queens, Geo. Ade and Thomas Meighan. But I will try and forget myself long enough to tell the fans that the score is said to be 4 to 2 in favor of the Yankees though it seems so improbable that Judge L-s has called a meeting of the umpires and official scorers to go over the game inning by inning and see if it was legal.

They's a man in our crowd of admirers that says this is not the first time the Yankees ever win from the Giants but he has got a long gray beard and may be all through from a mental standpoint.

The thing that probably beat the Giants today if the report is true that they was beat, was the terror struck in their hearts by this man Pennock. Before the world champions bat against a pitcher who they have never faced, Mr. McGraw makes them go to the library and look up all the books that bear on the subject. Well, they learned that Pennock is a man who has a country estate in Kenneth Square, Pennsylvania, and when he ain't pitching he rides to hounds.

"What does it mean?" asked Casey Stengel, "When it says a man rides to hounds?"

"All it means," replied Casey Dolan, "Is that you ain't going to hit against him."

A great many of the Giants, after witnessing Pennock's exhibition has made up their mind to spend the winter riding to hounds no matter what it is. Will say in this connection that Great Neck is a great place for riding to hounds and practically every time I go out in my costly motor I run over a couple of them.

Last year I predicted that Babe Ruth was going to be the hero of the world serious and a good many people thought I meant the world serious which I was then writing about. They must have been crazy.

Arthur Robinson says that the Babe is now two up on Cy Williams[1] and Cy ain't got no chance to catch up this season unlest they can get some Shelby Mont banker to arrange a city serious in Philadelphia.

Well when Mr. Pennock took his turn in the Yankee batting practice indicating that he was going to pitch, Casey Stengel's dogs was heard to give a loud bark of relief, knowing they would not be sent on another long trip as long as a left hander was working. The dogs was probably pulling for Pennock to last through the game but Casey was not. The official announcement that Herb was going to start caused quite a discussion on the Giant bench. Some of the boys wanted to go up to bat without their bats as the only Yankee lefthander they had ever faced before was Harry Harper.

The experts who had picked Arthur Nehf to work was greatly surprised when the well-known organist never even warmed up. Bently and McQuillan were out and in McQuillan's first inning it looked like the Yankees was the ones that might as well of left their bats on the bench, but after Hugh had throwed eight of the wildest balls ever seen to Dugan and Ruth somebody pointed out the plate to him and he made Meusel hit into a double play.

By the time the next inning started the Giant hurler's control was so good that he hit Ward's bat right in the middle. He done the same thing to the Babe's big bludgeon in the fourth. If anybody had been riding on the ball Babe hit they could of got right on the elevated without climbing the stairs. Before this round was over word was sent to McQuillan from the club house that his tub was ready. The Yankees was leading by three runs at the end of the fifth and the game begun to look like a even bet with the Giants a slight favorite.

Along about this time it was announced that Mrs. Caroline Dorsey, the Traverse City, Michigan, fan was still in her seat at the Yankee stadium, thinking the game was being played there. It is thought that standing in line so long has infected the lady's mind which wasn't so good to start with. It is even whispered that her ambition is to be come a pinch baserunner for the Yankees.

The monotony of the general situation was relieved in the Giant half of the sixth by the interspersal of a bit of football.

With Young on the first base, Will Meusel tried to hit into a double play, Scott tossed the ball to Ward and forced Young, but Ward could not throw to first as Young was setting on him. The Yankees claimed interference, but the umpires refused to allow same and for a time the fans thought he was the same party that refereed the Dempsey–Firpo fight. Mr. Stengel's dogs began to whine in the eighth when Manager McGraw sent them at least one inning. They were obliged to carry the old boy on the two fast defensive trips, the second of which landed him under Ruth's long fly which would have been the Babe's third homer if he had aimed it pretty near any other direction.

After the game the writer visited the rival club-houses to interview the rival managers.

"Mr. Huggins," I said, "Have you anything to say about the game?"

But it seems that Mr. Huggins had left the club-house. So had Mr. McGraw.

Note

1. The first National League hitter to hit more than 200 home runs, Williams's 251 career homers was the league record for a time. He is one of three players, along with Babe Ruth and Rogers Hornsby, born before 1900 to hit 200 home runs.

Nehf Is The Pitcher Sent to Well Once Too Often, Ring Lardner Opines

Bell Syndicate, Oct. 15, 1923

Polo Grounds, N. Y.—Arthur Nehf is the pitcher that went to the well once too often. That line is as old as Arthur Nehf felt after working his head off for several innings in his second assignment in four days. It was almost as old, in fact, as we experts feel after six days of being admired, bumped into, and walked on by loving fans. And when a man feels old he can't help from writing old stuff, but the details that the Yanks is world Champs is enough new stuff for one day.

Giant fans should not ought to feel bad about loosing this game. At least the National League champs was not disgraced, which they might have been if the heroes had won till Tuesday and forced Mr. McGraw to show us the rest of the pitching staff again. There would have been no chance of working Arthur Nehf another heat and the scribes, to add to their troubles, would of probably got cramps trying to write down the full list of those taking part in the parade from the club house to the box and back.

As I walked across the field when it was all over, I noticed that the grass was covered with a substance of a peculiar gray tint that looked something like mildew. Putting some of it in my brief case I left it with a bootlegger to be analyzed. He predicted it to be brains, which had evidently been spilled by Bob Meusel's single to center in the eighth inning.

Before the game I had the lukewarm pleasure of meeting Mrs. Caroline Dorsey of Traverse City, Mich. For the benefit of persons of doubtful tastes who have not been reading this column will state that Mrs. Dorsey is a lady who has stood in line in front of the general admission window for two or three years, hoping vs hope that she would be able to procure one of the coveted pasteboards. Half witted by this, she had been further influenced by different things that happened in the first game and had spent the entire next day in her terrible seat at the Yankee stadium though the scene of action had been transferred to the Polo ground.

"How do you do, Mrs. Dorsey," was my method of approach after we had been introduced by a garbage vendor from upper Montana. "Are you enjoying your stay in New York?" The garbage man then beckoned me to one side or the other and indicated that Mrs. Dorsey was stone deaf and just as dumb.

"Mrs. Dorsey," I said, "are you enjoying your stay in New York?"

I learned afterward through doubtful friends that Mrs. Dorsey had spent the last three days in a traffic jam, having got caught facing the wrong way on a one-way street. She decided tonight to stay over for the final game and was put on a train for the south at the request of her Michigan relative. Mrs. Dorsey's mind is not the only one that is cracked under the strain of this series.

When George Levy, the silver tongued announcer, told us that Nehf would start for the Giants and Pennock for the Yankees they was a long conference in the press stand at which it was decided to call this game either a dual of the southpaws or a battle of the left handers. Some of the experts nearly came to blows holding out for other titles, showing what a high state of tension the boys had reached.

The ball players was barking at each other and their umpires all through the early inning and even the gents who own stock in the rival clubs seemed to of left their usual winsome smile.

The ball game might have of been a whole lot closer if somebody had sent word to Herbert Pennock that the Giants was hitting the first ball. He seems to think that was against the rules and kept sticking them in there with results that can be seen on any score board.

In the medium thrilling eighth inning, when the master mind of Bob Snyder was working at fever heat, the Giants put up so much time running back and fores to and from the bench with and without that Mr. Huggins finely consumed a few more minutes kidding when he asked for the extreme penalty, a loss of yards, but Hank would not allow it.

As if they had not wasted enough hours this and last week, the Yankees tried some more in the ninth, trying to get their gummed up batting order straightened out. Even the newspaper men knew what the right order was without asking and yet, they say we are half witted. Well, hoping we will be the same next year.

Barney Dreyfuss to Present Saginaw's Mayor Little Gift

Out of Appreciation or What Citizen Cuyler Did for the Pirate Team, Thursday

Bell Syndicate, October 9, 1925

PITTSBURGH, PA. – MR. BARNEY DREYFUSS[1] IS BUSY FIGURING ON A present for the mayor of Saginaw, Mich., and, when Mr. Dreyfuss is figuring on giving somebody a present there is some good reason for the same. Some of the boys have told Mr. Dreyfuss that it was a man from Saginaw who saved the Pirates Thursday.

"If that is the case," said Mr. Dreyfuss, "I will not spoil his career by giving him a raise in salary because that is a very bad influence on you ball players. Look at Babe Ruth, I will send the mayor of Saginaw a present, something that would remind him of Pittsburgh—a box of stogies, maybe."

The name of the young man who won Thursday's ball game is Mr. Hazen Cuyler[2] and he is only 24 so he doesn't know anything except to swing and miss them most of the time. But he busted one and it went into one of the new stands that Mr. Dreyfuss had out in what they call middle field in Pennsylvania in order to be different from the other ball parks.

It brought in two runs and one of those runs was the one which won the ball game. Moore is playing second base because Johnny Rawlings broke his leg and Mr. Dreyfuss and Bill McKechnie decided they would not play with no one-legged second baseman. Some teams does, but Mr. Dreyfuss and Bill McKechnie are kind of particular about such things. Besides Fred Clark, who has been consulting with them, advised very strongly against having a one-legged second baseman.

Of course, Pittsburgh did very well when they had a bowlegged shortstop. But during the argument, the point was brought up that Hans Wagner had two legs even though they were as bowed as the Brooklyn bridge. And the majority vote kept Johnny Rawlings out of the series with the exception of getting his share.

The thing started to happen because old Roger Peckingpaugh was too anxious. He started to throw to first base because he thought he had the ball in his hand. But it wasn't in his hand at all. It was sliding down his neck and Roger is ticklish. When he was able to stop laughing Moore was on first base.

Mr. Peckingpaugh is one of those shortstops who makes an error about once a year and those are just the kind who pick the world's series to make their errors in.

I think Mr. Dreyfuss is a little hasty in buying the stogies for the mayor of Saginaw because I got in strict confidence from a man who was in Saginaw once the real story. Why he was in Saginaw is his own business, but anyhow, he was there.

He told me how Frank Haller, the Pittsburgh scout happened to get Cuyler for the Pirates. It seems that Mr. Haller went to Saginaw on his honeymoon and when he got to Saginaw he went to the ball game. While they was out at the ball game and the Mrs. says, "Look at that young man in the clean suit. He is the only man in the park who has on clean clothes. A boy like that is bound to succeed. Why don't you sign him?"

The scout tries to sidestep and explain that the boys with the dirt on them and tobacco in their faces make the best ball players. But the Mrs. is starting to get firm early in the game. She says, "I do not see why ball players have to be slobs." Or something like that.

So the scout bends his neck for the yoke and he looks at the young ball player. He is surprised to see that he is good though neat and having no bad habits. So he recommends him to be hired and farmed out. That is the way the Pirates came to get Hazen Cuyler and win that ball game here.

We are on our way to Washington where I may have to see Mr. Coolidge on important business and I may be late for the next game of the world series which is becoming so exciting now that people are starting to wake up right in the middle of it.

Notes

1. Owner of the Pittsburgh Pirates.

2. Lardner is being coy here. KiKi Cuyler—it's doubtful anyone other than his mother called him Hazen—was hardly an untested young player by the time he helped the Pirates beat the Senators in seven games in the 1925 World Series. Cuyler was coming off one of the best seasons of his 18-year-career, with a .357 batting average, 102 RBI, and a league-leading 144 runs scored. In the Series, he drove in six runs and scored three.

Blizzards and Politics Hit Pirate Punch

Bell Syndicate, Oct. 11, 1925

WASHINGTON, D. C.—They had better get this over quick or there won't be space enough in the District of Columbia asylums to hold all those who are going to apply for a room without bath.

In the first place the people who came to the ball park without being obliged to can be voted a little off color as it was no place to be for a person with any regard for health.

The cold seemed to go to everybody's head in the eighth inning. It was in this wild session that Sam Rice fell into the right field seats after a terrific smack by Earl Smith and, sooner or later, came up with the ball.

Whether or not Sam caught the ball will always be between him and his Maker. I am not his maker.[1]

Several of those setting in those seats were in position to tell the truth, but it is kind of hard to reach people by phone in Washington this week especially when you don't know their name and don't want to.

A moment later, Washington sent Marberry to bat in somebody else's turn. At least that was what we thought in the iceberg they have nicknamed the press box. I mean those of us who weren't too congealed to think. Nobody in the playing field seemed to agree to us and maybe we were all wrong. It wouldn't be the first time or yet the last time.

Anyway, it didn't make a difference in the result and neutral element is tickled to death that the pastime didn't go into extra innings, in which event they would have had to chip one and all out of the ball park with ice picks.

Washington is supposed to be far enough south to get out of October blizzards, but if that is the case it is just as well for our widows and kiddies that the American league pennant was not won by Philadelphia.

If any of the ball players or umpires are accused of having cold feet at this game they can justly retort, "Who didn't?"

Oswald Bluege may consider himself unlucky, left at home in a warm bed, waiting for somebody to come and replace the chunks Vic Aldridge had sliced out of his head.[2] But, Oswald, there are hundreds who would gladly have changed places with you, including the undersigned.

The leader of the greatest band we have ever heard at a serious seen president Coolidge approaching down the aisle and ordered his men to play "I'll See You in My Dreams." They say it is very difficult for lots of people to see him any other way.

No sooner had the president got seated when they played the "Star Spangled Banner" and he had to stand again. He seemed to be singing under his breath and it is said that he was making up a parody line dedicated to the Washington players who failed to get some very important hits in Pittsburgh Thursday.

The line was as follows:

"The bums popping in air gave proof through the afternoon that Vic Aldridge was still there."

Judge Landis went and set in the president's box for a moment. The president was decked out in a beautiful new salmon colored hat, while, with all due respect to the judge, it must be admitted that his own Fedora looked like it had spent two or three days in Pittsburgh.

The visiting boys scored a run in the second because J. Harris tried to make a catch of Pie Traynor's short Texas leaguer to right. Pie dashed around to third and came in on Wright's long fly to J. Harris whose throw home might have caught somebody who was in no special hurry.

The Senators lost a slim chance to score in their half when Max Carey dropped Peck's fly with two out. Max should not be found fault with for this little slip. He has been smacked three times with pitched balls in his throwing arm and was beginning to wonder whether a world serious is worth while after all.

Oswald Bluege was wondering the same thing with what Vic Aldridge left of his wondering apparatus.

Max stopped wondering in the fifth long enough to take two bases on a single which is against rules in polite leagues.

When the score was 3 to 1 in favor of Pittsburgh in the sixth, Goslin smacked a home run into the right field seats. Anybody but a goose would have waited till there was a man on base, in which case the wallop would have tied the score.

However, his mighty blow gave the Pirates such a crop of goose flesh that they stood flat footed and watched him beat out a bunt when he came up in the seventh inning calamity. Those of us up in the exposed press box were enjoying the same ailment for another reason.

A good many of the experts were expressing mystification in regards to the manner in which Peck and other star members of both clubs had shown a tendency to juggle ground balls and to nearly throw them away after once picking them up. Also why some of the big hitters had been accumulating batting averages that won't never cause their wife and kiddies to shout with joy and sing look what my red hot papa done.

It seems to me like the solution is to be found in the boys' literary efforts. A bat feels awful big and awkward in your hands after you have set up half the night juggling a pen. And it is a difficult matter to pick up a ball clean and throw it straight when suffering with writer's cramp.

Never in my experience of world's series have I seen or heard of so many athletes devoting themselves to authorship. If there is any member of either team who ain't dashing off literature during the present brawl, why it must be the nephew of the 3d assistant bat boy.

As a result of this situation a movement has been started amongst the regular baseball writers to have the players set in the press coop next year while us boys take their place on the field. This would insure the serious being indefinitely postponed during the first game to permit of the removal and disposal of the bodies.

One of the sensations of today's pre-game episodes was the big cheer that went up when the writer of these lines entered Mr. Griffith's stadium. It was learned later that I had been mistaken for President Coolidge's father.

As we struggle out of the park there is a report that Bill McKechnie has protested the game. My reply to Bill is, "So do I."

Notes

1. Rice would be questioned about whether he caught what looked like a home run by Earl Smith for the rest of his life. His usual answer was, "The umpire said I caught it." He left a sealed letter at the Baseball Hall of Fame to be opened after his death. It said "At no time did I lose possession of the ball."

2. Bluege, the Senators' third-baseman, had been hit in the head by one of Aldredge's pitches two days earlier.

Lardner Gets More Time to Locate Shirt

Bell Syndicate, Oct. 14, 1925

PITTSBURGH, PA.—THE SERIES WILL HAVE TO GO OVER FOR another day to give the Hotel Schenley more time in which to find my lost shirt. The following notice was placarded all over Pittsburgh tonight by Sheriff Honus Wagner.

"Lost, a gray shirt with pin stripe and collar attached. Size 16 neck, 35 sleeves and a long nose. Looks like it had been in a world series in Pittsburgh. Owner will give finder a cuff."

Owner will make good but it must be admitted that Honus ain't yet been elected sheriff. He is running for that office on his record. According to Bugs Baer,[1] a bear for statistics, Honus' world series record was broken today by Roger Peckinpaugh when the last named threw a ball loose. This makes five or six errors for Peck in one series as opposed to Honus' four or five errors or what have you? Peck has been in more world series, but has never ran for sheriff. If he and old Honus would both run, I would not know how to bet unless against either. But still, sheriff is easier to get to than first base.

Speaking of Bugs Baer, this was his anniversary. Himself and wife were married six months today and still cheerful, though the madam told me in the middle of the game that she wanted to get home and see what had become of their cat, christened Strongheart. Strongheart, it seems, was left at home in New York a week ago with plenty of milk bottles but no opener.

"He is liable to be a wild cat by the time we get home, and even when he, she or it is a tame cat, she always scratches me in an affectionate way when I come home off a trip. I bet you I have got a thousand marks from that cat."

"But," I retorted, "suppose Bugs would die tomorrow, what is a thousand marks in American money?"

The ball game started off great today when I found myself sitting alongside of Miss Dorothy Juss of Kildale, Pa. This Is Miss Juss' first world series.

"This my first world series," said Miss Juss. "I am Juss 5 years old. My father found this ticket which may have been in your shirt pocket which you claim to have lost. But, anyway, I am setting beside you and I have ambitions to become a poet, and I want you to look over this poem, which I have dubbed the naïve poem of a eight-year-old girl, remembering, of course, that Lee Meadows' little boy is experting. My poem is dedicated to one of the Washing pitchers, who wields the suit ball. They tell me his name is Coveleskie. I wrote this about him after he had lost that game in Washington."

"Let me hear the poem without further adieu," I prompted.

"Here is the poem," said little Miss Juss, and repeated it to me as follows:

"Old Covey was brutal.
His soup bone was brittle.
His fast ball was futile.
And so was his spittle."

"There is my poem," said Miss Juss. "You can take it or leave it."

"I leave it," I replied, and turned my head away to the business of the ball game.

The first batter to come was Sam Rice. He was loudly booed by the crowd for no other reason than that he made a grand catch in Washington and robbed Earl Smith of a home run. He was booed every time he came up. The way not to get booed In Pittsburgh, or perhaps elsewhere, is to ignore fly balls or muff them.

It seemed that the home boys scored a couple of runs in the third, but at that moment I was listening to a new argument in regards to how

Max Carey always gets to next base. The explainer was a flapper from Diletante, Tex., and her theory was this:

"Max," she said, "constantly faces back to the base whom he has just left. That leads the other club to believe that it is a one way street, they have no idea that he would be daring enough to disregard the traffic rules."

The next time I looked up, time was being called while Erick Owens ejected a spectator on the grounds that he had come to the ball park when he might have stayed at home.

The umpire was right, as usual.

Along came the ninth innings and Washington still one run behind.

Goslin hit four balls into the right field stands, all foul. Then he flied out. Why not have hit one of those four balls into the right field stands? That's why they call him Goose. Joe Harris smacked one into dead center and Max Carey climbed a tree trying to reach it. It was a two-base hit and would have been a home run in any other parish. The next two boys were Red Hot Popas and Popped.

Your correspondent found Bucky Harris as he was practicing card tricks for tomorrow's game in the bell hops' gymnasium at the Schenley.

"Who are going to pitch tomorrow?" I asked him.

"Old Barney," was his retort.

"As long as he is on your club," I said, "the adjective is redundant."

Note

1. Arthur "Bugs" Baer, cartoonist and journalist, who also wrote for Broadway, Hollywood, and continuity for the *Mutt and Jeff* comic strip. One of his most famous quips about a runner thrown out at second base—"His head was sure full of larceny, but his feet were honest"—so amused William Randolph Hearst that he hired Baer to work for him at the *New York American*.

Ring Hears the Game He Is Seeing

Bell Syndicate, Oct. 5, 1927

PITTSBURGH—WELL, FRIENDS, YOU CAN SEE FOR YOURSELVES THAT I am back in the city where I lost my shirt just two years ago and swore at the time that I would never come here again, but it is the inalienable right of every free born partly white American citizen to change his mind, if any, especially when one's dear public demands it.

Furthermore, this is one world's series which I am interested in personally and my nerves has been so shattered during the last couple weeks that I can't risk the lives of my wife and kiddies by listening with them to the play by play account over the radio, even though same be recited by the always engaging and generally accurate Graham MacNamee.

On Friday, the 23rd of September, I set in front of the loud speaker while somebody at WNYC reported the third battle between the Giants and Pittsburgh and when Freddy Lindstrom broke up the game with a hit that hopped over three or four of the Waner boys' heads, I kicked our darling dog Peter through a costly plate glass window and called the parrot everything but Polly. If any of my little ones had been in the room I would have knocked them for a Chicago count, and the madam herself would not have escaped without her quota of contusions.

No doubt you are in a fever to know the reasons for this renewal of the baseball rabies in a torpid old stiff like the undersigned. Well, last spring, before the season opened, I wagered a pretty penny at odds of 3 to 1 that Pittsburgh would win the pennant and another pretty penny that Pittsburgh would beat out the Giants. But that ain't nowheres near the half of it. Pittsburgh's present manager and I broke into the national pastime in the same league, the same year, and I have always felt toward him the way you feel toward whoever shared with you the griefs and mortifications of harassed saphood.

Veteran ball players in that league, the Central, used to take inhuman advantage of Donie Bush's unsophistication and mine and kid us to such an extent that we almost wept together, evenings, into steins of South Bend's best beer. That was 22 years ago, when the hick shortstop was 19 years old and the hick reporter 20. Which would make him 41 at the present writing and me 42; that is if we hadn't aged 10 years apiece since last April. Jack Hendricks, whose Cincinnati Reds scrunched St. Louis Thursday, had the best ball club in that Central league and Bush would have been a member of it if Jack hadn't been blessed with Champ Osteen, one of the greatest of minor league shortstops.

Just the same I claim credit for first calling a big league scout's attention to Donie. The scout was George Huff, athletic director at the University of Illinois and ivory hunter for the Boston Red Sox. George had an engagement one afternoon at Notre Dame, but I persuaded him to come out to the South Bend ball park and take a look at Bush. It was Donie's bad day. Hitting three times left-handed and three-times right-handed, he amassed one home run, two triples and three singles. George wired that night to John I. Taylor, who owned the Boston club. John I. wired back that be was perfectly satisfied with the shortstop he had. Which was reasonable enough, his shortstop being Heinie Wagner.

(Editor's note: Why don't you talk, about yourself a little?)

(Author's note: All right. I will)

Donie was drafted by Detroit, sent to Indianapolis for a year's seasoning and then recalled by Hughey Jennings. He had several run-ins with Ty Cobb. I met him in Chicago one time and asked him what the trouble was.

"Nobody in the world," said Donie, "can get along with that so-and-so. He's driving me crazy. He's handed me 26 signs to remember, and if I miss one, he rides me. He's a so-and-so."

"I'm supposed to be writing a story about him for the American Magazine," I said.

"Well, then," said Donie, "you're writing about the greatest ball player that ever lived or ever will live."

And be proceeded to give me 15,000 words of instances of Ty's superiority over all other ball players, past, present and to come.

Donie hasn't had what you would call a perfect year. In April, with an eye to economy, Barney Dreyfuss took a long-term lease on a stretcher to carry his stars to and from the hospital. It was what the railroads call a two-way haul. The athlete who was pretty near all right again would ride from the hospital to Forbes Field, where the stretcher would pick up the one who had just got hurt and take him to the hospital.

The club went along without a left-handed pitcher, and Ray Kremer, one of the best right-handers in the league, was injured most of the season. Johnnie Morrison dropped out of sight. Earl Smith was set down 30 days for smacking Dave Bancroft, and there was an argument with Kiki Cuyler which resulted in the latter's enjoying the cool shade of the bench all through August and September. On the other hand, Bush hasn't been obliged to do the managing single-handed. A great many baseball writers have helped, and without his even having to ask them to. If he is half the guy I think he is, he will repay us all next year by telling us how to write our stuff.

Well, it's over now and I can forget recent nightmares about Giants chasing me all over the room, nightmares from which I awoke to behold a White-sheeted figure at my bedside moaning, "I am the Spirit of St. Louis." I will admit that the New York bunch had me scared when (if they were quoted correctly) they began talking like Jack Sharkey, to the effect that they would "blow Pittsburgh right out of the league." They came close to doing it, too, but the trouble with them was that they contracted the blowing habit and blew in Philadelphia against a club that hardly ever beats anybody on purpose.

There is a good deal of talk always about this club being game and that club being yellow, but the club that wins is usually the club which, on a given day, gets the best hitting, the best pitching, the best fielding and the best luck. The Giants are a good, game ball club, handicapped by erratic battery work. Their gameness didn't get them anywhere when they couldn't hit Petty and Ulrich and when the Phillies could and did hit Grimes.

(Editor's note: Have you forgotten yourself entirely?)

That reminds me. I telephoned John Heydler last Thursday morning and asked him what would happen if the Thursday game between St. Louis and Cincinnati had to be called off on account of wet grounds.

"I'm glad you brought that up," said John. "I suppose you didn't think I had enough to worry me already. Well, if the game is called off, St. Louis, which has no game scheduled for Friday, will insist on playing Cincinnati Friday morning. Pittsburgh will protest and it will be up to the board of directors. And while you are looking for trouble, I may as well tell you that this pennant race is likely to end with three clubs tied for first place. In that event, there will be a series of three-game series before the world's series and the next time you want to play golf, you can tee off on snow drifts."

For the benefit of those who have just tuned in, the club that is going to oppose Pittsburgh is the New York American League club. I am going to bet on them, a very small percentage of my winnings. And I hope I lose, but please don't repeat that to the Babe or Mr. Huggins. It's a tough series to guess. You can't tell how the Yankees will act in a regular ball game after playing exhibition games all season. Anyway I have decided that the only way to keep a shirt in the World Series is to keep it on, and this shirt is going to remain right where it is till the series is over. So may the best club win quick.

Enid Has Its Fair Fan

Bell Syndicate, Oct. 6, 1927

PITTSBURGH—I WISH TO STATE AT THE OUTSET THAT I WATCHED the game under a severe handicap. Possibly my more senile readers will recall that amongst those attending the World Series of 1921 was a Mrs. Vera Thake, nicknamed "Ducky," because her husband was a quack doctor in Enid, Oklahoma. The town of Enid had conducted a popularity contest and the winner was to be sent to the series, which Enid hoped would last a long time.

Mrs. Thake won the contest and was given a ticket to New York, but no ticket to the series. She stood in line in front of a ticket window at Madison Square Garden for three days before she found out that, the games were being played at the Polo Grounds. In some way or another she got ahold of my telephone number and from then on she draped herself around me. There was no vacant seat in the press box, so she sat in my lap and I had to read about the game in the papers next day.

Well, when, I took my seat yesterday afternoon, a terrible-looking woman to my left started a one way conversation and who should she turn out to be but Mrs. Thake's daughter. She said her name was Helma and she had been christened that because it was what she replied every time her mother spoke to her.

She did not win any popularity contest, but came to the series as the result of a wager. Last spring she bet with a girl friend that Cleveland would beat out Pittsburgh, thinking they were in the same league. The loser was to ride here on a surf board, rolling a peanut in front of her. Miss Thoke started from Enid in July, when it became evident that

Cleveland could never do it, and arrived today just too late to wash her face and hands before the game began. She had a anonymous letter of introduction to me and was pretty much of a pest all afternoon.

If it had not been for she and the fact that Donie Bush got beat, I would have had a pretty good day. Directly behind me was Graham MacNamee and his microphone and I could hear every word he said, so it was just like eating your cake and having it.

I mean here I was watching a World Series game and listening to the broadcast of it at one and the same time. You might almost say I attended a doubleheader, the game Mac was describing and the game I was watching.

I suppose my millions of radio fans will want to know what Mr. MacNamee looks like and I only wished I could tell you, but I cant. It ain't because he is indescribable, but I couldn't turn around on account of a stiff neck which I caught from Wilbert Robinson of the Brooklyn club coming over on the train Monday night. Robbie contracted the ailment during the regular season from looking straight up in the air at his ball club's line drives.

The Hotel Schenley was: kind of crowded at the noon hour so I decided to make a lunch of hot dogs at the ball park. I found out that they don't call them hot dogs here, in Pittsburgh. They call them "wieners" in honor of Lloyd and Paul.

I ran into Dan Howley, manager of the St. Louis Browns. He said he was disappointed in only getting Catcher Manion in the draft. He wanted to get Ed Wynn too, which would have rounded out his ball club.

"I had a tough break a while ago," said Dan. "My team were all at the ball yard when the tornado hit St. Louis and it didn't kill a one of them."

Early in the morning a dense fog hung over Pittsburgh and in the afternoon some of the ball players acted like they was still in it. A good many of we experts thought the two clubs wasn't Pittsburgh and New York at all, but the Phillies and Browns disguised as Lon Chaney.

Waite Hoyt and Ray Kramer seemed to be betting on each other. Both these gents are a whole lot better than they looked in this battle. If they ain't, I am going to take up pitching.

I could still continue my art. In fact, pretty near every ball player in this series is experting on the side and at one juncture in the game they asked a ten minutes recess so as they could refill their fountain pens.

Earl Smith complained that it was hard work to typewrite while wearing a mask, protector and shinguards and Judge Landis has state that hereafter a stenographer will be permitted to set on the home play and take the catchers' dictation.

To add to the confusion, in the excitement of the third innings, Miss Thoke jumped up on a press table and did a cartwheel. The swish of her skirts blew away the first 6,000 words of Charley Herzog's story and Charley's only hope is that it blew them toward Baltimore.

I guess I forgot to mention that Miss Thoke is betting on the Yankees. She has got them mixed up some way with the Notre Dame football team and at frequent intervals all afternoon, she would holler, "Hurrah for Rockne" and "touchdown, touchdown."

In the last half of the ninth, some of the fans wanted Donie to send Cuyler in to hit for John Miljus, but Donie picked Brickell. Mr. Cuyler remained on the bench, where he has spent the last two months because, so rumor hath it, he did not choose to run or slide in 1927.

The 1927 World Series was the last one Lardner attended in person. Five years later, he wrote a column purporting to "cover" the 1932 Series by listening to it on the radio. It is the last thing he ever wrote about baseball. Lardner died almost exactly a year after it appeared in newspapers around the country.

Lardner Agrog About Series

Bell Syndicate, Sept. 28, 1932

NEW YORK—The world is agog and I am agrog over the World Series, which opens here Wednesday between the New York Yankees and the Chicago Cubs. I have made a most careful study of the two clubs. The most careful part of the study was not to see the manager of either ball club. During the middle of the season I did talk to Rogers Hornsby over the telephone and he gave me this interesting dope:

"I have got the fastest right-hander in baseball in the person of Lonnie Warnecke. He throws them right down at your knees where nobody wants them; he is as fast as Vance with a great and invincible fast ball to right-handers or left-handers when he's got his control. I've got Woodie English who is improved so much you wouldn't believe it; a kid named Herman; this Hemsley, and you know the rest of the gang." All right, I know the rest of the gang. And Rogers is gone and Charlie Grimm is manager and the outcome depends on whether Gehrig flops in a pinch or Woody English throws an autographed baseball from here to Toledo.

Now then, these games are going to be attended by the oversigned via radio. He ain't going to see them, but will hear them as he has heard them for the past three years—by air—and he will therefore be in competition with the Messrs. Husing, McNamee, Manning, Tatten et al, and my contention is that one of us will wind up in a tie.

To begin with, I will give the boys a start by asserting that the series is going to be between Washington and St. Louis. The pitchers for the opening game will be William Watson Clark and Rube Waddell. Both of them are kid left-handers and it is just a question of nerve. Behind the bat will be Mickey Street and Lou Criger, This is just a question of nerve.

Now, let's get to the infield. Beginning on first base, the Phillies have Charlie Grimm. He sings, plays, writes, is a born comedian and, unfortunately, monkeys with a ukulele. He bats left handed, sings left handed, tells his jokes left handed, throws left handed and talks left handed. His opponent, Lou Gehrig, lives in the Bronx left handed, plays no instrument with either hand, carries a sandwich in both hands and, as luck would and does have it, hits long drives into right center and dead right field. It looks like a what-up.

At second base we have the young Herman boy and the veteran Tony Lazzeri. Tony once took a passed ball and won a World Series against Pittsburgh. I don't know whether he sang on the passed ball or took it silently. Being of his race, he probably sang. Herman, being of almost any race, probably would sing, too, under those circumstances. It looks like a walk-up.

At shortstop we have two Germans, Herman Long and Honus Wagner. Neither of these kids can sing, but both are born croakers. The third basemen are Woody English and Joe Sewell, neither of whom is English or Sewell. They are both very steady, except English and Sewell. So you can look on it as a walk-up.

Now we come to the outfields and the less said about them the better, especially Babe Ruth.

Just before the game Ohio State University will parade across the field and form the alma mater "W." then it will be Middlebury's turn. The officials will then call the rival captains to the center of the field for the toss of the coin.

Whoever tosses the coin the highest will be entitled to the choice of what time to start the game. Capt. Babe Ruth is a pretty high coin tosser. High tossing is a big advantage in a short series like this, because the winner has the choice of what time the game shall start, early or late, and naturally the club that has the pitcher with the fastest ball wants the game started at the same time; otherwise he will have nobody to pitch to, which is a big advantage. With Ruffing on one club and Bush on the other, this makes it even. The toss will be watched with plenty of lethargy.

SOME FINAL THOUGHTS ON THE GAME

Oddities of Bleacher "Bugs"

Boston American, July 23, 1911

IF REPORTERS OF BASEBALL DIDN'T HAVE TO SIT UP IN THE PRESS BOX they would probably like their jobs better. Not that said box is such a dull place, with all the repartee of the scribes, operators and "critics." But it would be much more fun to listen to, and take part in, the conversations in the bleachers, where the real "bugs" sit.

Time was when we liked nothing better than to pay our two bits, rush for a point of vantage back of first or third base or out in the neighborhood of right or left field, invest a nickel in a sack of peanuts, another nickel in a score card, and then settle down to try to prove, by our comments and shouts, that we knew more about baseball than anyone around us.

That was when we spoke of "inshoots" and "outs" and "drops" and "outdrops"; wondered who that was hitting in place of So-and-So and thought ball players were just a little bit better than other people, because they wouldn't pay any attention to us if we drummed up nerve enough to speak to them outside the park.

It was before we knew that there's no such thing as an inshoot, that "outs," "drops" and "outdrops" are merely "curve balls"; before we could identify a substitute batter or a new pitcher by just glancing for an instant at his left ear, or his walk, or noting the way his hair was brushed in the back; before we were absolutely positive that the players are just common human beings and that some of them are really no better than ourselves.

But it was lots more joy in those days. There may be a certain kind of pleasure in brushing majestically past the pass-gate man, strutting along the rear aisle of the stand in the hope that some one will know you are a baseball writer, speaking to a player or two and getting answered, finding your own particular seat in the press box and proceeding to enlighten the absent public regarding the important events on the field, in your own, bright, breezy style. But what fun is all that compared with scraping up the necessary quarter, or half dollar, and knowing you are going to SEE a game, not report it?

The man who is on intimate terms with the ball players, who calls at their hotel and takes them out in his machine, goes to the station with them to see them off, gets letters from them occasionally, and knows they are just people, isn't the real "fan" or "bug," even if he does have to pay to get into the park.

The real article is the man who knows most of the players by sight, as they appear on the field, but wouldn't know more than one or two of them if he saw them on the street, struggles hard to keep an accurate score and makes a mistake on every other play, or doesn't attempt to score at all, disputes every statement made by his neighbors in the bleachers whether he knows anything about said statement or not, heaps imprecations on the umpire and the manager, thinks something is a bonehead play when it really is good, clever baseball, talks fluently about Mathewson's "inshoot," believes that Hank O'Day has it in for the home team and is purposely making bad decisions, and says, "Bransfield is going to bat for Moore" when Walsh is sent in to hit for Chalmers.

He doesn't know it all, but he's happy. He is perfectly satisfied when the folks around him believe what he says, and sometimes he almost gets to believing it himself. He's having a thoroughly enjoyable afternoon, if his team wins. If it doesn't, he knows just why and can tell his wife, his brother or his pal, that evening, how the tables could have been turned if only Manager Tenney had used a little judgment.

His imagination is a wonderful thing. Without it he would be unable to make any sort of an impression on his fellows. He must talk unhesitantly, as if he had all the facts, and never stammer or back up when his assertions are questioned.

Pat Moran is catching for the Phillies. Everybody knows Pat. He is getting a chance to work because President Lynch has set down Charley

Dooin for a "bad ride." A tall foul is hit. Pat gets under it but makes a square muff.

"He's a rotten catcher," says a nearby fan.

"He's a mighty good catcher when he's right," replies our friend.

"Why isn't he right?" queries the nearby one, sarcastically. "He's had time enough to get in shape, hasn't he?"

"No ball player can keep in shape and drink the way Pat does," is the come-back. "I was down town last night and I saw the whole Philadelphia bunch. Pat was certainly pouring in the strong stuff. He's a regular reservoir."

This remark is greeted with silence because no one has nerve enough to come out with a positive denial of the tale. As a matter of fact, Pat never touches the "strong stuff," and if he bunched all his annual drinking into one night, he'd still be thirsty. But that doesn't make any difference with our friend. He has scored a point by seeming to know why Pat dropped the foul ball.

Charley Herzog is on first base. He starts for second with the pitch. Kaiser, at bat, takes a healthy swing and fouls one over the third base seats. Charley crosses second, but is called back.

Our friend is in a rage.

"He had it stole," he roars, "and that bonehead Kaiser went and spoiled it by fouling off that ball. It was a bad ball, too. They must have chloroformed Tenney when they handed him that guy."

If you'd tell the angered one that Kaiser and Herzog were trying to work the hit and run, and that Kaiser would have been "called" if he hadn't swung, you would be laughed at or treated with contemptuous silence. It never happens, on a hit-and-run play, where the pitch is fouled, that some one doesn't say "He had it stole," and storm at the batter.

The Rustlers are at bat in the last half of the ninth. The score is 5 to 3 against them. Jones singles, and Spratt, batting for Mattern, sends a double to right. "Buster" Brown, coaching at third, makes Jones stop there. There is a pretty good chance for him to beat Schulte's throw to the plate. There is also a small chance that Schulte's throw will beat him. Coacher Brown's act raises a storm of protest.

"You BONEHEAD. He could have walked in. Get somebody out there that knows something."

And just because Brown DOES know something, he has held Jones at third. What he knows is that a 5 to 4 defeat is just as bad as a 5 to 3 beating, that Jones's run isn't worth six cents if Spratt doesn't score, too, and that Jones's run is almost sure to be scored if Spratt's, the needed one, is.

Sweeney fans, Tenney fouls out and Hoffman takes Herzog's long fly. The fan goes home convinced that "Buster" Brown has an ivory dome. If he stopped to think, he would realize that Jones's record of runs scored was the only thing that possibly could be affected by the act of Mr. Brown, and that there was just a chance that Schulte's throw would have hastened the end.

The argument that Schulte might have thrown wild and thus allowed Spratt also to score doesn't hold water, for good outfielders aren't taking any chances of overthrowing in cases like that. They are just getting the ball back into the diamond, so that some one can prevent liberties on the bases.

Here's one that actually did happen. It was at the Detroit game on the Huntington Avenue grounds on the twelfth day of June. With one out, Nunamaker singled through Bush. Hall sent a grounder to O'Leary, who tried to nail the catcher at second, but was too late. Hooper popped a fly which Bush gathered in.

Gardner hit a slow one over second. O'Leary picked up the ball, but saw that he had no chance to throw out Gardner. He bluffed a peg to Delehanty, who was playing first, and then uncorked a throw to Moriarty. Nunamaker had reached third and wandered a few feet toward home. He tried desperately to get back, but it was too late, and Moriarty tagged him for the third out.

Almost simultaneously the following storms broke from two real fans:

"Well, what do you think of that stone-covered, blankety-blank Irish Donovan letting him get caught like that?"

"Well, that fat-headed bum of a Dutch Engle. Who told him he could coach?"

Bill Carrigan was the coacher, and Bill has no strings attached to Mr. Nunamaker's feet. Nor had he done anything to deserve being called a stone-covered Irish Donovan or a bum of a Dutch Engle.

However, Bill and "Buster" Brown and Pat Moran and all of them are still alive and happy, and the fans are even happier. They go out there to have a good time and they have it. Things are often done which don't please them at all—things that would be done differently if they were in charge. But, believe us, they wouldn't have half as much fun if they were in charge, or if they got in through the pass gate.

Kill the Umpire

Bell Syndicate, July 23, 1922

SPORT COLUMNS IN OUR DAILY NEWSPAPERS IS BEGINNING TO READ LIKE the official communiques that use to be printed on Page 2 dureing the late war except that the papers used to publish the communiques from both sides so that which ever side you was pulling for, why you could read that side's communique and feel like your favorite team had got the best of it, whereas amongst all the stories you see about the battles between the umpires vs. the ball players and bugs, you don't never find a case where the umps claims near as good as a draw and in most cases the said umps don't claim nothing because he is either still unconscious or hideing in a hollow tree when the reports is sent out.

Maybe my readers has overlooked the quaint little incidence that has been coming off lately in different leagues around the U.S. and our neighbors to the north. Well to begin with they was a couple of cuties staged in the Eastern Canada League and the scene of action was Three Rivers which lays about 1/2 way between Montreal and Quebec.

This little city couldn't use to support a ball club, but a franchise was recently boughten by public spirited citizens who became wealthy dureing the Stillman spat. Well they was a umpire named Bruneau who made the rash remark that one of the Three Rivers players was out and the crowd amused themself by tearing off pieces of the grand stand and throwing them at the umps.

After the game they waited for him outside the park and was going to present him with a necktie made entirely of rope but the police got him and his Adam's apple out of town and nothing happened till later in the same wk. when another ump named Mahoney said in a jokeing way that a certain player in the visiting Montreal club had reached his base ahead of the throw.

Catcher Bailey of Three Rivers knocked Mr. Mahoney for an afternoon nap and when he woke up he fined Bailey $50.00 and canned him out of the game whereupon the bugs took up a collection amounting to $65.00 which they gave to Bailey, netting him a profit of $15.00. The bugs left the park before the game was over and adjourned to the hotel where Mahoney was staying and they went right up to his room and waited for him and gave him a house warming that is said to have been very carefully thought out.

Mr. Mahoney afterwards sent a telegram to Eddie Guest[1] the poet asking him to please not forget Three Rivers wile he is writeing hymns of praise in regards to different cities.

Well about a wk. after the Three Rivers incidence they was a ball game played in Crisfield, Md., in the Eastern Shore League and the bugs let the game go three full innings before one of them jumped out of the grand stand and cracked Umpire Knowlton on the chin. The ump was a game bird and umpired the last 6 innings from the hospital.

Down in Durham, N.C., where you would think there would be plenty of bulls, the crowd lit into a couple of policemens that was trying to escort Umpire O'Keefe from the ball yard to his hostelry. The policemens was allowed to escape with a couple of bruises, but the gang toyed with O'Keefe. Boys will be boys.

And in that same wk. Catcher Allen of St. Paul got mad at Umpire Shannon in Milwaukee and tore off the ump's mask and smacked him but the umps managed to stay on his ft. and continue to render perilous decisions.

This is the gen. lay of the land in the north, south, east and middle west with several California precincts still missing.

Well, Judge ain't it about time you done something a specially with dog days coming and conditions libel to go from bad to worst. Next thing you know some of these fans and ballplayers will lose their temper and make trouble for some umpire.

The 1st thing that has got to be realized is that the present system of umpireing is all wrong. Men in charge of our national pastime has made the mistake of insisting on the umpires studying the baseball guide and mastering the laws of the game with the result that they have finely became monomaniacs on the subject of haveing games played according to the rules.

Practically all the fans and a big majority of the players ain't read the rule book since pitchers wore a mustache and therefore they can tell a umpire what is what without being hampered by no printed code.

Another mistake is for the umpires to try and umpire from right down there on the field where they are too close to the game to see it good. The place to umpire a ball game is either up in the grand stand or on the players' bench and the umps should either be made to set in one of them 2 places or else give up their job entirely and leave the fans and bench warmers take turns giveing decisions.

A good many experts is in favor of the umpireing being done by who ever is catching as the catchers generally always seems to know when a decision is wrong, but this scheme would result in practically everybody strikeing out which the fans don't like to see.

Whatever is decided on it is to be hoped that they will be some radical change, but if the moguls is stubborn and hangs on to the present system, why the lease they can do is fix it so as when a umpire makes a decision vs. Three Rivers or Durham it won't be necessary for either athletes or bugs to soil their hands on same.

Every ball park should ought to be equipped with a expert sniper that could pick off the umps the minute he went wrong and then the ground keeper's staff could rush out and roll him out of the way like a canvas infield cover.

Note

1. Edgar Guest wrote some 11,000 sentimental poems that appeared in the *Detroit Free Press*, were syndicated nationally, and collected in more than 20 books. I briefly emerge from these notes to say I attended the Edgar Guest elementary school while growing up in Detroit.

Why Ring Stopped Covering Baseball

Bell Syndicate, July 17, 1921

I GOT A LETTER THE OTHER DAY ASKING WHY DIDN'T I WRITE ABOUT baseball no more as I usen't to write about nothing else, you might say. Well friends, I may as well admit that I have kind of lose interest in the old game, or rather it ain't the old game which I have lose interest in it, but it is the game which the magnates has fixed up to please the public with their usual good judgement.

A couple yrs. ago a ball player named Baby Ruth that was a pitcher by birth was made into an outfielder on acct. of how he could bust them and he begin breaking records for long distants hits and etc. and he become a big drawing card and the master minds that controls baseball says to themselfs that if it is home runs that the public wants to see, why leave us give them home runs so they fixed up a ball that if you don't miss it entirely it will clear the fence and the result is that ball players which use to specialize in hump back liners to the pitcher is now amongst our leading sluggers when by rights they couldn't take a ball in their hands and knock it past the base umpire.

Another result is that I stay home and read a book.

But statistics shows that about 7 people out of every 100 is ½ cuckoo so they's still some that is still interested in the national pastime so for their benefit I will write a little about it as long as I don't half to set through a game of it to get the material.

Well, I was in a certain town a little while ago and run acrost a friend of mine that is a big league ball player which I won't say which club he is on, but he made the remark that now days when his club comes to the

Polo Grounds, N.Y., he don't never see me setting in the press coop no more, and I says I was working pretty hard and he says:

"You would be surprised the number of people that is too busy to come and watch us play ball."

So I said it wasn't only his club that I didn't have no time for but it was all the clubs and I couldn't get steamed up over them no more and maybe it was because I was getting old.

"Well," he says, "they's a lot of others getting old, too, and if they keep on ageing like they have so far this season, why pretty soon we will be haveing secret practice at 3:30 P.M."

Well, I finely got up nerve to ask him where his club stood in the race.

"We are a good eighth," he says, "and we are proud of it. A club that is out in front in this race hasn't got nothing to brag about as you can't see how they can help it. But when you look at the 8 clubs in this league, you will half to own up that it takes genius to be worse than the other 7, and believe me we got genius."

"Listen," he says, "why don't you come out and set on our bench some day and get an education? They's 2 of the new boys that was overseas together in the war and after they got back to America they didn't see each other till this spring when they both joined our club. So one of them asked the other where he played last season and he says he didn't play only a couple months. He says he was laid up with a long sledge of sickness.

"Then one day one of the boys was talking about a pitcher on another club and we hadn't seen this pitcher yet, but this boy had been in the same league with him last season. So we asked this boy what this here pitcher had and he says he has got a great curveball that ain't fast or it ain't slow, its just mediokum."

"Listen," says my friend, "they use to say that Connie Mack had intricate signs that it took smart ball players to learn them. Well, you ought to try and learn the signs we are useing. For inst. say the other club has got men on second and third base and it's a close game and their best hitter is up and we don't want to take a chance on him.

"Well, Bill sets there on the bench and yells at the pitcher and finely the pitcher looks and Bill holds up four fingers. This means he wants the pitcher to give the man four balls. Then Bill points to first base. That is to show the pitcher that it is first base and not third base that he wants the man passed to. Then the pitcher is as libel as not to stick one right in the groove and the star batter knocks it cock eyed and we lose the ball game and Bill asks the pitcher what was the matter and the pitcher is libel to say he thought Bill only held up three fingers, meaning to try and strike the guy out."

"Listen," says my friend, "you think Schalk and Killefer and them babies is brainy catchers and they are supposed to outguess the batter and etc. Well, our catchers has to outguess the pitchers too. Like for inst. take Schalk. If he signs for a curve ball, why he can get ready to catch a curve ball. But if one of our catchers signs for a curve ball and the pitcher says all right, why he is just as libel as not to be kidding and the catcher has got to guess what he is going to throw and most of the time, when it comes it is a big surprise.

"A little uncertainty like that is what keeps us from going to sleep out there, as they's never no uncertainly in regards to who is going to win the game.

"But we have other excitement, like for inst. they's a big thrill every time we are in the field and somebody on the other club hits a fly ball. We know 2 or 3 of the boys is going to have a collision but we don't know which ones or whether they are going to get hurt or killed. So far they ain't none of them been killed, but the season ain't only half over and this is no time to give up hope."

Br'er Rabbit Ball

The New Yorker, Sept. 13, 1930

In spite of the fact that some of my friends in the baseball industry are kind enough to send me passes every spring, my average attendance at ball parks for the last three seasons has been two times per season (aside from World's Series) and I probably wouldn't have gone that often but for the alleged necessity of getting my innumerable grandchildren out in the fresh air once in a while. During the games, I answer what questions they ask me to the best of my knowledge and belief, but most of the afternoon I devote to a handy pocket edition of one of Edgar Wallace's sex stories because the events of the field make me yearn for a bottle of Mothersill's Remedy.[1]

Manufacturers of what they are using for a ball, and high officials of the big leagues, claim that the sphere contains the same ingredients. mixed in the same way, as in days of old. Those who believe them should visit their neighborhood psychiatrist at the earliest possible moment.

When I was chasing around the circuit as chronicler of the important deeds of Cubs or White Sox, it was my custom and that of my colleagues to start making up our box scores along about the seventh inning in cases where one club was leading its opponent by ten runs. Nowadays the baseball reporters don't dare try to guess the answer even if there are two out in the last half of the ninth inning and the score is 21 to 14.

I have always been a fellow who liked to see efficiency rewarded. If a pitcher pitched a swell game, I wanted him to win it. So it kind of sickens me to watch a typical pastime of today in which a good pitcher, after an hour and fifty minutes of deserved mastery of his opponents, can suddenly be made to look like a bum by four or five great sluggers who couldn't have held a job as bat boy on the Niles High School scrubs.

Let us say that the Cubs have a series in Brooklyn. They get over there at eleven in the morning so they can find the park by the time the game begins. The game develops into a pitchers' battle between Charlie Root, Bud Teachout, Guy Bush, and Pat Malone for the Cubs and Dazzy Vance, Jim Elliott, and Adolfo Luque for the Robins. The last half of the ninth inning arrives with the score 12 to 8 in Chicago's favor—practically a no-hit game in these days. Somebody tries to strike out, but Malone hits his bat and the ball travels lightly along the ground toward third base. Woody English courageously gets in front of it and has two fingers broken. This is a superficial injury for an infielder of the present, so Woody stays in the game. The Brooklyn man is safe at first. The next Brooklyn man, left-handed and a born perpendicular swatsman, takes a toehold and crashes a pop fly toward Charlie Grimm. The pellet goes over the right-field fence like a shot and breaks a window in a synagogue four blocks away.

Manager McCarthy removes Malone and substitutes Blake, hoping the latter will give a few bases on balls and slow up the scoring. But Blake gives only two bases on balls and then loses control. He pitches one over the plate and the batsman, another left-hander who, with the old ball, would have been considered too feeble to hit fungoes on one of these here miniature golf courses, pops it over the fence to the beach at Far Rockaway, where it just misses a young married couple called Rosenwald. The victory is Brooklyn's and the official puts the names of a lot of pitchers, including Rucker and Grimes, into a hat and the first name drawn out gets the credit.

I mean it kind of upsets me to see good pitchers shot to pieces by boys who, in my time, would have been ushers. It gnaws at my vitals to see a club with three regular outfielders who are smacked on top of the head by every fly ball that miraculously stays inside the park—who ought to pay their way in, but who draw large salaries and are known as stars because of the lofty heights to which they can hoist a leather-covered sphere stuffed with dynamite.

Those who are cognizant of my great age ask me sometimes what Larry Lajoie would do in this "game." Well, he wouldn't do anything after one day. Larry wasn't a fly-ball hitter. When he got a hold of one, it usually hit the fence on the first bounce, travelling about five feet three inches above the ground most of the way and removing the ears of all infielders who didn't throw themselves flat on their stomachs the instant they saw him swing. They wouldn't have time to duck this ball, and after the battle there would be a meeting of earless infielders, threatening a general walkout if that big French gunman were allowed in the park again, even with a toothpick in his hand.

But without consulting my archives I can recall a dozen left-handed batsmen who hit fly balls or high line drives and who hit them so far that opposing right and centre-fielders moved back and rested their spinal columns against the fence when it was these guys' turn to bat.

I need mention only four of this bunch—two from each league—to give my contemporaries a talking point when their grandchildren boast of the prowess of the O'Douls, Kleins, and Hermans of today. The four I will select offhand are Elmer Flick and Sam Crawford of the American League and Harry Lumley and Frank Schulte of the National.

In the year 1911 (I think it was) Mr. Schulte led the National league in homers with a total of twenty-one. Such a number would disgraceful in these days, when a pitcher gets almost that many. Just the same, I am willing to make a bet, which never can be decided, that Frank, with the present ball in play, would just about treble that total and finish so close to the Babe himself that it would take until December to count the ballots. I have frequently seen, in the dim, dead past, the figures of Fielder Jones and Eddie Hahn backing up against the haywire when Flick or Crawford came to bat, and on one occasion, when we travelled east on the same train as the Detroit club, I overheard a bit of repartee between Jones and Samuel. That afternoon Jones had caught three fly balls off Sam without moving more than a yard out of his position, which was a comfortable one, with the fence for a back rest.

"Why," said Sam grumblingly, "were you playing pretty near out of the park for me?"

"Why," said Jones, "do you always hit to the same place?"

Right-fielders were constantly robbing Lumley and Flick of two-base hits or worse by lolling against the bleacher wall—and it must be remembered that in those ancient times bleachers were far enough from the playing field so that the first and third-base coachers couldn't sit in them.

Speaking of Mr. Lumley (if you've heard this before, don't stop me), we (the Cubs) came east one season and we had a pitcher named Edward Reulbach, who was great when he had control and terrible when he lacked it. On this trip he lacked it to such an extent that Manager Chance ordered him to pay forenoon visits to each hostile battlefield and pitch to the rival batsmen in their practice. The latter had no objection—it just meant somebody to hit against without wearing out one of their own men.

Well, we got to Brooklyn and after a certain game the same idea entered the minds of Mr. Schulte, Mr. Lumley, and your reporter, namely: that we should see the Borough by night. The next morning, Lumley had to report for practice and, so far as he was concerned, the visibility was very bad. Reulbach struck him out three times on low curve balls inside.

"I have got Lumley's weakness!" said Ed to Chance that afternoon.

"All right," said the manager. "When they come to Chicago, you can try it against him."

Brooklyn eventually came to Chicago and Reulbach pitched Lumley a low curve ball on the inside. Lumley had enjoyed a good night's sleep, and if it had been a 1930 vintage ball, it would have landed in Des Moines, Iowa. As it was, it cleared the fence by ten feet and Schulte, playing right field and watching its flight, shouted: "There goes Lumley's weakness!"

Well, the other day a great ballplayer whom I won't name (he holds the home-run record and gets eighty thousand dollars a year) told a friend of mine in confidence (so you must keep this under your hat) that there are at least fifteen outfielders now playing regular positions in his own league who would not have been allowed bench-room the year he broke in. Myself, I just can't stomach it, but Brooklyn recently played to one hundred and ten thousand people in four games at Chicago, so I don't believe we'll ever get even light wines and beer.

Note

1. A pill to relieve motion sickness that was popular at the time.

Acknowledgments

Some years ago, I came across an article James Lardner wrote for the *New York Times* in 1985 at the time of the Ring Lardner centennial celebration at Olivet College in Olivet, Michigan. In that piece, James casually mentioned that most of his grandfather's journalism had never been collected. Of such casual mentions are anthologies born. James and his cousin Susan Lardner offered their encouragement and support from the moment I suggested a collection of Ring's journalism to them and granted me the rights to reprint his work. I am grateful to them both.

A third person whose help was invaluable is Richard Layman, who is the Ring Lardner of Ring Lardner scholars. The vice president of Bruccoli Clark Layman Inc., which publishes the *Dictionary of Literary Biography* and other reference works, Layman graciously sent me *Ring W. Lardner: A Descriptive Bibliography*, a book he and Matthew J. Bruccoli published in 1976 that has an entry for every piece of fiction and journalism Lardner ever wrote. It is a heroic work of scholarship that proved indispensable in assembling this book. Layman read the manuscript and made a number of valuable suggestions. He is not responsible for any mistakes I may have made in the introductory material or notes, and of course, the opinions expressed in them are mine alone.

Dan O'Brien, journalist, sportswriter, and archivist extraordinaire, was extremely helpful in providing readable copies of Lardner's "Pullman Pastimes" pieces in *The Sporting News* and the columns he wrote for the Bell Syndicate. O'Brien supplied me with many of these pieces and directed me to a website where I was able to find the rest. I'm most grateful to him, and to Pete Cava, who wrote a fine article on Lardner for the *Dictionary of Literary Biography*, for pointing me in his direction.

Lardner is the subject of two excellent biographies that provided some of the background information in this book: *Ring Lardner* by Donald Elder, which was published in 1956, and *Ring: A Biography of Ring Lardner* by Jonathan Yardley, published in 1977. Elder's book, which is out of print but worth seeking out, benefits from interviews with Lardner's wife and children as well as a number of his friends. It provides a fascinating look at his early years in Niles, Michigan, and describes the influence of his remarkable mother. It also paints a fine portrait of Lardner's later years as with his health failing, he roamed the streets of New York.

Yardley, a Pulitzer Prize–winning critic, approaches Lardner from a greater distance, which allows him to step back and assess his work in detail. His portrait of the state of professional baseball when Lardner covered it, and how the game shaped his views and his writing, is particularly interesting. Both books offer generous samples of Lardner's work and the critical assessments of their authors.

Biographical information of another sort can be found in *The Lardners: My Family Remembered*, a clear-eyed, yet sweetly evocative memoir by Ring Lardner, Jr., a two-time Oscar winner for screenwriting, which tells what it was like to grow up as part of the remarkable Lardner family. We are fortunate that when it came to storytelling skill and the ability to see things straight, "Bill" was every bit his father's son. More recently, the third Lardner generation has produced another first-rate memoir that carries the family story into the twenty-first century. *Shut Up, He Explained* was written by Kate Lardner, whose father was David, the youngest of Ring's sons, but who was raised by her mother and Ring, Jr., who were married after David's death.

The most current and thorough anthology of Lardner's fiction is *Ring Lardner: Stories and Other Writings*, which is part of the Library of America series, which reprints the work of the country's greatest writers. The book also includes samples of Lardner's plays, song lyrics, letters, and sketches.

In seeking out Lardner's work, I visited a number of libraries around the country, both in person and online. Fortunately, the entire run of the *Chicago Tribune* is available through the Chicago Public Library's website, while microfilm copies of the *Chicago Inter-Ocean* and *Chicago Examiner* are at the Harold Washington Library Center. I found microfilm of the *Boston American* at the Boston Public Library and located other articles Lardner wrote for newspapers and magazines at the New York Public Library, the Los Angeles Public Library, and the Santa Monica Public Library.

I am grateful to Gary Johnson, the president of the Chicago History Museum, and Ellen Keith, the museum's director of research and access, for their assistance. Thanks also to Tim Wiles and Bill Francis at the Baseball Hall of Fame; Sreenath Sreenivasan at the Columbia University Graduate School of Journalism; and Alex Belth, David Israel, and Robert Kimball.

Many thanks as well to my friend John Schulian, who has collected John Lardner's work in *The John Lardner Reader*, for lending a patient ear, and more thanks than I can properly express go to Barbara Isenberg for her many valuable suggestions and ideas and her constant support.

Thanks to my agent, Tim Hays, for his efforts on this book's behalf and to Rick Rinehart at Lyons Press for giving it a happy home. And thank you to senior production editor Alden Perkins for her help in preparing the manuscript for publication and to assistant marketing manager Jason Rossi for his assistance.

Finally, it should be noted that this book is a smaller version, dedicated solely to Lardner's baseball journalism, of *The Lost Journalism of Ring Lardner*, which I edited and was published by the University of Nebraska Press in 2017. That book includes not only Lardner's writing about baseball, football, boxing, and other sports but also his articles about many other topics of American life—and his own.

Selected Bibliography

Berg, A. Scott: *Max Perkins: Editor of Genius*. New York: Penguin, 1978.

Bruccoli, Matthew, and Richard Layman: *Ring W. Lardner: A Descriptive Bibliography*. Pittsburgh: University of Pittsburgh Press, 1976.

Bruccoli, Matthew, and Richard Layman, ed., *Some Champions: Sketches and Fiction by Ring Lardner*. New York, Scribner's, 1976.

Carruthers, Clifford M. *Letters of Ring Lardner*. Washington: Orchises, 195.

Elder, Donald. *Ring Lardner*. Garden City, NY: Doubleday, 1956.

Lardner, Kate. *Shut Up, He Explained: The Memoirs of a Blacklisted Kid*. New York: Ballantine, 2004.

Lardner, Ring. *Ring Lardner, Stories and Other Writings*. New York: Library of America, 2013.

Lardner, Ring Jr. *The Lardners: My Family Remembered*. New York: Harper & Row, 1976.

Rapoport, Ron, ed., *The Lost Journalism of Ring Lardner*. Lincoln and London, University of Nebraska Press, 2017.

Yardley, Jonathan. *Ring: A Biography of Ring Lardner*. Lanham, MD: Rowman & Littlefield, 1977.